IMAGES
of America

LIBERTY COUNTY

I0806140

On the Cover: First cousins Otis Amason and Laura Stevens play with a pet fawn, Maribou, near their grandmother's home at Springfield Plantation in the 1930s. Both cousins became Liberty County preservationists. Otis restored the historic Midway Church and Dorchester Presbyterian Church, and Laura restored over 18 historic structures including the Eddie Bowens Farm and Sam Ripley Farm, which are listed on the National Register of Historic Places. (Courtesy of the Springfield Legacy Foundation.)

IMAGES
of America

LIBERTY COUNTY

Meredith R. Devendorf

ARCADIA
PUBLISHING

ISBN 978-0-7385-6609-2

Published by Arcadia Publishing
Charleston, South Carolina

Printed in the United States of America

Library of Congress Control Number: 2009924230

For all general information contact Arcadia Publishing at:
Telephone 843-853-2070
Fax 843-853-0044
E-mail sales@arcadiapublishing.com
For customer service and orders:
Toll-Free 1-888-313-2665

Visit us on the Internet at www.arcadiapublishing.com

For those who cherished our memories—Clement Stevens Sr., John and Luretha Stevens, W. W. Law, Lillie Gillard, and my grandparents John and Martha Stevens

Contents

ACKNOWLEDGMENTS

A special thank-you to Glenn Fox, a selectman of the Midway Society and beacon of calm, for introducing me to Nicky Clark. Mr. Clark, in turn, arrived at my office door with a box of treasures—a collection of full-sized halftone films from the *Liberty County Herald*. His father (M. F. Clark Jr.), mother (Lollie Gill Clark), and brother Pete Clark ran the newspaper for many years, and Nicky began working as the last editor when he was still a teenager.

At the Midway Museum, where I began my history career at age seven, I had the pleasure of working with longtime curator Joanne Clark and her daughter Dianne Clark Behrens. Because of them, I will never look at an image of Button Gwinnett the same way again.

Florence Tate Roberts, indefatigable site manager for Seabrook Village, allowed me full access to photographic materials and her keys.

Arthur Edgar of Fort Morris Historic Site provided the town plan for Sunbury and valuable historical information.

Sallie Walthour Richardson, a shipmate in all things historical, provided images and insight for Midway Congregational Church and the Union Brotherhood Society.

Each day, waiting at the security checkpoint, was made worthwhile by working with Buck Meeks at the Fort Stewart Museum. Helen Wyatt Snapp and Robert Steinen, who captured so much of early life at Camp Stewart, gave remarkable gifts in the donation of their photographs to the U.S. Army.

Thanks also goes to Mayor Bill Austin who tried diligently to acquire photographs for this project. My editor Katie Stephens Shayda showed unflagging support through the many incarnations of this project. We have been together so long—she even changed her name!

For Carlos, I thank you for your unquestioning friendship. I can never repay you for your patience. As ever, I thank my mother, Laura, for her unflagging support and belief in my abilities. Without her patience and slack uptaking, I could never have finished this project. And I thank my late father, Don, for supporting my work and, in particular, for not staging one of his infamous technological poltergeist jokes at a sensitive moment.

Introduction

Nestled on the Georgia coast halfway between the Savannah and Altamaha Rivers, Liberty County stretches from the white sands of St. Catherine's Island to the piney sandhills of Fort Stewart, Gum Branch, and Hinesville. Originally settled by Guale Indians, the land has witnessed every period of American history.

In the early 1500s, Spanish explorers visited the coast, which became Liberty County, and were entranced by the free-flowing springs and abundance of lush green. In 1526, San Miguel de Gualdape, the first European colony in what later became the United States, began somewhere near Sapelo Sound. Plagued by disease, famine, and violence, the colony ended violently within months of its founding.

Challenged by a new Protestant English queen, Elizabeth I, who wanted North America and La Florida, the Spanish returned in the 1560s and successfully established St. Augustine. From there Spanish missionaries radiated out across the southeast and set up missions from the Chesapeake to Mobile Bay and inland to the Appalachian Mountains. On St. Catherine's Island, Franciscan brothers built Mission Santa Catalina de Guale, which existed for 100 years.

In 1630, a band of Puritan dissidents left their home in Dorchester, England, for the Massachusetts Bay Colony where they established the town of Dorchester. By 1695, they began to run out of land in their township, and one group of colonists moved to South Carolina where they founded a new settlement, west of Charleston, called Dorchester. In South Carolina, the Dorchester Puritans began a conflicted relationship between conscience and practicality by owning African slaves.

Rice slaves, too, had a distinctive heritage. As Europeans did not possess the tools or experience to grow rice, South Carolina colonists began importing Africans more familiar with the crop. As a result, slaves from the Senegambia region of coastal West Africa came from particular cultural groups such as Yoruba and Ibo who cultivated rice. These Africans largely stayed within the rice-growing region that ran from near Wilmington, North Carolina, through the Georgia coast and inland up to 25 miles. Even when sold, these slaves remained in the rice region where, though from different cultures, they developed customs and dialect peculiar to the Sea Islands.

When the Spanish withdrew from the northern reaches of La Florida, the English began protecting their assets in South Carolina. With slaves outnumbering whites nearly four to one, colonial fear of slave revolt was palpable, and the English crown believed the Spanish might attempt to instigate a rebellion. Gen. James Edward Oglethorpe had a solution to set up a colony in which men who had been thrown into London debtors' prisons could work off their debts as indentured servants to Protestant freeholders. Essentially, Oglethorpe proposed the establishment of an all-white colony between South Carolina and Spanish Florida. The Royal crown agreed, and Oglethorpe landed on a high bluff overlooking the Savannah River in 1733. He met Mary Musgrove, born Coosaponakeesa, a half-Creek woman married to an English trader. She agreed to work as an interpreter and negotiator for Oglethorpe in return for a generous grant of land.

Oglethorpe was true to his word and left instructions for Mary's land grant. The Georgia Trustees, on the other hand, did not wish to honor the agreement. After several years of negotiation, Mary Musgrove, now married to her third husband, Reverend Thomas Bosomworth, declared that she was Empress of the Creeks and she would cause a war if she did not receive her grant. She received St. Catherine's Island, the largest land grant made outright to a woman in Georgia's colonial history.

Among the Protestants recruited to Georgia were the Dorchester Puritans who settled in South Carolina. In 1752 faced with forced conversion to Anglicanism by the South Carolina royal government, the Puritans moved to an area halfway between Savannah and the Scottish outpost of Darien. Through the colonial period, the area was known as St. John's Parish, and the Puritans started a new meetinghouse—Midway.

Within a decade of settling in Georgia, the Dorchester Puritans found themselves concerned with the Seven Years War and the aftermath of taxation and tea parties. When Georgia assembled a delegation to represent colonists at the Continental Congress in 1776, two of the three members hailed from Midway. Dr. Lyman Hall and Button Gwinnett, accompanied by George Walton of Augusta, signed the Declaration of Independence. During the American Revolution, British troops made a special excursion to Midway to burn the church that belonged to the upstart Puritans.

When the war concluded, the former parishes were broken into counties. The southern part of St. John's Parish, which contained Darien, became McIntosh County, named for the Revolutionary War hero Lachlan McIntosh. The northern part, however, was named in honor of its independent spirit and became Liberty County. Out of the 159 counties in Georgia, Liberty, Peach, and Union are the only counties not named for individuals or groups of people.

From the moment the county began, the people of Liberty suffered and prevailed through wars, storms, and social change. Many famous names called Liberty home throughout the years. Brig. Gens. Daniel Stewart and James Screven were heroes of the Revolutionary War. Samuel F. B. Morse, inventor of the telegraph, Pres. Theodore Roosevelt, and First Lady Eleanor Roosevelt all had roots in Liberty. John Elliott Ward, the first U.S. ambassador to China, called Liberty home and is buried in the Midway cemetery. Alexander Stephens, vice president of the Confederacy, taught school in Liberty prior to the Civil War. Supreme Court Justice Clarence Thomas played with his cousins during summers in Seabrook and Trade Hill. There are countless judges, ministers, authors, politicians, teachers, scientists, and professors whom Liberty claims.

But, for every famous name, there are hundreds of everyday people living in Liberty. This book is not about the famous, the infamous, or the unknown but everyone. Together, their individual threads weave the tapestry of Liberty County. This book is by no means comprehensive. In fact, a dozen books would just begin to cover the complex story of Liberty. This little volume is designed only to provide a glimpse of the county.

One

Exploration to Reconstruction

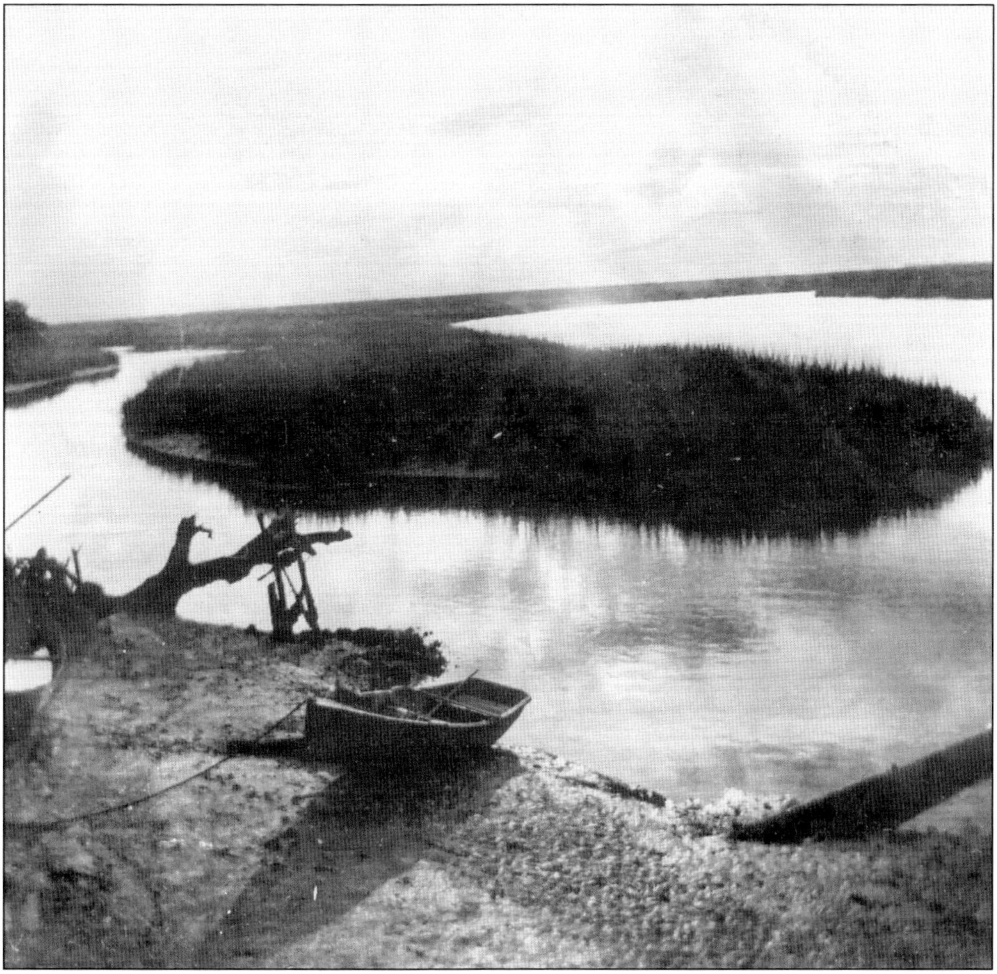

When Columbus arrived in the New World in 1492, a small American Indian cultural group known as the Guale—pronounced "Wah-lee"—lived on Ossabaw, St. Catherine's, and Sapelo Islands and on the mainland immediately to the west. The tidal marshes provided diverse foods including shellfish, and shell middens—trash piles left by American Indians—still line the edges of these estuaries. Over the ensuing centuries, Europeans, Africans, and American Indians interacted with each other and the landscape to form the history of Liberty County. (Photograph by Julia Maxwell King; courtesy of the Springfield Legacy Foundation.)

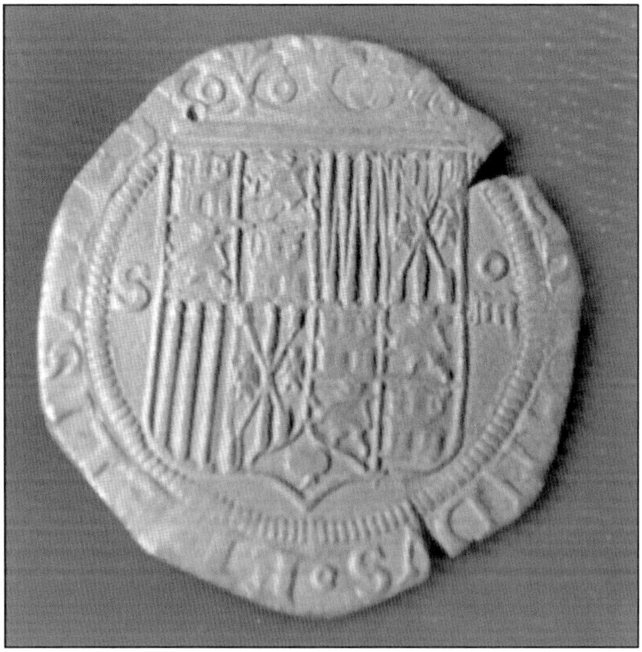

In 1526, Lucas Vasquez de Allyón landed near Sapelo Sound with a group of 650 Spanish colonists including the first Africans brought to North America. He established San Miguel de Gualdape, the first European colony in the future United States. Within months, famine and disease killed hundreds of colonists including Allyón, the African slaves fled, and 150 survivors returned to Santo Domingo. The coin pictured here is the only physical evidence of the San Miguel colony. (Courtesy of the Springfield Legacy Foundation.)

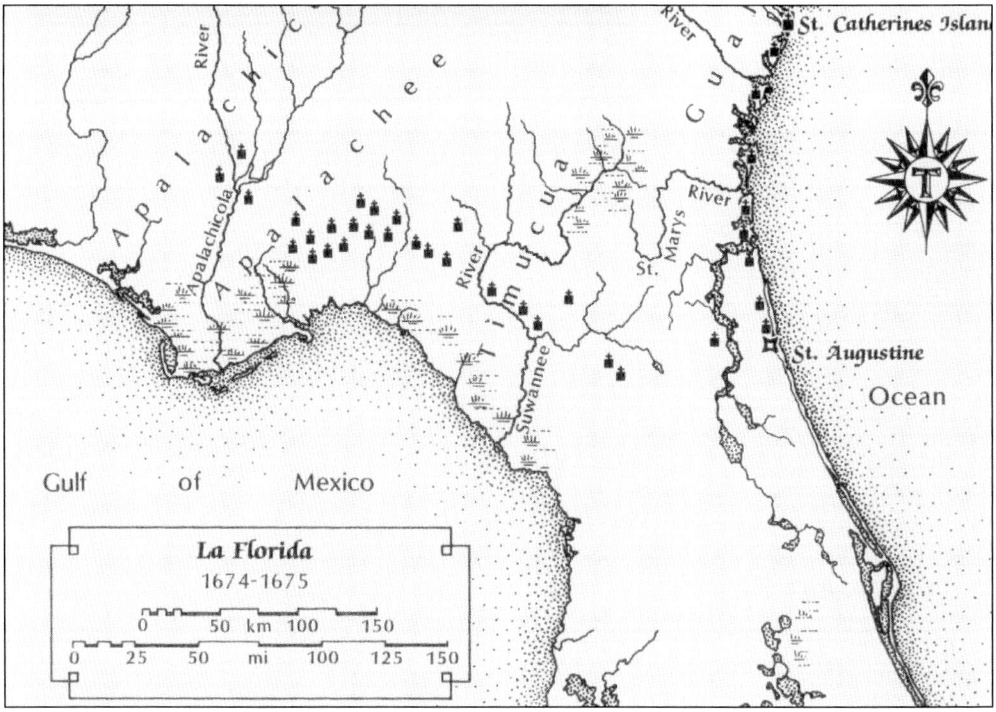

The Spanish did not attempt to colonize North America again until 1563 when they established St. Augustine. To further repel English incursions into La Florida and to protect the critical trade route along the Gulf Stream from the coast of the Caribbean to the Outer Banks, the Spanish built a system of missions. Stretching from Mobile Bay around the horn of Florida and north to the Chesapeake Bay, the Atlantic mission system was far more extensive than the mission system established in California. (Courtesy of the Springfield Legacy Foundation.)

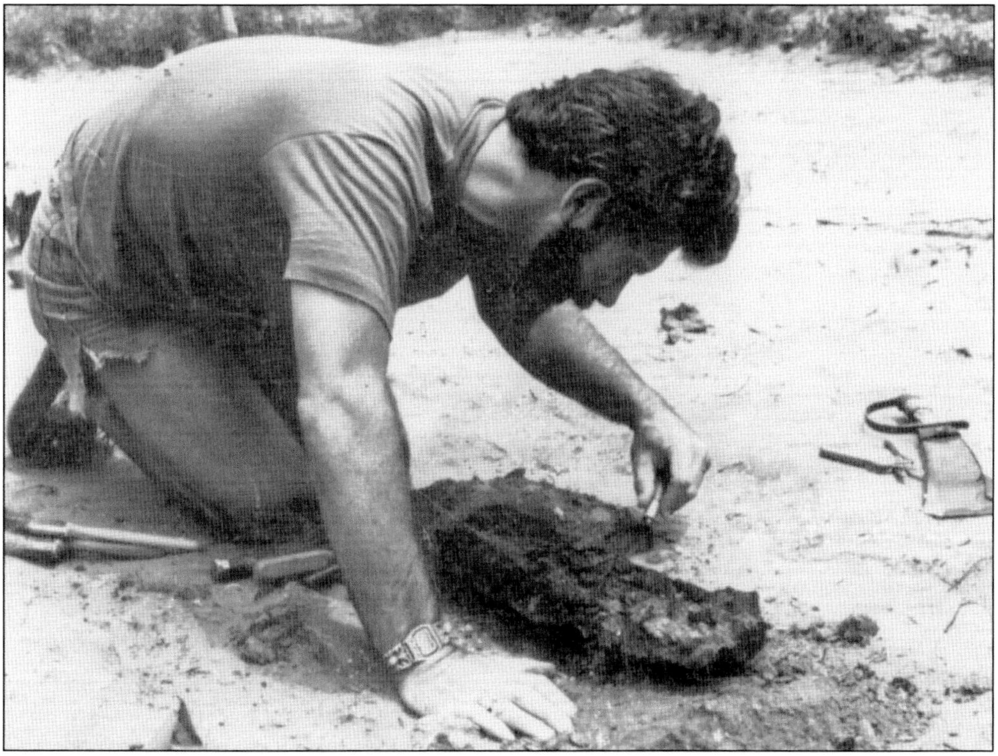

On St. Catherine's Island—or Santa Catalina, according to the Spanish—Franciscan priests established a mission in the late 1500s. The complex had a church, well, and support buildings for the missionaries who converted the Guales to Christianity. In 1597, two Franciscans were murdered after admonishing a tribal leader for taking a second wife. The Spanish abandoned the mission on St. Catherine's in the 1680s leaving their claim to the northern Georgia coast largely unprotected from the English. The mission was excavated by Dr. David Hurst Thomas, shown here, beginning in the 1970s. (Courtesy of the Edward John Noble Foundation.)

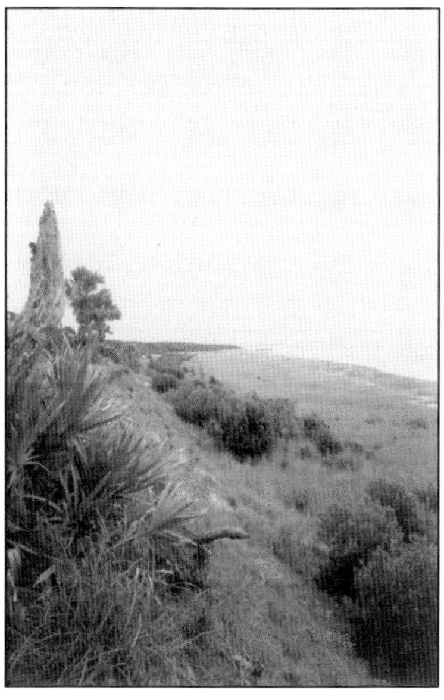

When Gen. James Oglethorpe organized the English colony of Georgia in 1733, he engaged the services of Mary Musgrove, who was born Coosaponakeesa, to negotiate with the Creek Indians. In return for her invaluable assistance, Oglethorpe promised her title to Ossabaw, St. Catherine's, and Sapelo Islands and then returned to England. When the Georgia Trustees refused to honor his offer, Mary Musgrove Bosomworth threatened to provoke a war. The trustees responded by granting her St. Catherine's Island, the largest land grant made directly to a woman in colonial Georgia. (Courtesy of the Springfield Legacy Foundation.)

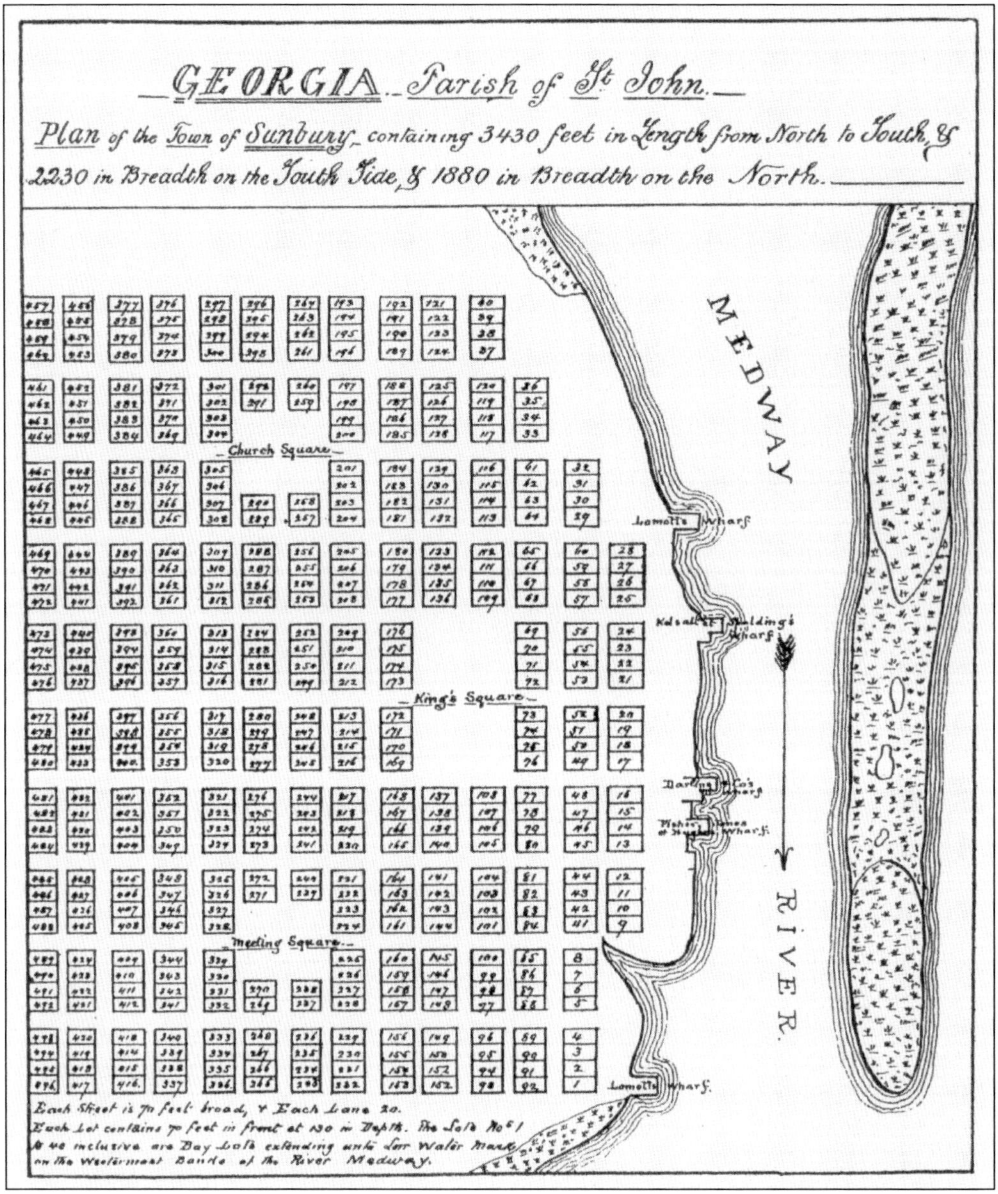

During the colonial period, the area that became Liberty, McIntosh, and Long counties was known as St. John's Parish. In 1757, a prosperous colonist, Mark Carr, began selling lots from lands he owned on a bluff on the Medway River facing the Atlantic Ocean and St. Catherine's Sound. Settlers established the town of Sunbury, named after Carr's ancestral home in Middlesex County, England. This map shows the town plan of Sunbury. Designed in the fashion of contemporary towns like Savannah, Georgia, and Lunenburg, Nova Scotia, Sunbury was organized with town lots situated on squares. Owners of town lots usually had larger plantation tracts for farming nearby. Sunbury became a port of entry for trade with the English, and within 20 years of its founding, the town rivaled Savannah with over 1,000 residents. Despite the sharp decline in Sunbury's fortunes after the Revolutionary War, the town became Liberty County's first county seat. Hurricanes and malaria further wreaked havoc on Sunbury in the 1800s, yet ships continued to make port in the town until the early 20th century. (Courtesy of Sunbury Historic Site.)

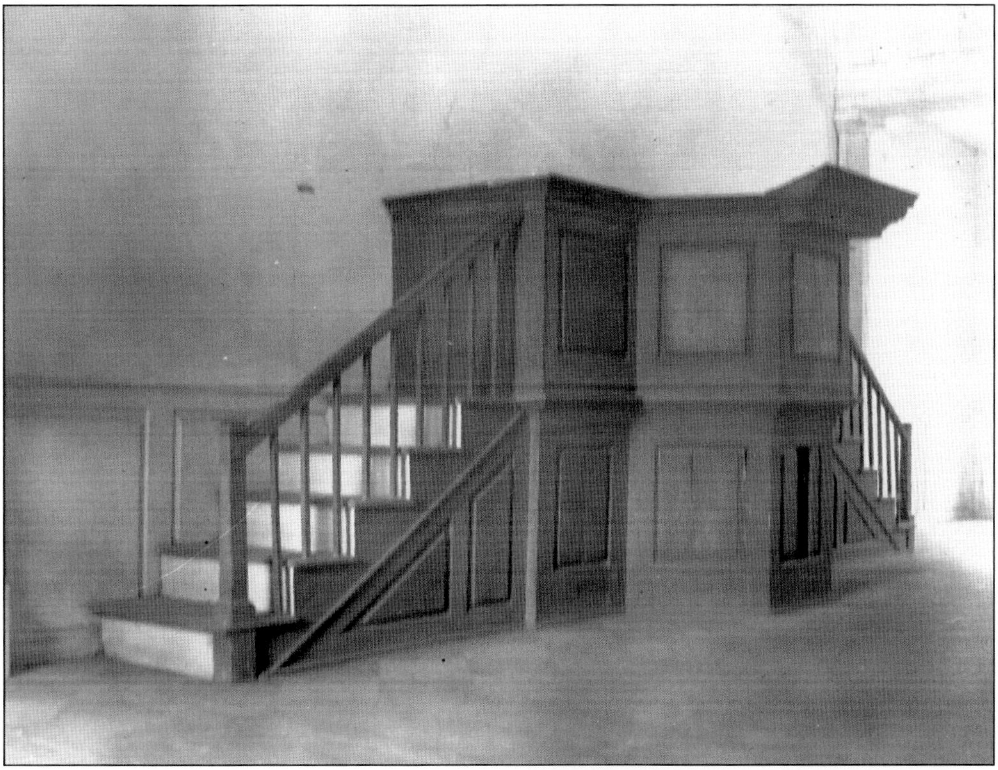

General Oglethorpe welcomed Protestant dissidents, persecuted for their religious beliefs, to settle on land grants in the new colony of Georgia. In 1752, three men representing Puritans in Dorchester, South Carolina, west of Charleston, visited lands in St. John's Parish situated midway between the Savannah and Altamaha Rivers. In possession of land grants from the English king, the Dorchester Puritans moved to the Midway district in the 1750s accompanied by their African slaves. The location for their meetinghouse—the place for worship and governance—was to be, according to Puritan custom, equally convenient for most of the parishioners. In 1756, John Stevens gave 2 acres of land bordering the Sunbury and Barrington Ferry Roads, now Martin Road and U.S. Route 17, and the first Midway meetinghouse was built. (Photograph by Julia Maxwell King; courtesy of the Springfield Legacy Foundation.)

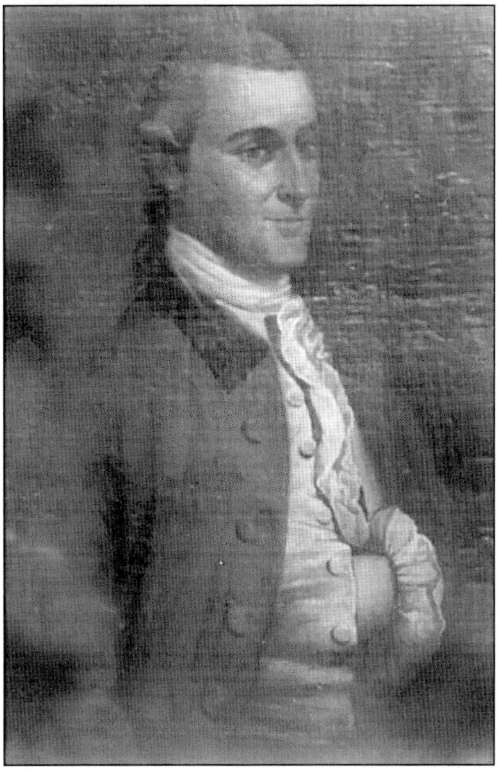

William Maxwell was an early settler of the Midway district. (Courtesy of the Springfield Legacy Foundation.)

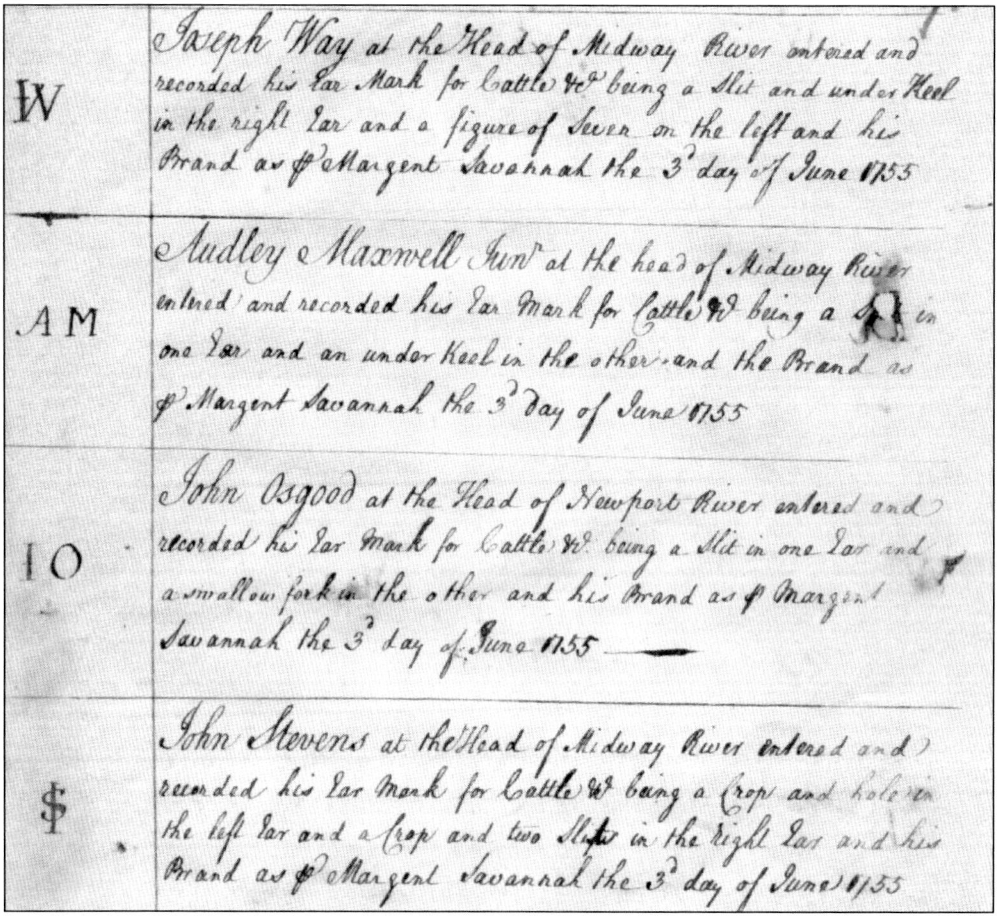

Brand	Entry
W	Joseph Way at the Head of Midway River entered and recorded his Ear Mark for Cattle &c being a Slit and under Keel in the right Ear and a figure of Seven on the left and his Brand as ℘ Margent Savannah the 3d day of June 1755
AM	Audley Maxwell Junr at the head of Midway River entered and recorded his Ear Mark for Cattle &c being a [illegible] in one Ear and an under Keel in the other and the Brand as ℘ Margent Savannah the 3d day of June 1755
IO	John Osgood at the Head of Newport River entered and recorded his Ear Mark for Cattle &c being a Slit in one Ear and a swallow fork in the other and his Brand as ℘ Margent Savannah the 3d day of June 1755
$	John Stevens at the Head of Midway River entered and recorded his Ear Mark for Cattle &c being a Crop and hole in the left Ear and a Crop and two Slits in the right Ear and his Brand as ℘ Margent Savannah the 3d day of June 1755

In addition to growing rice and upland crops, settlers also raised cattle. Until the mid-20th century, cattle roamed freely on the land. Pictured here is a sample of the registered brands used to mark and identify cattle in the 1700s in St. John's Parish. (Courtesy of the Springfield Legacy Foundation.)

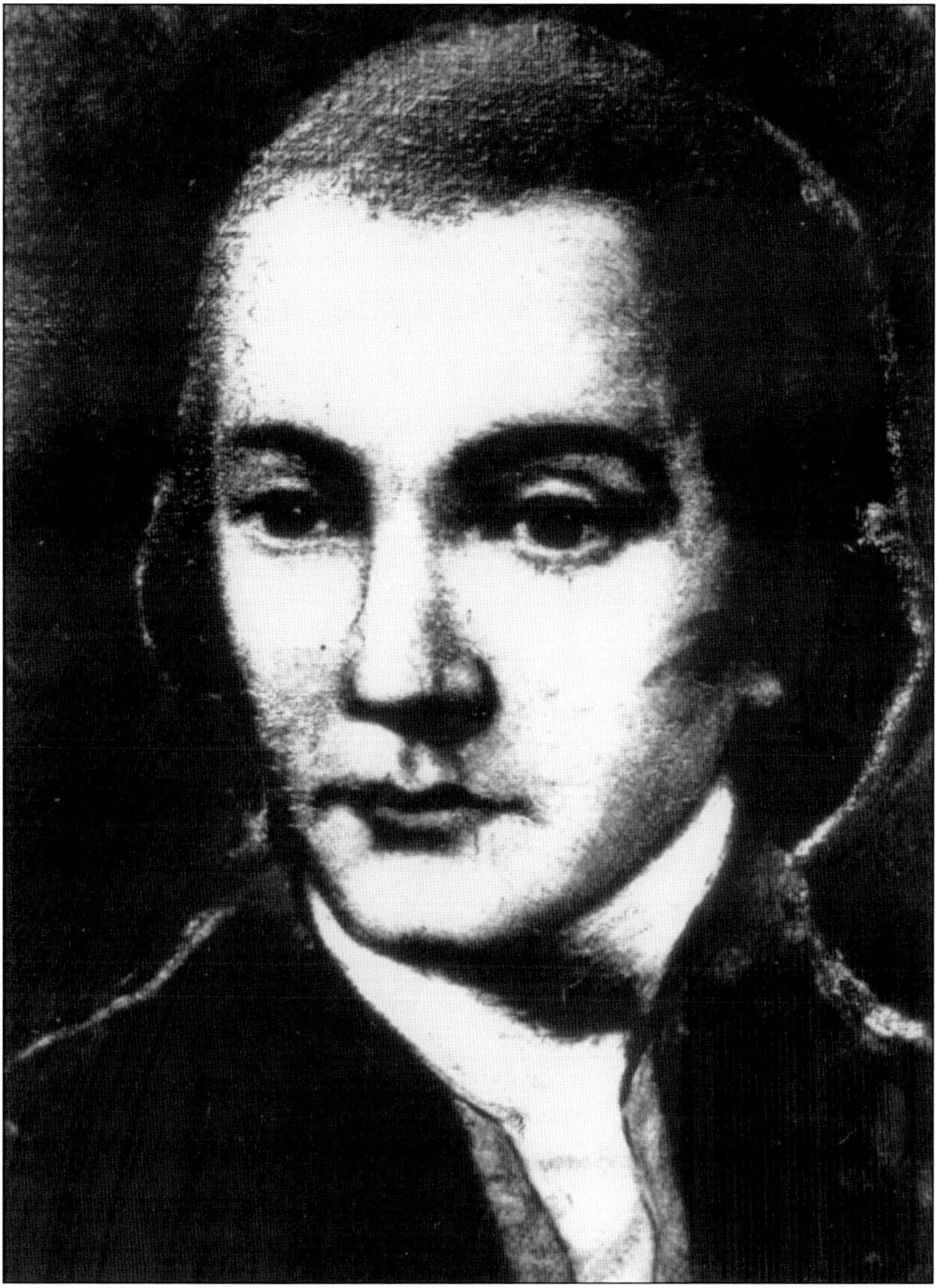

Dr. Lyman Hall was a crucial figure in the struggle for American independence. A physician by training, Dr. Hall lived at Hall's Knoll, his plantation atop a hill in the swamp northwest of the Midway meetinghouse. To ratify the Declaration of Independence, Congress required unanimous approval of all 13 colonies. A majority of Georgians were loyal to the king, but Dr. Hall convinced his fellow delegates to sign the Declaration of Independence. He is portrayed here in an oil painting of unknown date and origin. (Courtesy of the Midway Museum.)

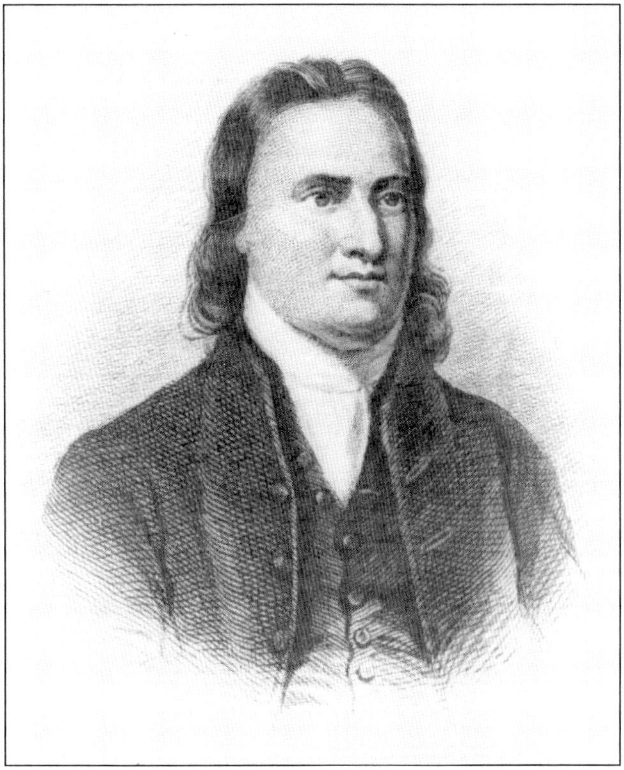

Also representing Georgia from St. John's Parish was Button Gwinnett, an English merchant who purchased St. Catherine's Island from Mary Musgrove Bosomworth's widower in 1774. Very different than Dr. Hall in mind and temperament, Gwinnett had a short career following his moment of fame in Philadelphia. In 1777, Gwinnett became Georgia's governor and immediately began to antagonize Col. Lachlan McIntosh, commander of Continental troops in Georgia. After Gwinnett's interference in a military campaign by Colonel McIntosh resulted in disaster, the two men participated in a duel held in Savannah on May 16, 1777. Gwinnett was wounded and died a few days later. (Courtesy of the Midway Museum.)

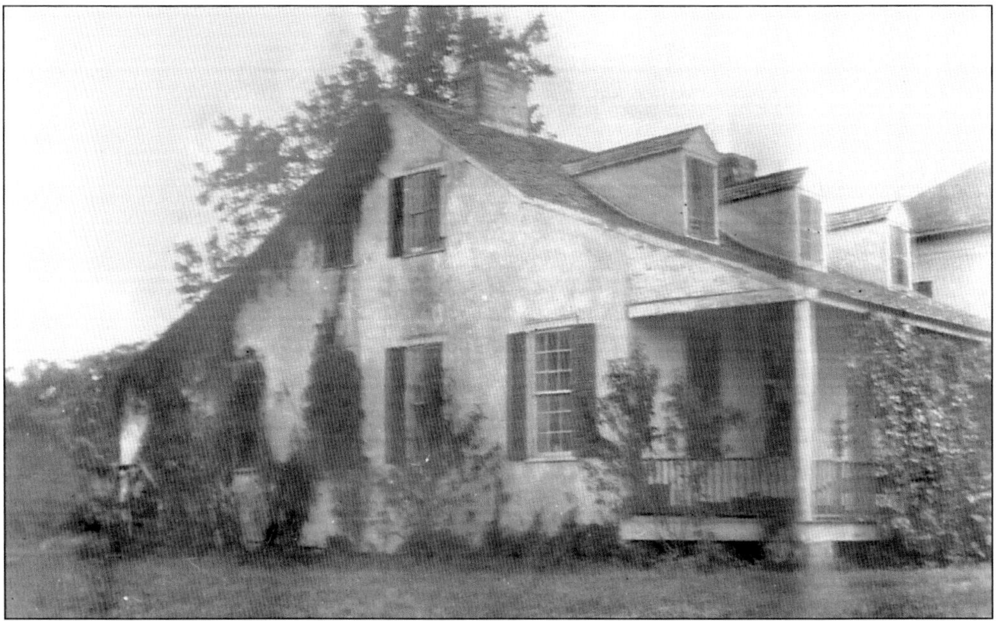

Known as the Button-Gwinnett House, this home faces west over Waldburg Creek on St. Catherine's Island. Gwinnett owned and lived on the island from 1774 until his death in 1777. Local tradition associates the house with Gwinnett. A source of debate, some legends maintain that the house was built by Mary Musgrove Bosomworth. The house is pictured here in the late 1800s. (Photograph by Julia King; courtesy of the Springfield Legacy Foundation.)

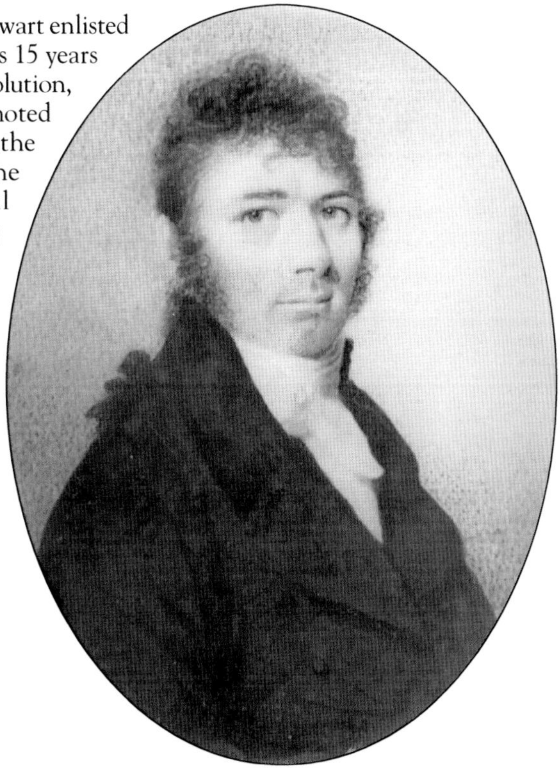

Born in 1761 in St. Johns Parish, Daniel Stewart enlisted in the general militia in 1776 when he was 15 years old. Before the end of the American Revolution, he organized a cavalry brigade, was promoted to the rank of colonel, and commanded the minutemen of Georgia. After the war, he attained the rank of brigadier general and served in many offices including Liberty County sheriff, state senator, and state representative. (Courtesy of the Midway Museum.)

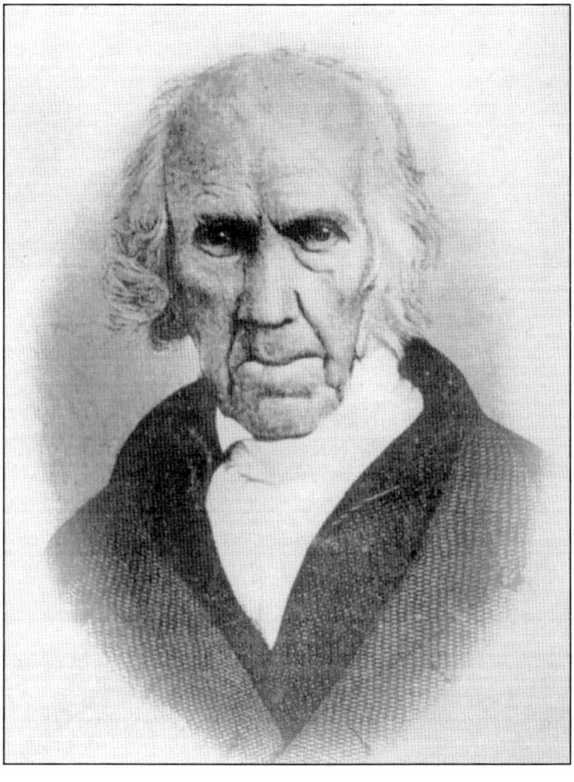

Rev. William McWhir became headmaster of Sunbury Academy, one of the first private schools in Georgia, in 1791. An Irishman by birth, McWhir immigrated to the United States in 1783. For several years, he served as principal at a school where George Washington served as trustee and sent his stepchildren. Through discipline and elevated academic standards, McWhir refined Sunbury Academy into one of the best schools in Georgia. (Courtesy of the Midway Museum.)

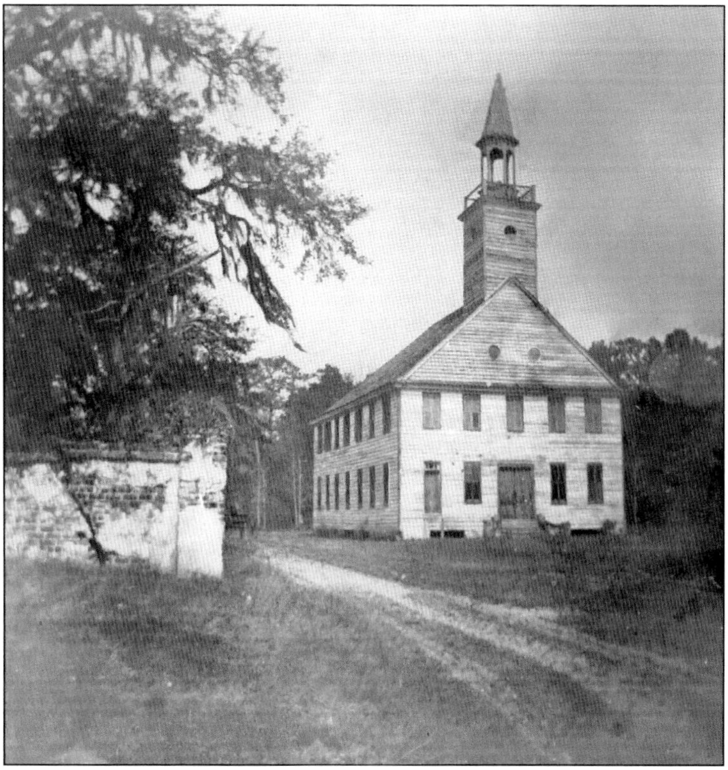

During the American Revolution, British troops visited St. John's Parish and burned the Midway Church. After the war, parishioners rebuilt their meetinghouse in 1792 and retained a congregational minister to fill the new pulpit. This photograph was taken when the rebuilt Midway Church was about 100 years old. (Photograph by Julia King; courtesy of the Springfield Legacy Foundation.)

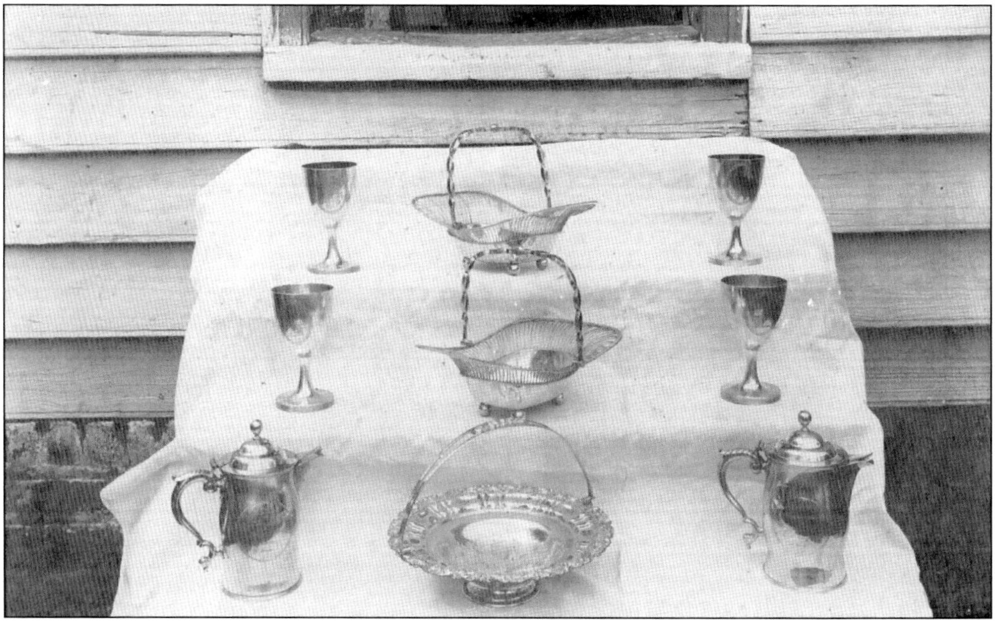

Congregationalists in the Midway district maintained strong ties with their Puritan roots and emphasized the tenets of education, faith, and hard work in their culture. Communicants at Midway Church attended religious services all day on Sunday. Many African slaves also attended services and became members of Midway Church. Pictured here is the original silver communion service from the 1792 Midway congregation. (Courtesy of the Midway Museum.)

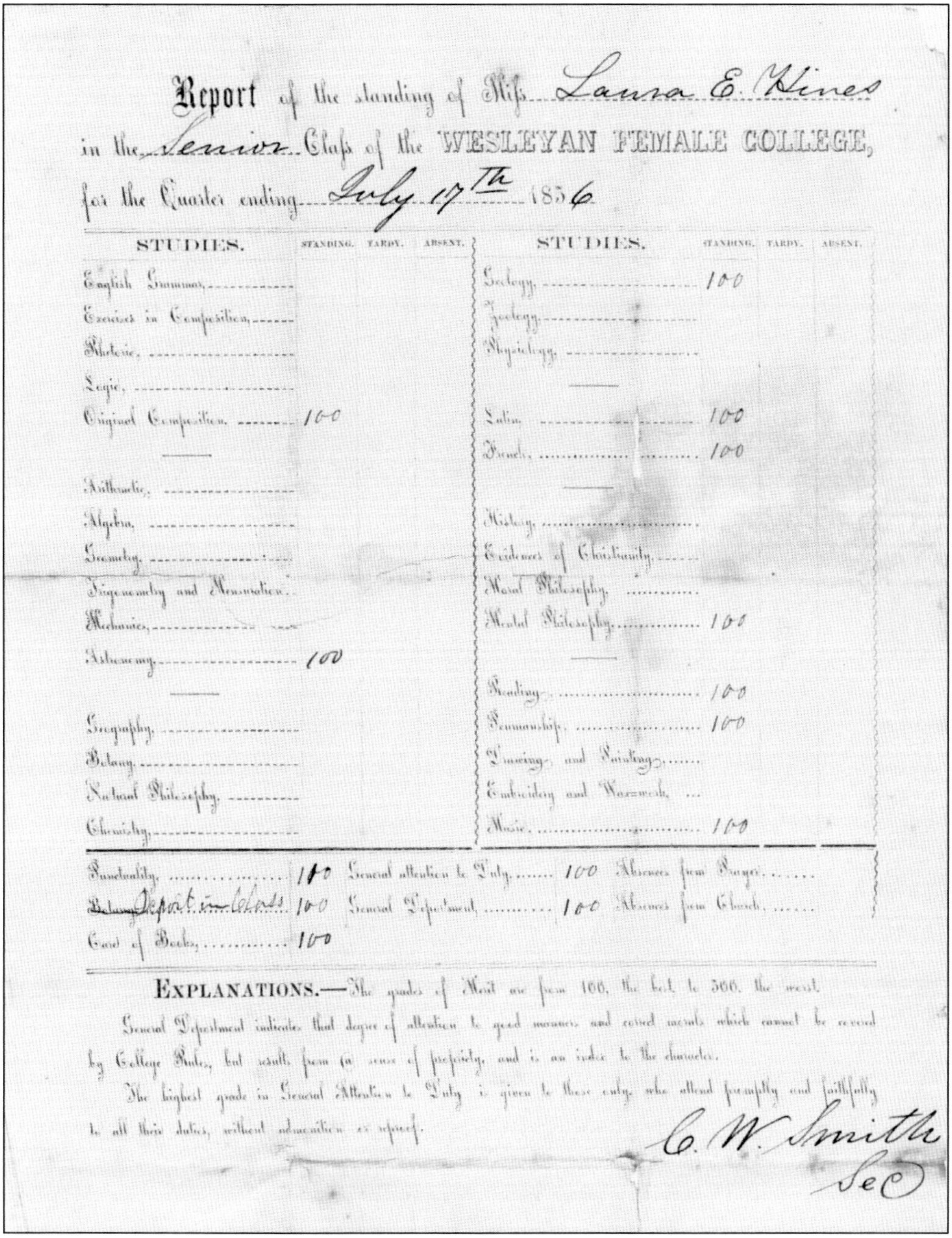
Report of the standing of Miss Laura E. Hines

in the Senior Class of the WESLEYAN FEMALE COLLEGE,

for the Quarter ending July 17th 1856

STUDIES.	STANDING.	TARDY.	ABSENT.	STUDIES.	STANDING.	TARDY.	ABSENT.
English Grammar,				Geology,	100		
Exercises in Composition,				Zoology,			
Rhetoric,				Physiology,			
Logic,							
Original Composition,	100			Latin,	100		
				French,	100		
Arithmetic,							
Algebra,				History,			
Geometry,				Evidences of Christianity,			
Trigonometry and Mensuration,				Moral Philosophy,			
Mechanics,				Mental Philosophy,	100		
Astronomy,	100						
				Reading,	100		
Geography,				Penmanship,	100		
Botany,				Drawing and Painting,			
Natural Philosophy,				Embroidery and Wax-work,			
Chemistry,				Music,	100		

Punctuality,	100	General attention to Duty,	100	Absences from Prayers,	
~~Behavior~~ Deport in Class	100	General Deportment,	100	Absences from Church,	
Care of Books,	100				

EXPLANATIONS.—The grades of Merit are from 100, the best, to 300, the worst.

General Deportment indicates that degree of attention to good manners and correct morals which cannot be reached by College Rules, but results from a sense of propriety, and is an index to the character.

The highest grade in General Attention to Duty is given to those only who attend promptly and faithfully to all their duties, without admonition or reproof.

C. W. Smith
Sec.

White boys and girls of the Midway district were highly educated and both sexes attended college. Boys attended schools such as Yale, Princeton, and Cambridge. When Wesleyan College opened in Macon, Georgia, the school became the first institution of higher education chartered for women in the United States. Shown here is Laura Hines's Wesleyan report card. A granddaughter of Charlton Hines, founder of Hinesville in 1837, Laura matriculated at the age of 14 and graduated as valedictorian in 1856. (Courtesy of the Springfield Legacy Foundation.)

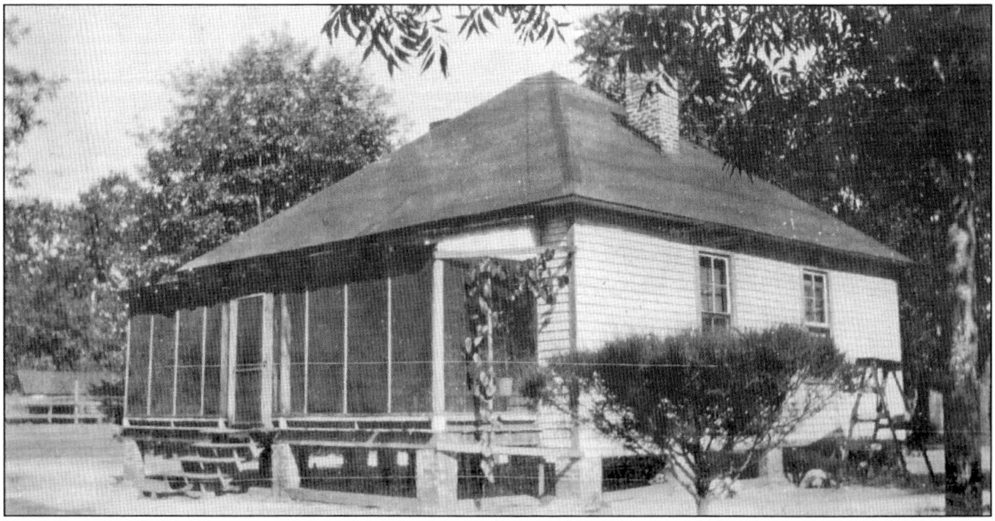

Plantation homes in Liberty County were not grand affairs as seen in other parts of the South. Partly because most whites did not remain in residence through the malaria season, homes tended to be small and were designed to remain cool and well ventilated. The house pictured here was built around 1840 at Palmyra Plantation and features four rooms and a central passage. Built almost exclusively of wood, few antebellum houses survive in Liberty County due to hurricanes or fire. (Courtesy of the Springfield Legacy Foundation.)

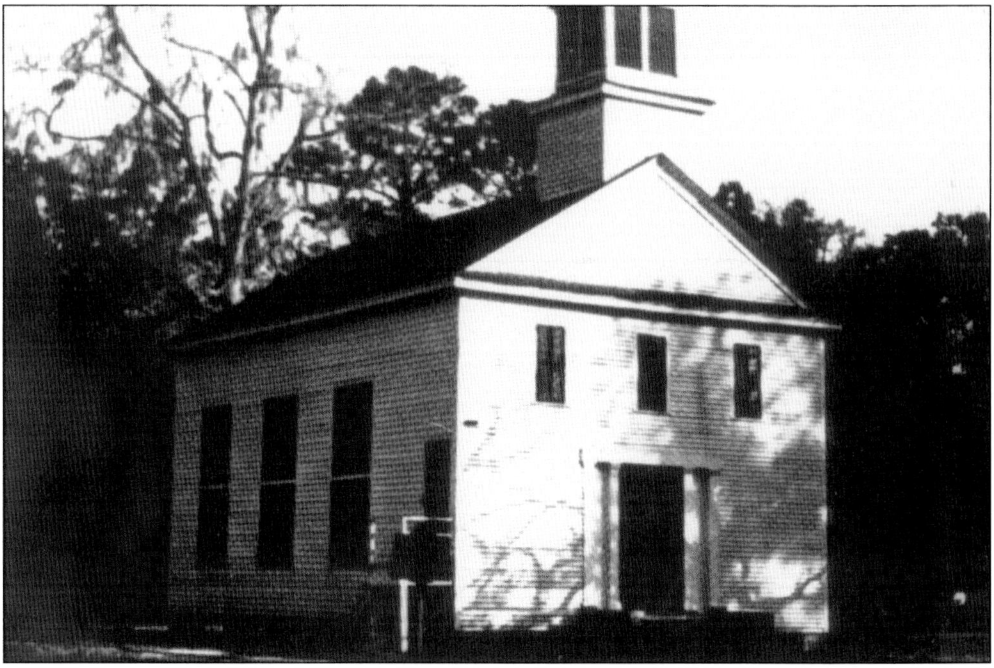

Built in 1854 on land donated by Bartholemew Busby, owner of the nearby Melon Bluff Plantation, the Dorchester Presbyterian Church served the antebellum communities of Colonels Island and Sunbury. After the Civil War, the remaining white families centered activities in Dorchester Village, which evolved around the church. Otis Amason restored the church in the late 20th century with assistance from Charles M. Jones and monthly services continued into the 21st century. (Courtesy of the Liberty County Herald.)

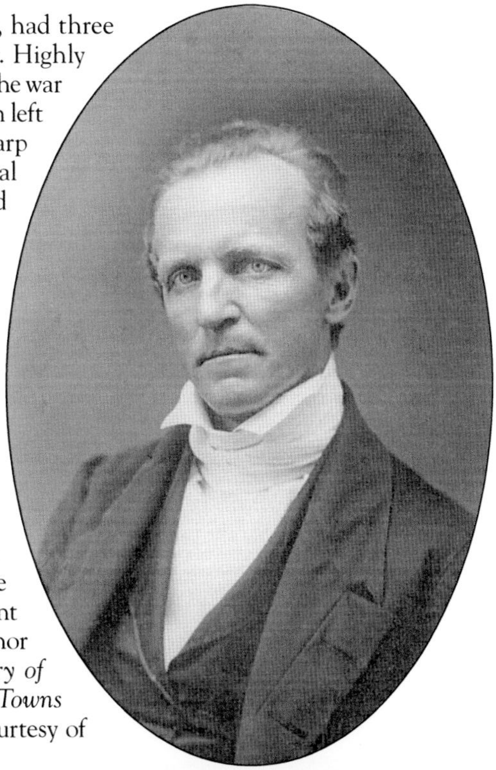

Rev. Charles Colcock Jones and his wife, Mary, had three children prior to the outbreak of the Civil War. Highly educated young adults, their lives were changed by the war and its aftermath. The three siblings (bottom, from left to right) were Charles Colcock Jones Jr., Mary Sharp Jones, and Joseph Jones. Joseph received a medical degree from the University of Pennsylvania and succeeded Joseph LeConte as professor of chemistry and geology at the University of Georgia. With the outbreak of the Civil War, Joseph and his brother, Charles Jr., served the Confederacy, the former working for the surgeon general of the Confederacy and the latter as the secessionist mayor of Savannah and chief of artillery for the military district of Georgia. After the war, Joseph attempted to keep the three Jones plantations—Montevideo, Maybank, and Arcadia—but found it impossible. He spent the remainder of his life in Louisiana studying tropical diseases and teaching medicine. His brother, Charles Jr. (top), a graduate of both Princeton and Harvard, became a prominent early southern archaeologist, historian, and author of many books including a four-volume *History of Georgia*, *Antiquities of the Southern Indians*, *Dead Towns of Georgia*, and a collection of Gullah tales. (Courtesy of the Midway Museum.)

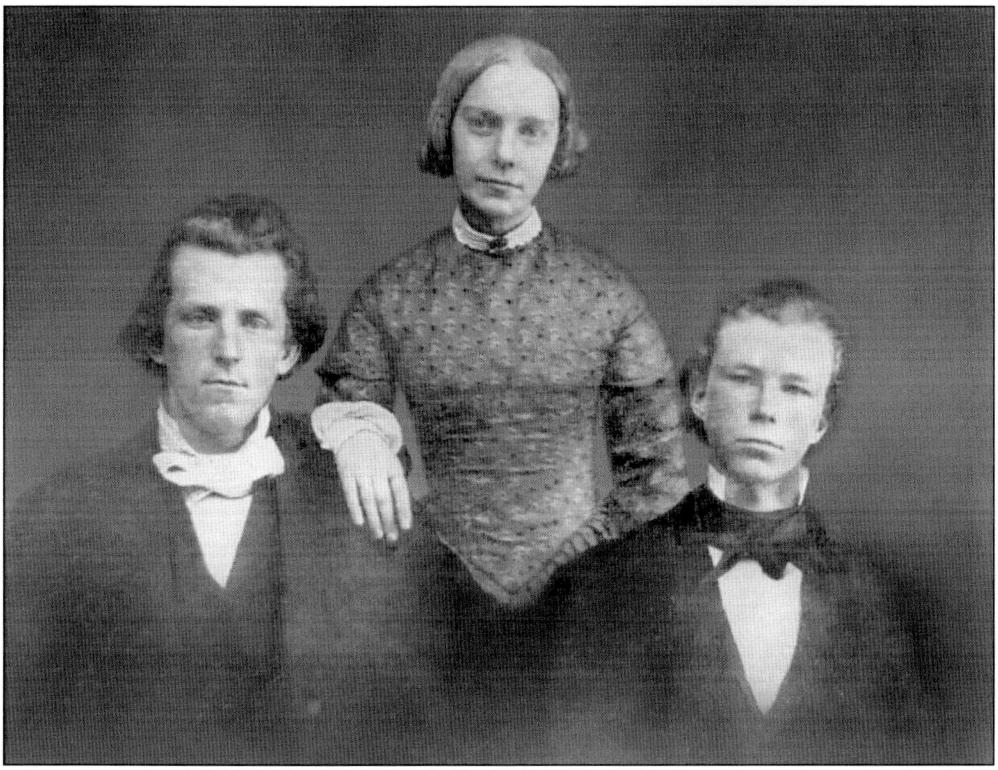

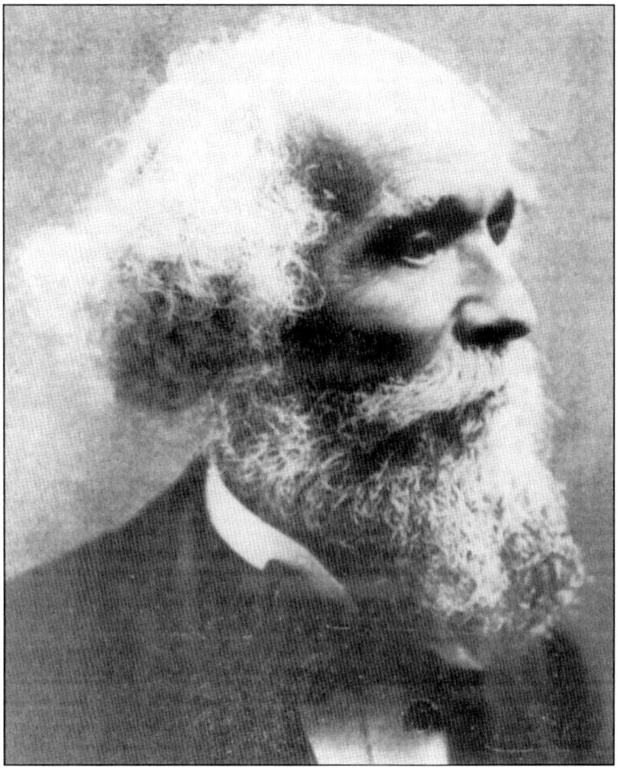

Among other highly educated young men caught in the Civil War era were John (top) and Joseph LeConte (bottom), sons of noted botanist Louis LeConte. Having grown up at Woodmanston—their father's expansive rice plantation near Riceboro—the brothers both relished the natural sciences. John earned an M.D. and taught physics and chemistry at the University of Georgia and the University of South Carolina. After the Civil War, the LeConte brothers left the South and helped establish the University of California at Berkeley. In June 1869, John was named acting president of the university. Among his many contributions to science, he measured the speed of sound and demonstrated that flames are sensitive to sound. (Courtesy of the Midway Museum.)

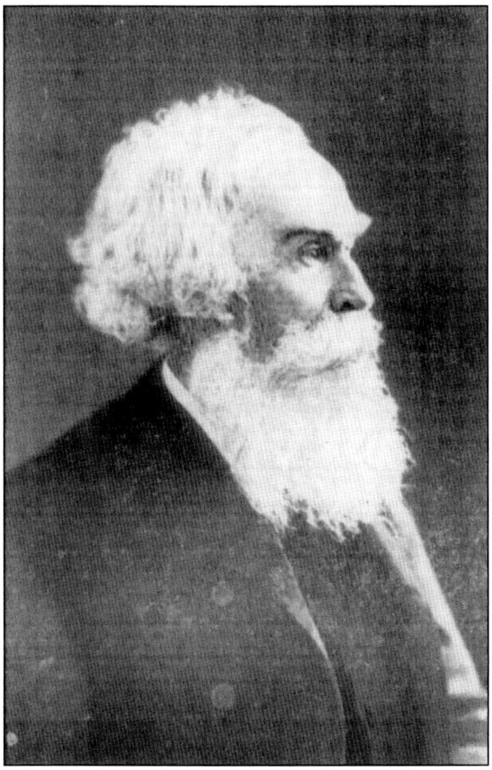

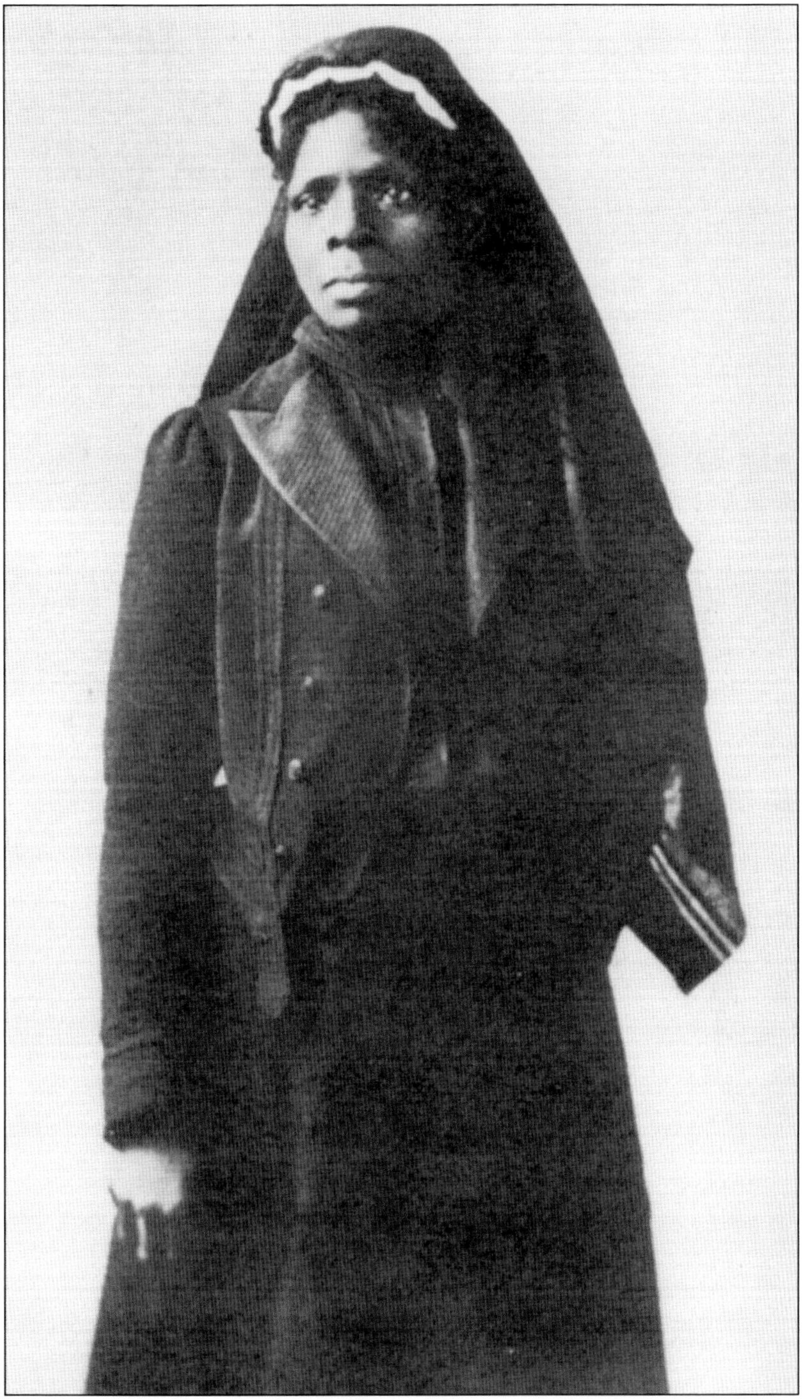

Born a slave at the Grest Plantation near Isle of Wight, Susie King Taylor moved to Savannah at an early age where she received an education, a rare and illegal occurrence in the antebellum South. During the Civil War, she married an African American Union soldier. Because of her education, Taylor worked as a teacher and as a nurse in federal camps. (Courtesy Susie King Taylor, *Reminiscences of My Life in Camp*, 1902.)

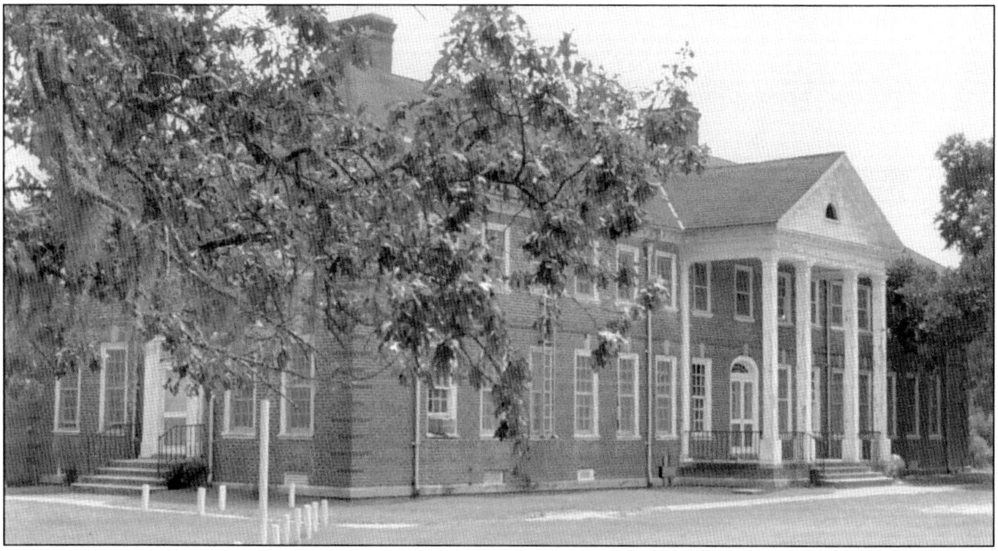

In 1892, W. A. Golden, an African American farmer, donated land for a new Congregational church and school just west of the Midway Church. Dorchester Academy flourished as a day and boarding school for African American students. This photograph was taken on the grounds of Dorchester Academy in the 1930s. In over 60 years, Dorchester grew from a boarding school to an autonomous center of African American social and economic activity. Pictured here are members of the Union Brotherhood Society standing in front of the gristmill used to convert corn into meal and grits. Founded in 1932, the society helped uninsured African Americans pay for proper burials to avoid being taken advantage of by lenders. Members pictured here during an anniversary—or "society turning out"—are (from left to right) Janie Stevens, Union Brotherhood Society founder William McKinley Walthour Sr., Rev. Richard W. Monroe, Joe L. Bowers, Frank Baker, Phillip Hartwell, William "Bill" Brown, Wilhelmina Walthour, Flossie Harley, and Augusta Martin. (Courtesy of Sallie W. Richardson.)

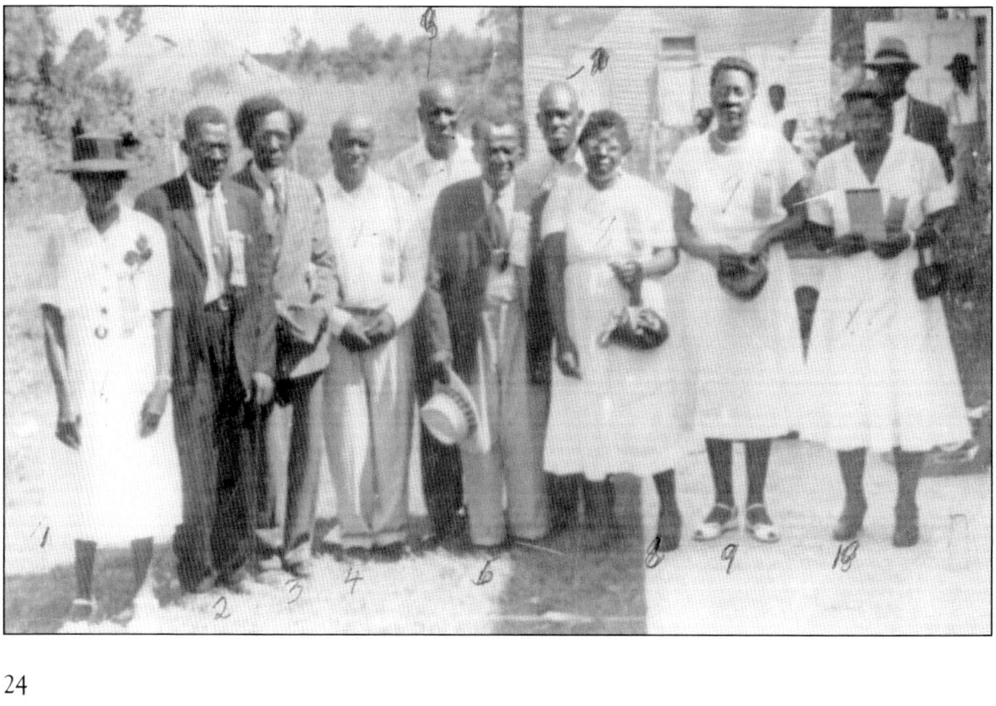

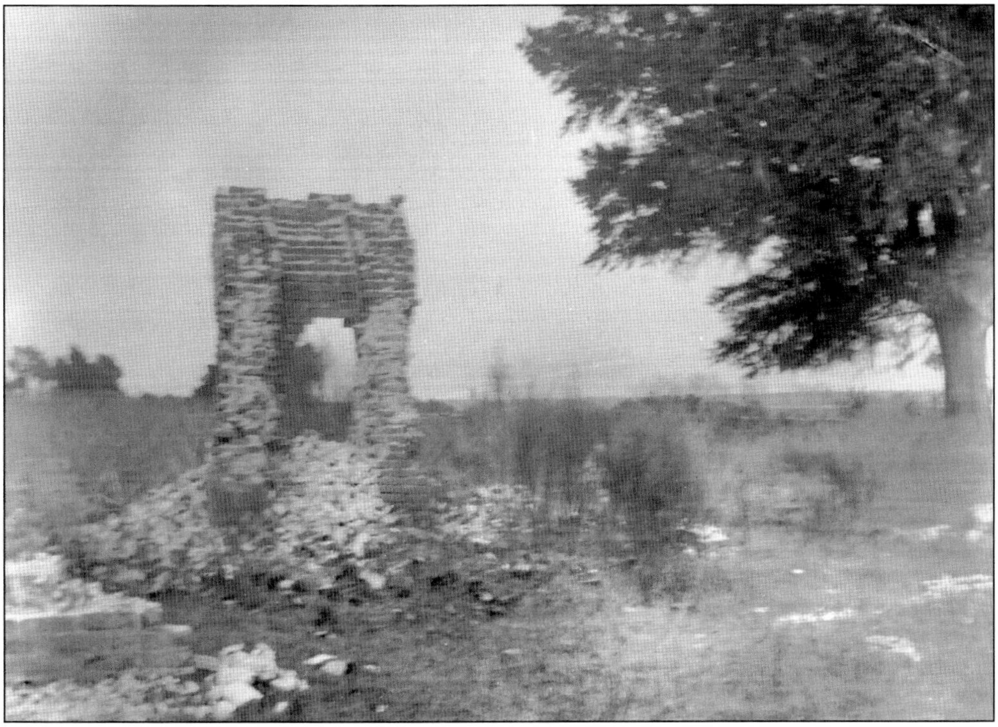

With the end of the Civil War, the plantation era came to an end. Some white families attempted to resume farming, but many abandoned planting. This photograph was taken on the C. C. Jones plantation, Montevideo, near Riceboro in the early 1900s. (Photograph by Julia King; courtesy of the Springfield Legacy Foundation.)

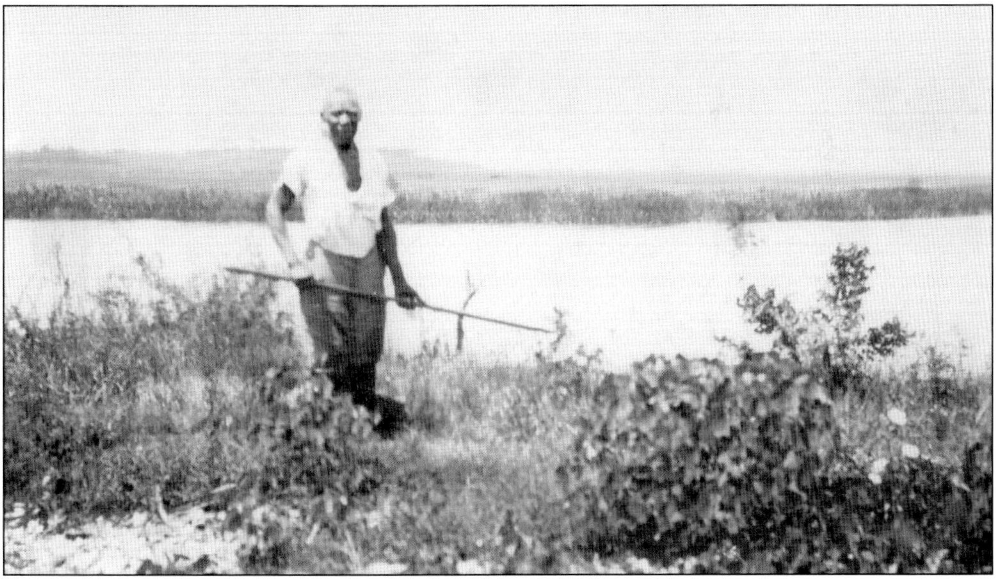

Photographed in the early 1930s and identified as "Uncle," Mr. Quarterman was reputed to be the last surviving former slave on St. Simons Island. He was born at Maxwellton, the Colonels Island Plantation of the King family in Liberty County. (Courtesy of the Springfield Legacy Foundation.)

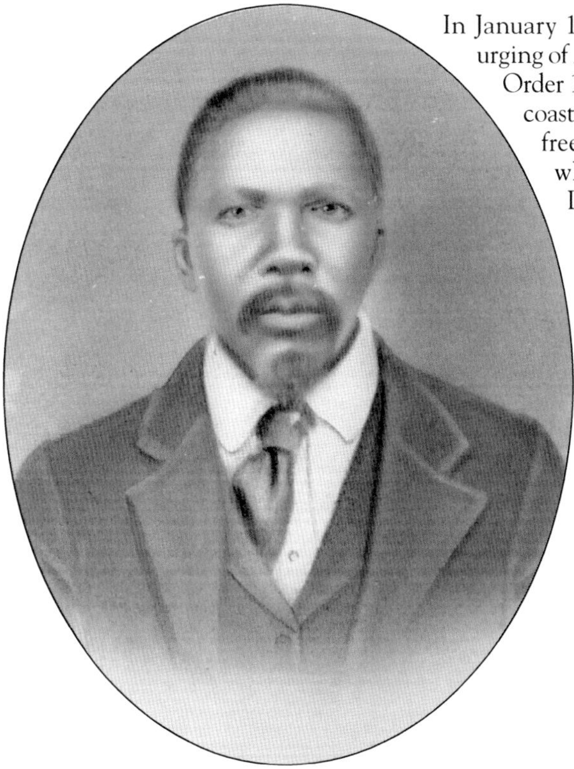

In January 1865, Gen. William T. Sherman, at the urging of African American ministers, issued Field Order 15, which distributed abandoned lands in coastal Georgia and South Carolina among the freedmen. Among Liberty County freedmen who became landowners was Richard Delegal, born a slave near Sunbury. He died in 1903. (Courtesy of the Seabrook Village Foundation.)

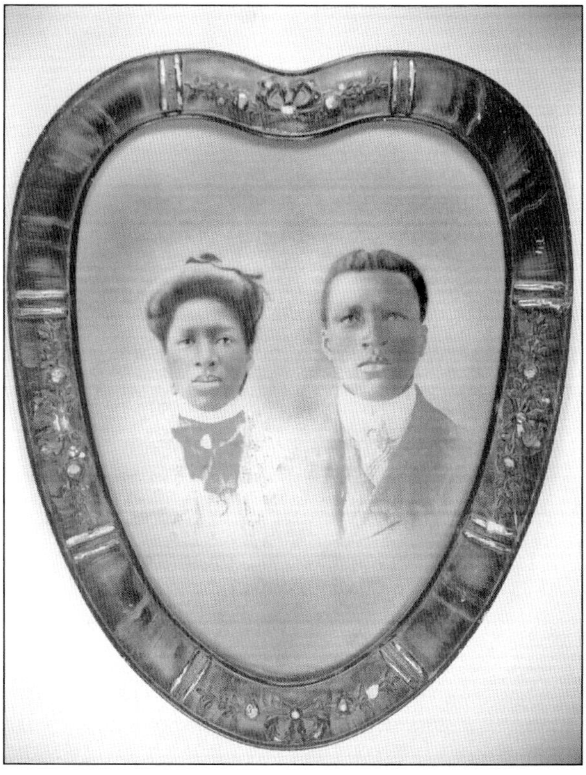

As slaves, Richard Delegal and his wife, Georgia Ann, were not legally able to receive an education. They understood value of education, however, and encouraged their children Helen (left) and John (right) to pursue higher education. Both attended college, and Helen Delegal taught at Dorchester Academy. The young siblings died in 1903 along with their father. (Courtesy of the Seabrook Village Foundation.)

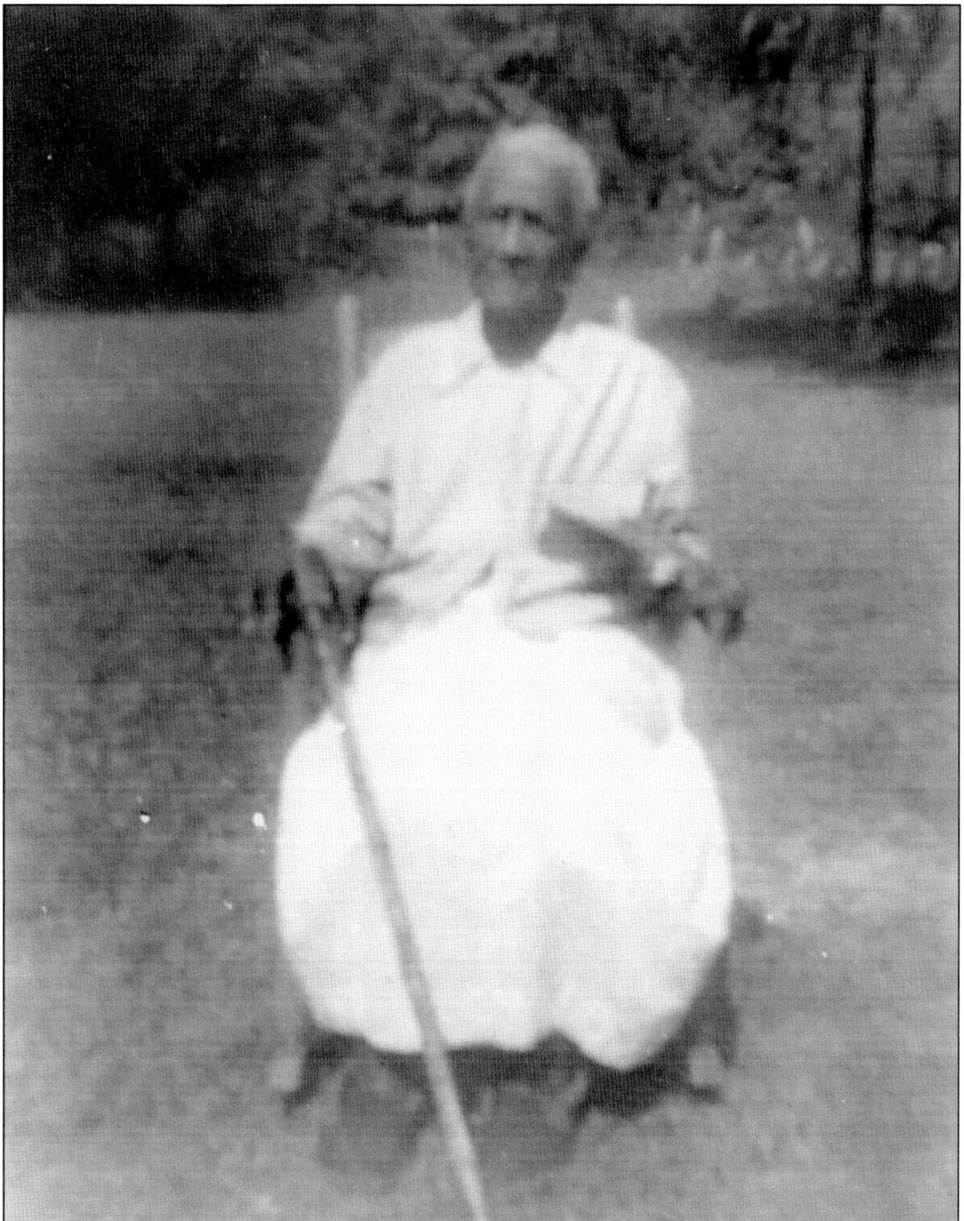

Georgia Ann Delegal was born a slave in 1856 and was 100 years old when this photograph was taken by her granddaughter Mamie Benjamin. She and her husband added to their postwar landholdings in the Trade Hill community west of Sunbury. In the 20th century, the Delegal estate included several hundred acres, a remarkable accomplishment but made more so by the fact that neither Georgia Ann nor her husband, Richard, had a formal education. Family tradition held that Mrs. Delegal was such a good seamstress she could make a dollar profit on each dress sewn. Land prices hovered around one dollar per acre, and in her long life, she managed to buy over 200 acres of land in her own name. Mrs. Delegal was a keen businesswoman and became a philanthropist in the Trade Hill and Seabrook communities, donating land for Seabrook School and the Sunbury Church and cemetery. (Courtesy of the Seabrook Village Foundation.)

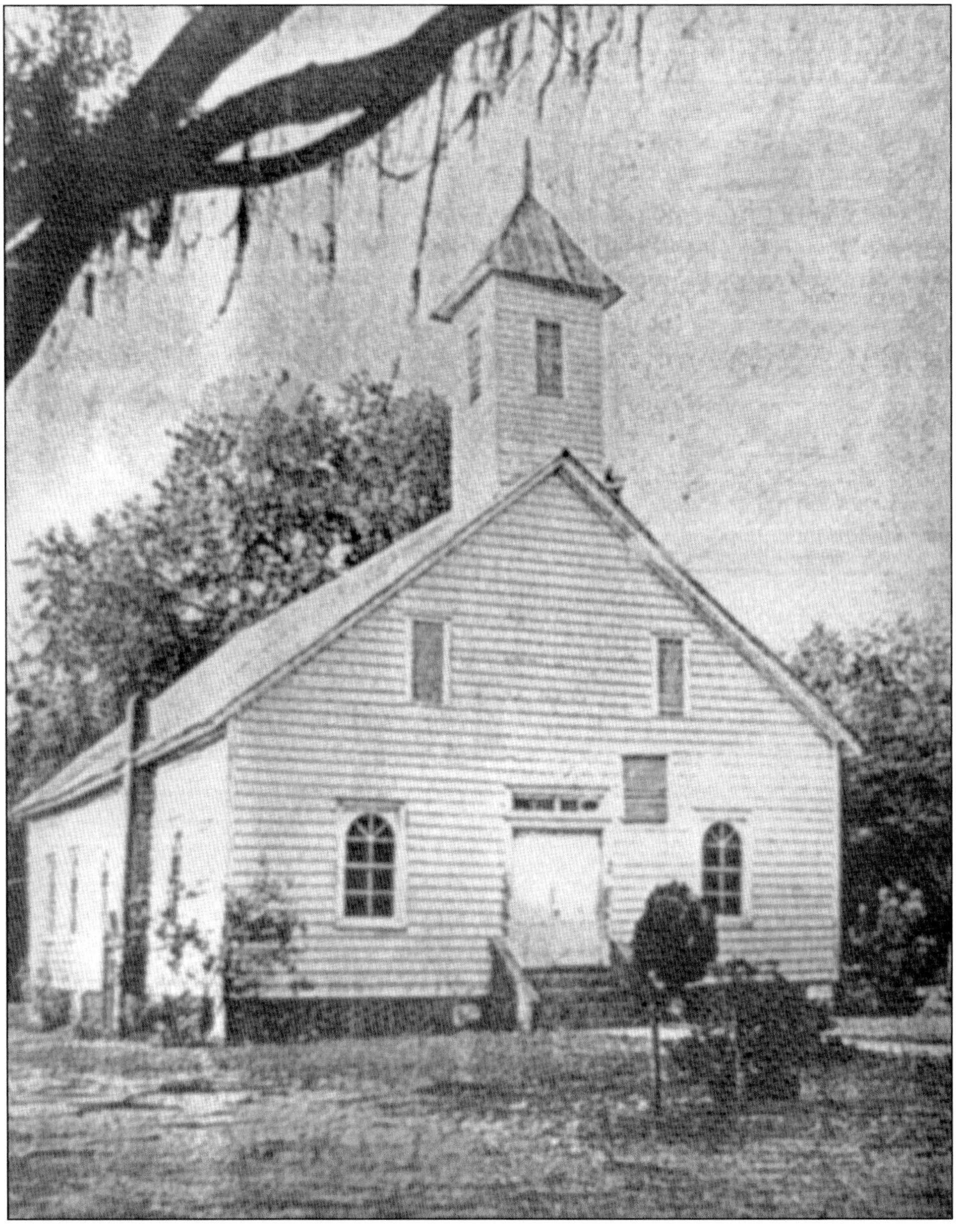

Created in 1806, the Sunbury Baptist Church was the heart of the Sunbury Baptist Convention covering the tidewater of Georgia and lower South Carolina. Originally located near Fort Morris at Sunbury, the church was burned in 1864 by Union troops led by Gen. James Kilpatrick as a signal to federal gunboats offshore. Black communicants rebuilt the church during Reconstruction and continued services at Sunbury until the early 20th century. After the Civil War, African Americans settled on farms 2 miles west of the church and established Palmyra Baptist Church at Trade Hill. In 1918, Sunbury Church members decided to move the building closer to the community, placed the large structure on logs, and rolled it from Sunbury to a piece of land in Trade Hill donated by Georgia Ann Delegal. Later renamed Sunbury Missionary Baptist Church, the wooden church was razed in the 1970s and replaced with a masonry building. (Courtesy of the Seabrook Village Foundation.)

Two

Between the Wars

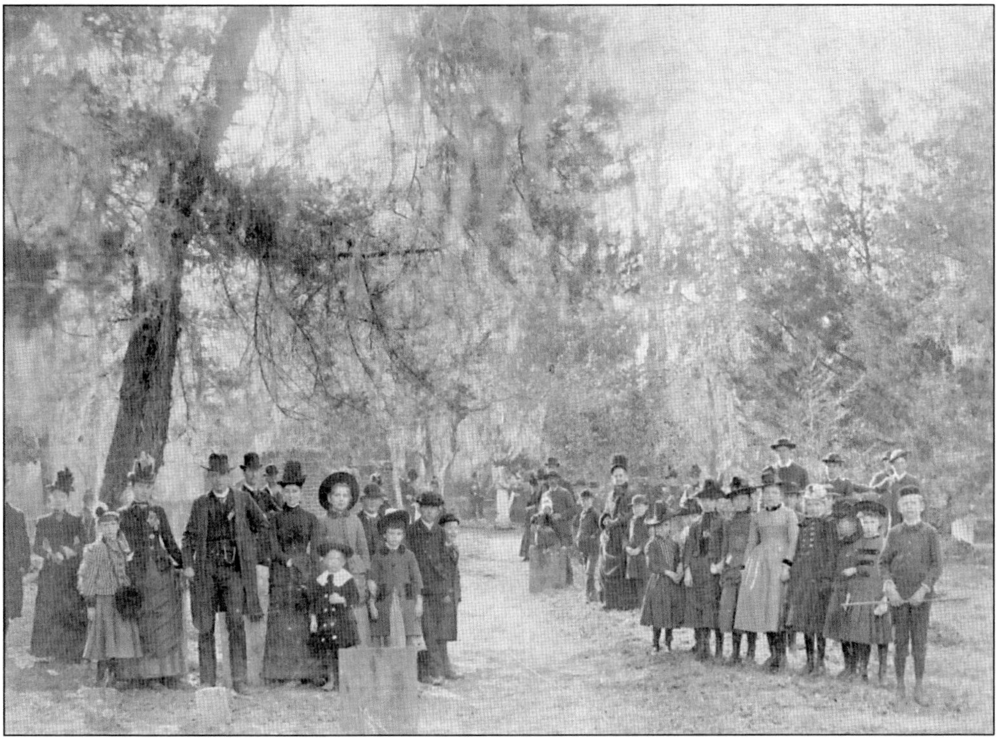

After Reconstruction, Liberty County settled into small-scale farming and a relatively isolated rural existence that persisted through the outbreak of World War II. After its African American members constructed Dorchester Academy and Midway Congregational Church at Golden's Grove in 1872, the Midway Church fell into disuse. Many white families who lived in the plantation district in coastal Liberty County left during and after the Civil War. Families, descended from the original Puritan settlers, gathered in 1887 to reorganize the Midway Society, which has maintained the church and cemetery since that time. (Courtesy of the Midway Museum.)

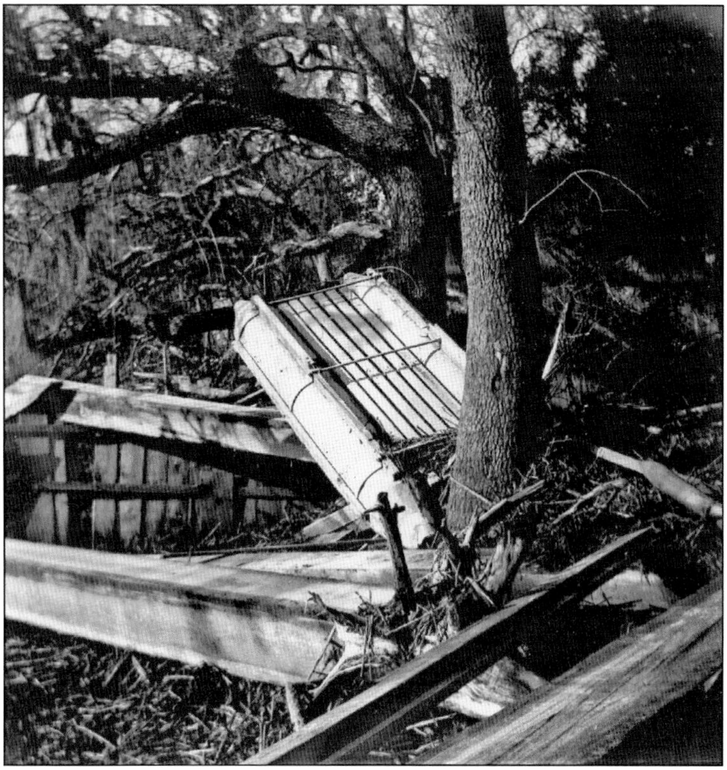

In August 1893, a massive hurricane struck the central Georgia coast. Damaging winds were nothing in comparison to the tidal surge estimated to have been anywhere from 20 to 36 feet in height. Striking just before a spring tide, among the highest of the year, the surge inundated Sapelo, Blackbeard, St. Catherine's, and Ossabaw Islands. This series of photographs by Julia King is the only known visual record of the damage in Liberty County. (Photograph by Julia King; courtesy of the Springfield Legacy Foundation.)

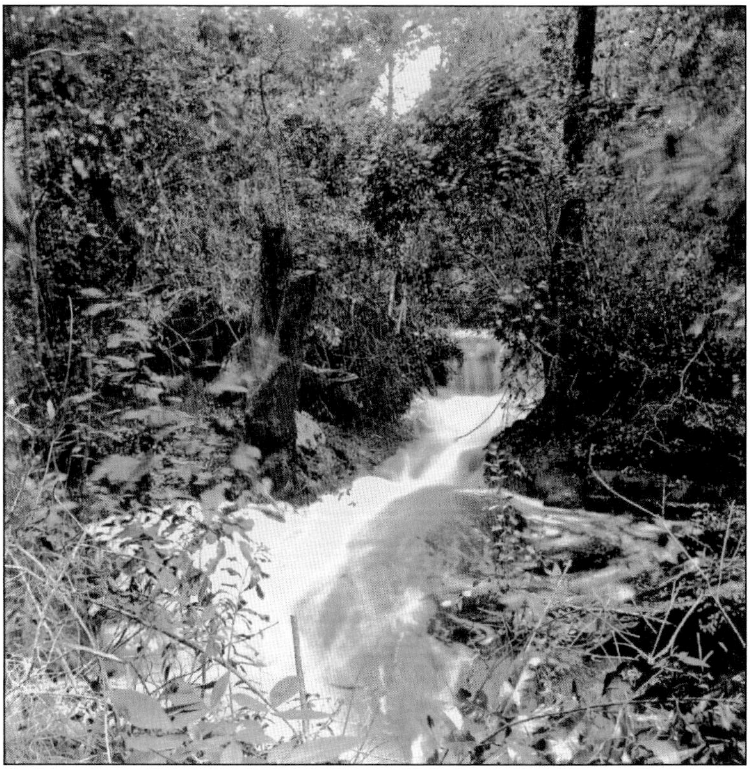

Lacking any warning system, the Sea Island Hurricane of 1893 caught residents completely unprepared. An estimated 2,000 to 3,000 people died, mostly from drowning. The number may have been much higher given the lack of communication in isolated areas of the islands and mainland. (Photograph by Julia King; courtesy of the Springfield Legacy Foundation.)

People clung to trees as the water rose relentlessly, and survival depended greatly on whether trees remained rooted or drifted away. In addition to human casualties, thousands of horses, mules, cows, and other animals drowned in the tidal surge. The stench of rotting flesh persisted for days following the storm. (Photograph by Julia King; courtesy of the Springfield Legacy Foundation.)

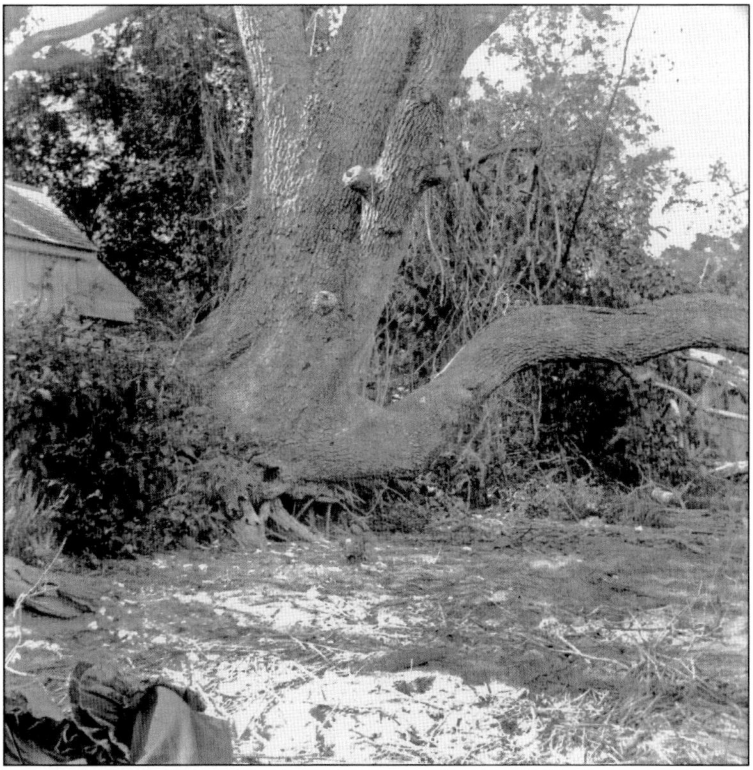

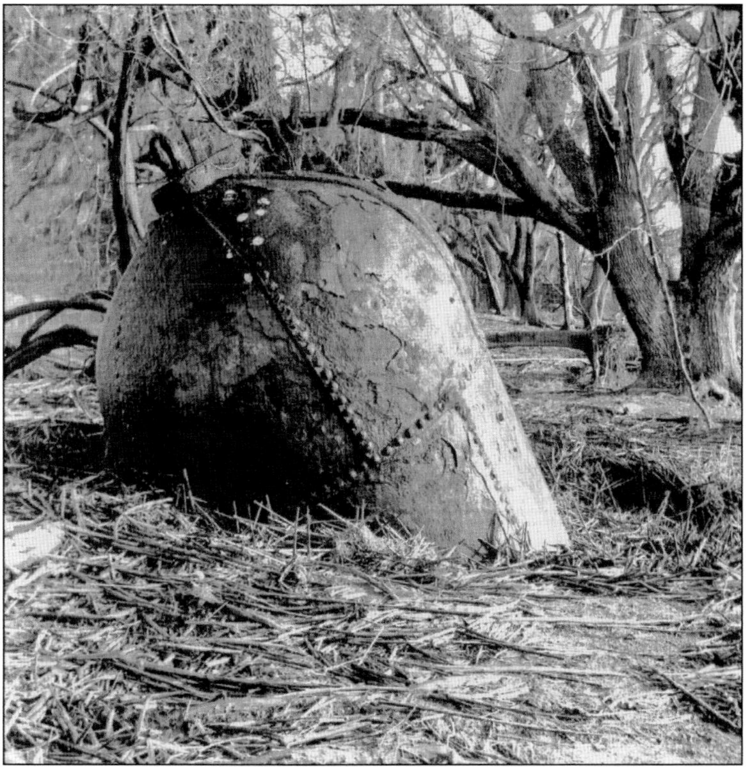

Although coastal Liberty County lies in the Georgia Bight and is generally thought to be "immune" from hurricanes, historical data shows that the area has suffered many strikes. So powerful was the collective memory of the Sea Island Hurricane that, when forecasters compared 1999's Hurricane Floyd to the 1893 storm, longtime coastal Georgians heeded the evacuation notice en masse. (Photograph by Julia King; courtesy of the Springfield Legacy Foundation.)

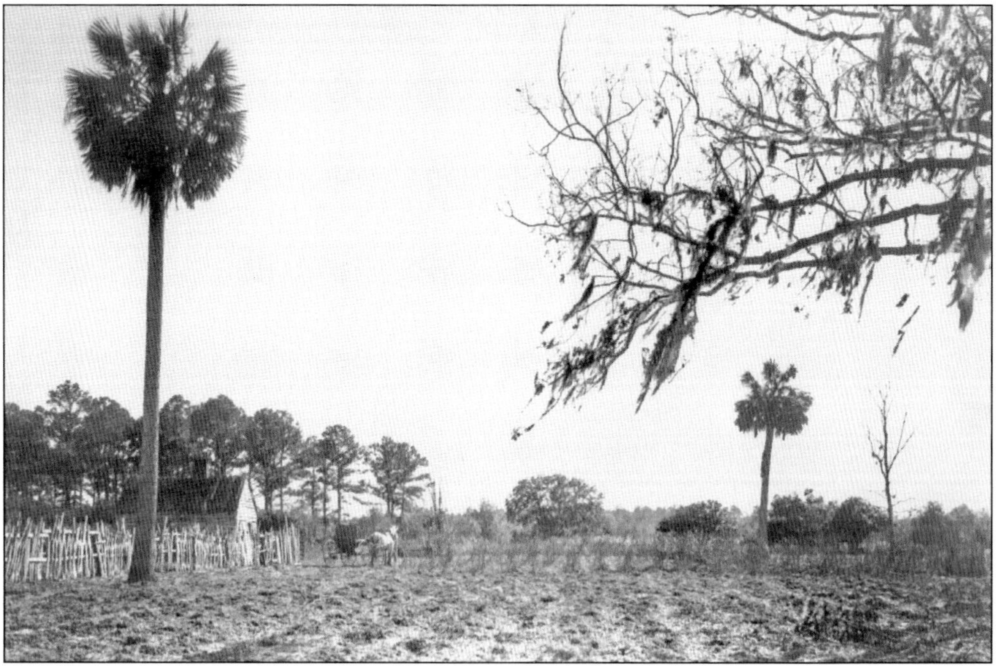

The Civil War and emancipation of slaves ended the viability of large-scale planting. Rice, in particular, was a highly labor-intensive crop. Some large planters attempted to resuscitate their antebellum operations, but most eventually abandoned their plans. With higher education, many young adults from planter families chose to move to new locales to pursue professional careers. Among those who left Liberty County were John and Joseph LeConte. In the top photograph, the LeConte's Woodmanston Plantation is pictured in 1897 during Joseph LeConte's last visit to his boyhood home. The land was still open, and LeConte poses next to a shrub in the bottom photograph. (Courtesy of the Midway Museum.)

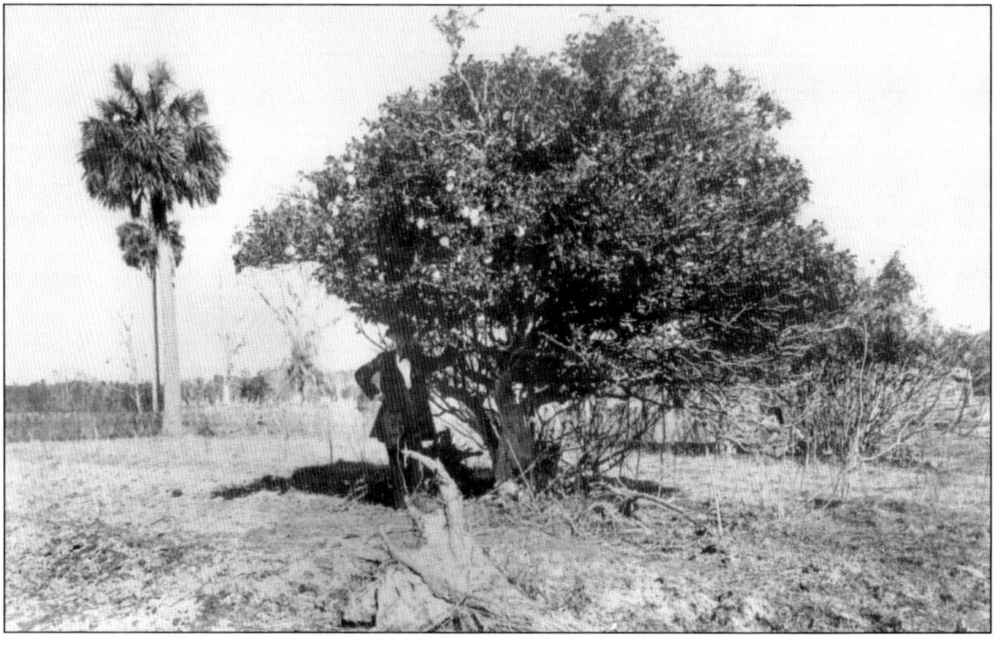

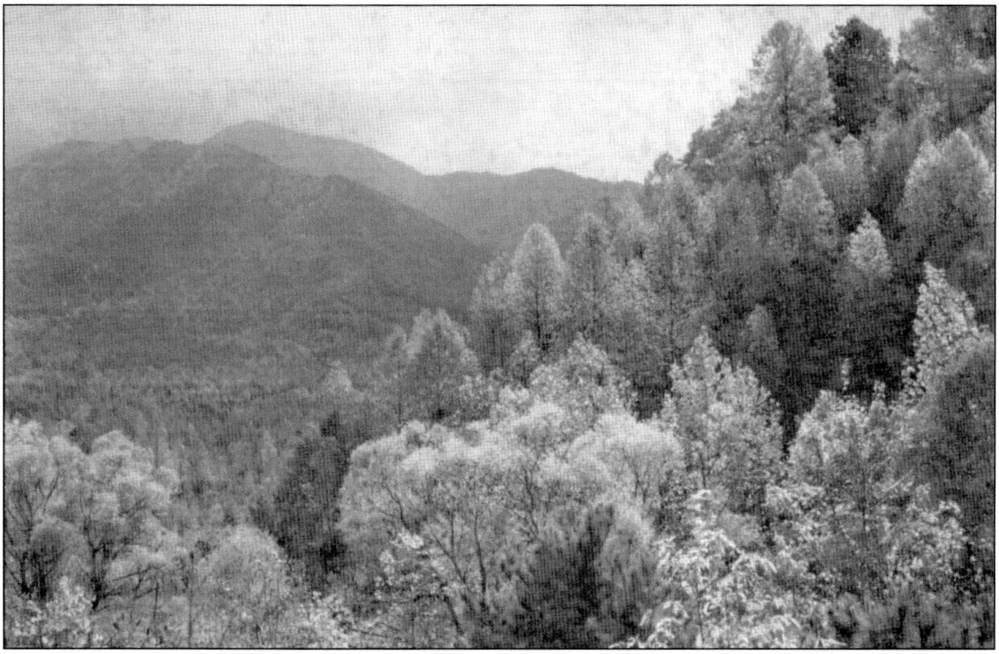

While some confusion exists over which brother inspired the nod, Mount LeConte, pictured here in the Great Smoky Mountain National Park, gained its name from the Liberty County natives. Additionally, birds, buildings, plants, streets, and geological formations have all borne the LeConte name. (Courtesy of the Midway Museum.)

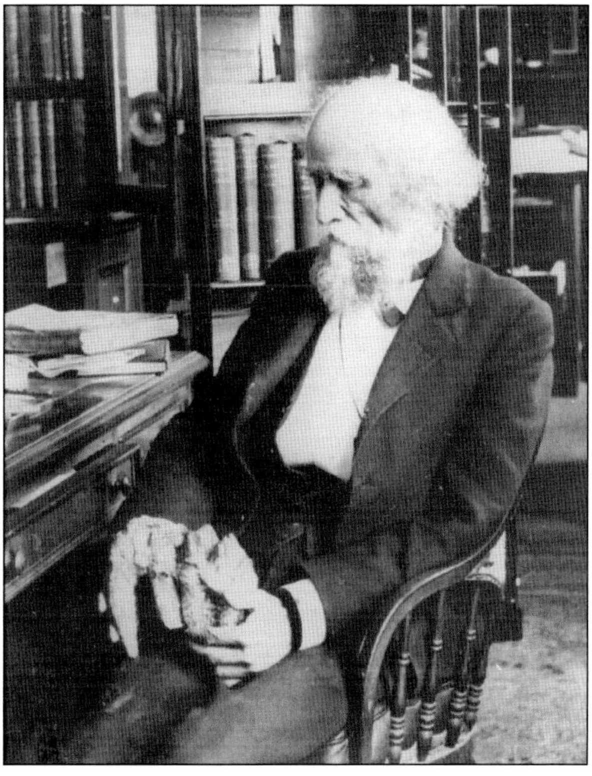

Joseph LeConte, photographed here in his Berkeley office, was the first botanist, geologist, and natural historian appointed to the faculty of the University of California at Berkeley. A friend of John Muir, LeConte was a founding member of the Sierra Club. LeConte's son Joseph Nesbit LeConte became a famous nature photographer and captured the Hetch Hetchy Valley before it was dammed, sparking one of the first public debates about preserving natural areas and catapulting the Sierra Club onto the national policy stage. (Courtesy of the Midway Museum.)

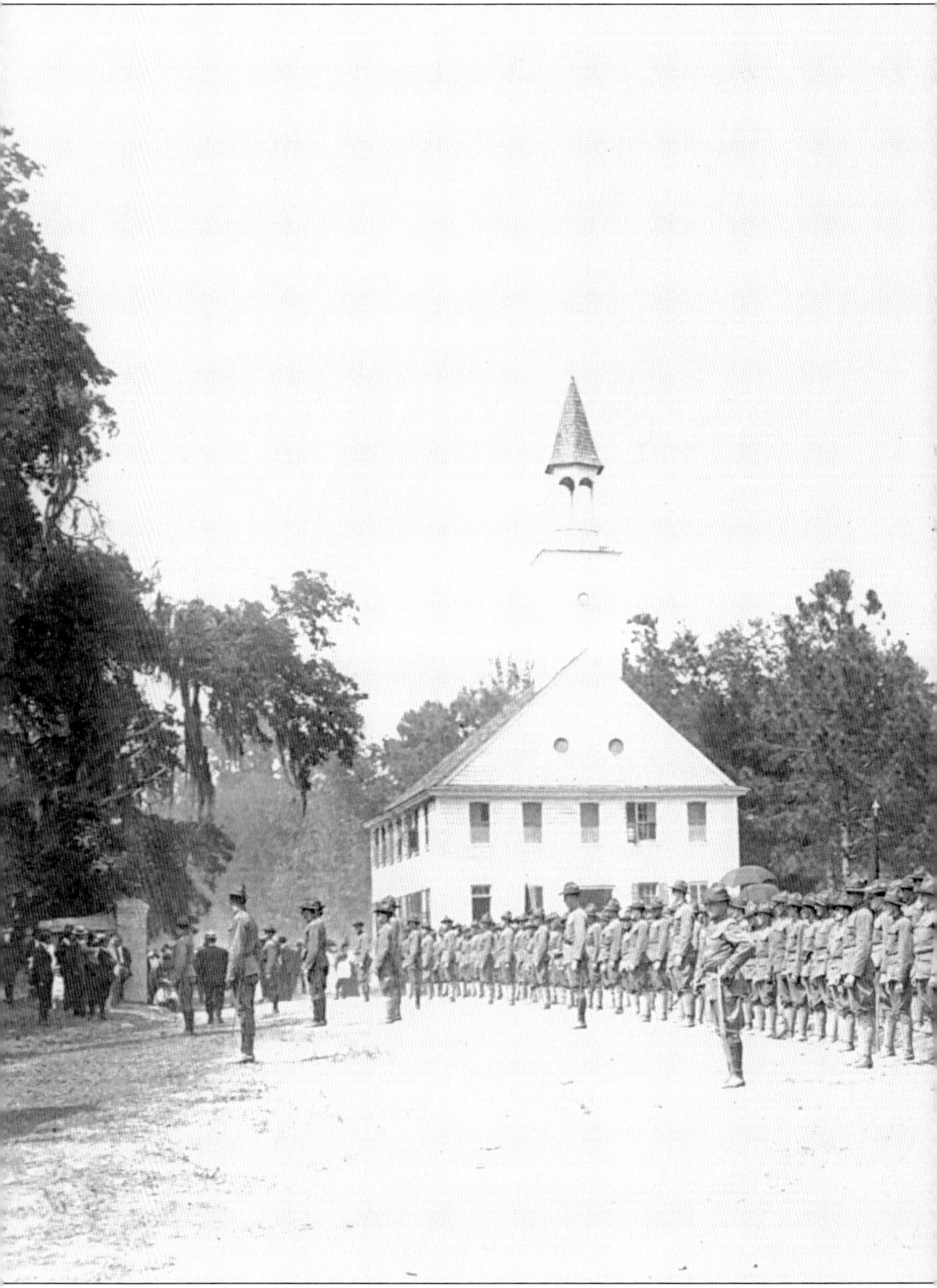

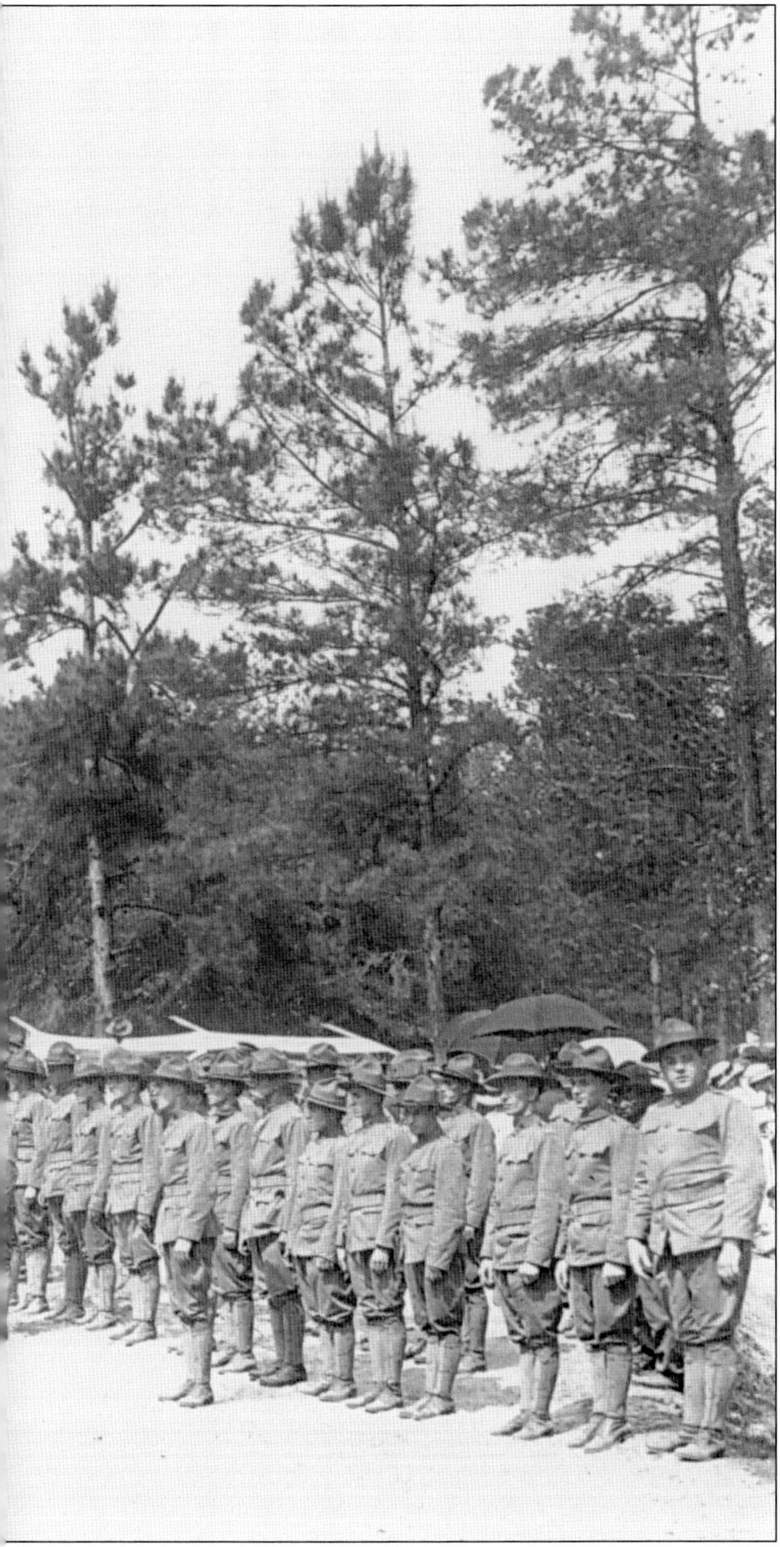

On April 26, 1915, the U.S. Congress erected a monument in the Midway cemetery. Dedicated to the memory of Brig. Gen. Daniel Stewart and Gen. James Screven, local heroes of the American Revolution, the monument stood at the center of the old burying ground. Troops representing the Savannah Guards, Georgia Hussars, Chatham Artillery, Liberty Independent Troop, and U.S. Army stationed at Fort Screven, Tybee Island, Georgia, massed in front of the Midway Church. Over 5,000 people attended the dedication ceremony. On behalf of the Midway Society, Joseph B. Way of Flemington said, "We are told by our church that from 1752 to 1865 there were buried in this historic place 1,200 people—one governor, one U.S. senator, two generals of the American Revolution, one commodore, one scientist of worldwide fame, one diplomat, and 11 ministers of the gospel." (Courtesy of the *Liberty County Herald*.)

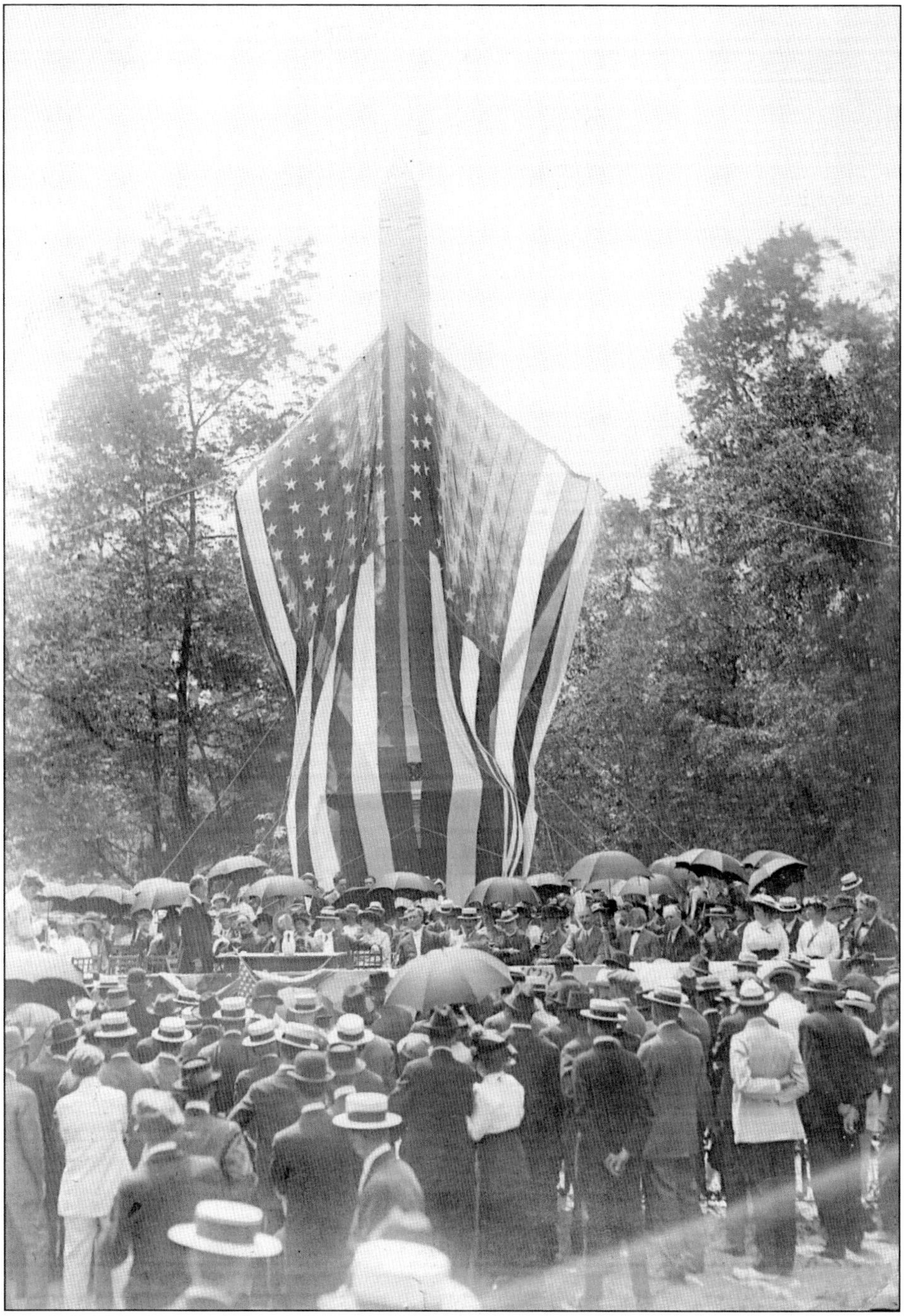

The monument was covered in two enormous American flags, and 13 young ladies, descendants of the Puritan settlers of Midway, served as sponsors of the dedication. At the critical moment, Mary Helen Quarterman and Eliza Maxwell Stevens pulled the cords holding back the flags and unveiled the obelisk as a double brigadier general's salute was fired by Battery A and Battery C, First Coast Artillery Battalion. The crowds picnicked on the grounds, and Western Union set up a telegraph station within the cemetery for celebrants to send commemorative telegrams. (Courtesy of the Springfield Legacy Foundation.)

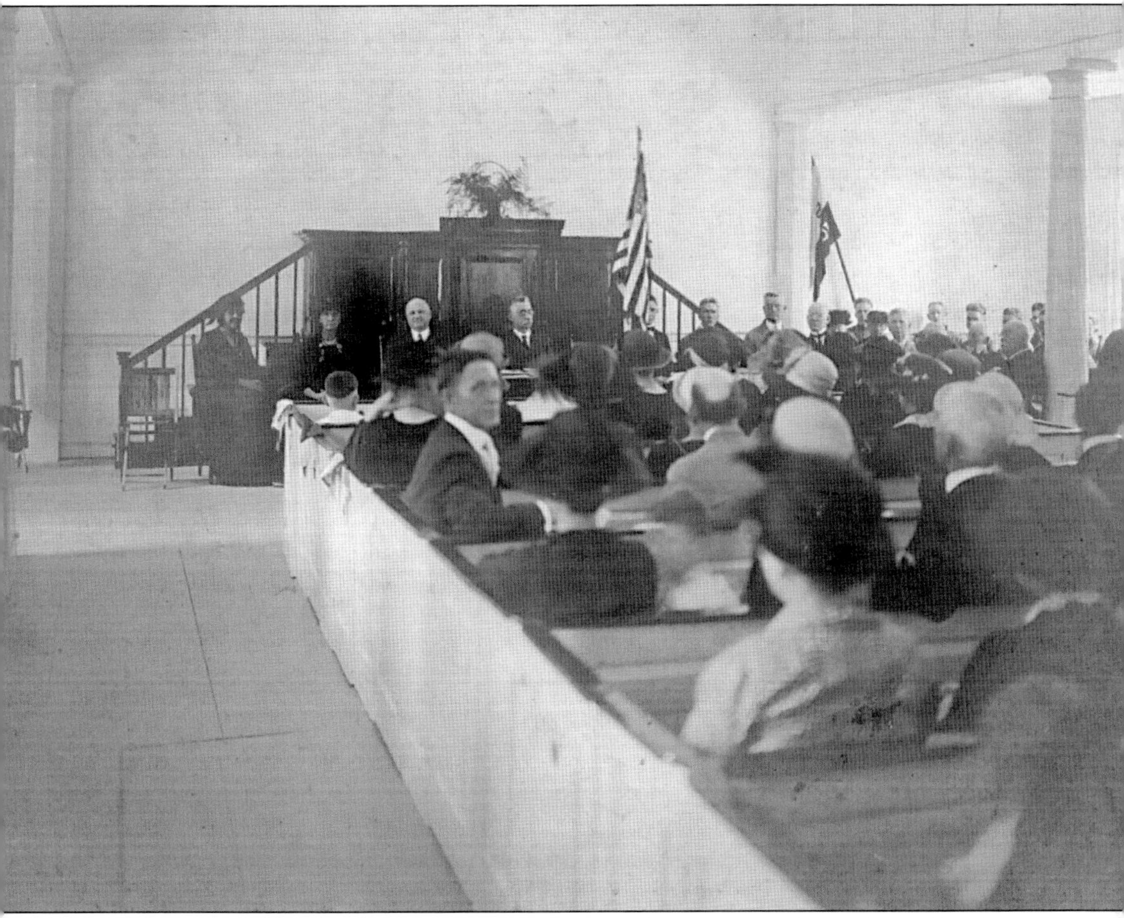

Taken on April 26, 1915, this photograph provides a rare glimpse inside the Midway Church during the annual Midway meeting. (Courtesy of the Springfield Legacy Foundation.)

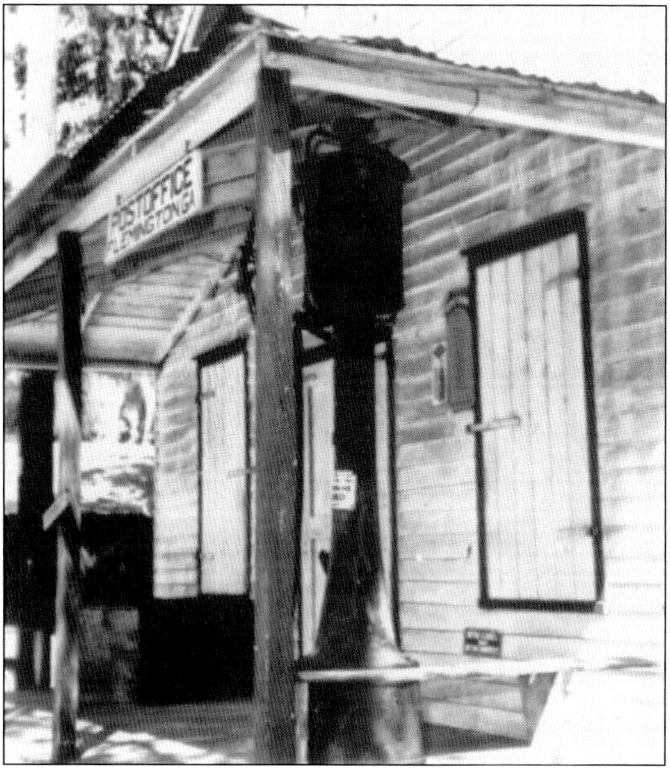

The Flemington Post Office was located next to Stacy's Store on the Old Sunbury Road. After the post office closed, the store handled mail for the village until Hinesville took over delivery. The building was still standing in the early 21st century and has been used for many purposes. (Courtesy of the *Liberty County Herald.*)

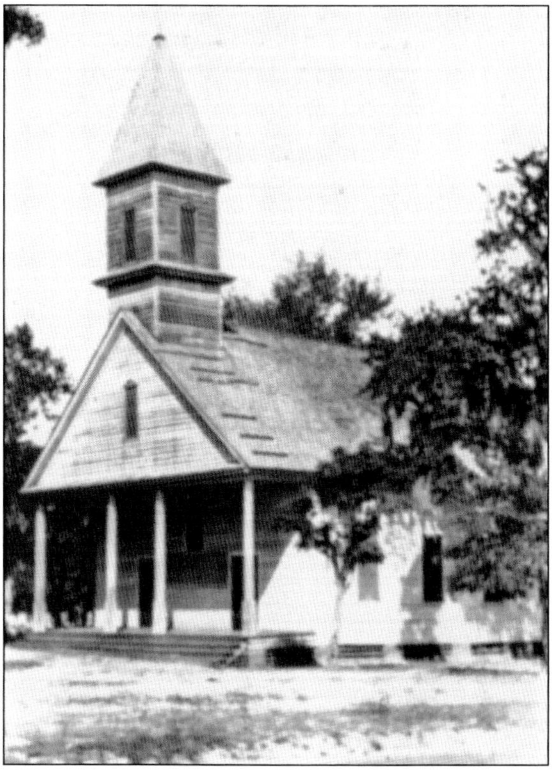

Early churches in Liberty County were similar in form to the Midway Church. These houses of worship were built of wood and simple in form such as Walthourville Presbyterian Church, Flemington Presbyterian Church, and Taylors Creek Methodist Church, pictured here. Communicants from surrounding areas gathered on Sundays and considered church-going the primary social event. (Courtesy of the *Liberty County Herald.*)

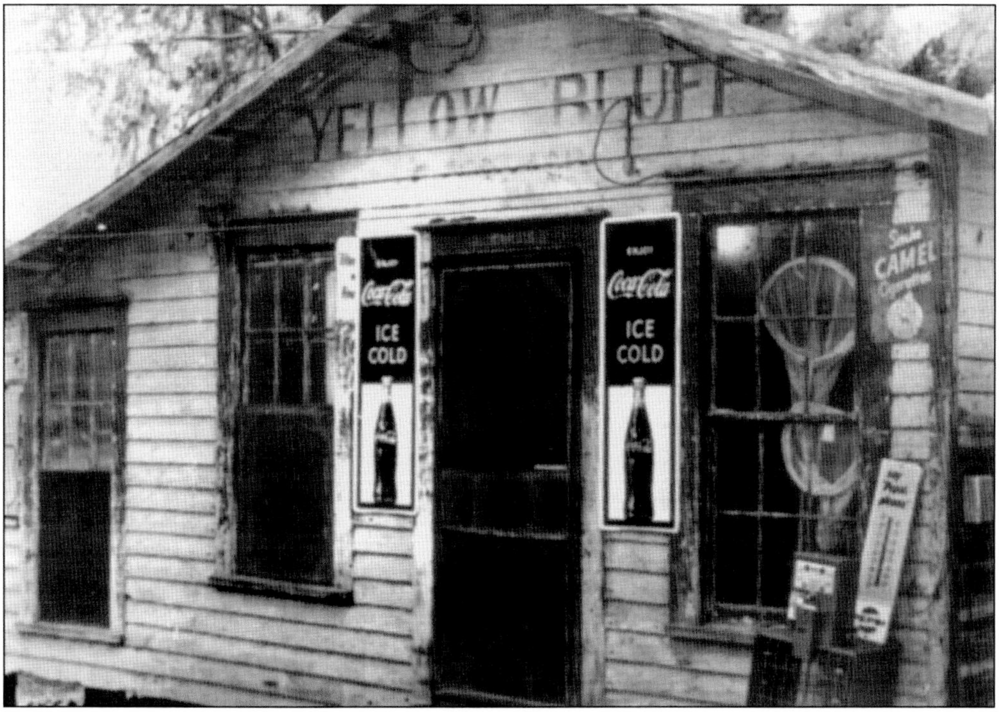

Arthur Goodman operated a familiar sight for generations of Liberty County fishermen, the Yellow Bluff Store, located on the eastern shore of Colonels Island—overlooking St. Catherine's Island—for many years. Part of a fish camp established around 1906, the store sold bait, supplies, and refreshments. Visitors rented cottages, and locals enjoyed dances in the tearoom housed in a refurbished oyster house. (Courtesy of the *Liberty County Herald*.)

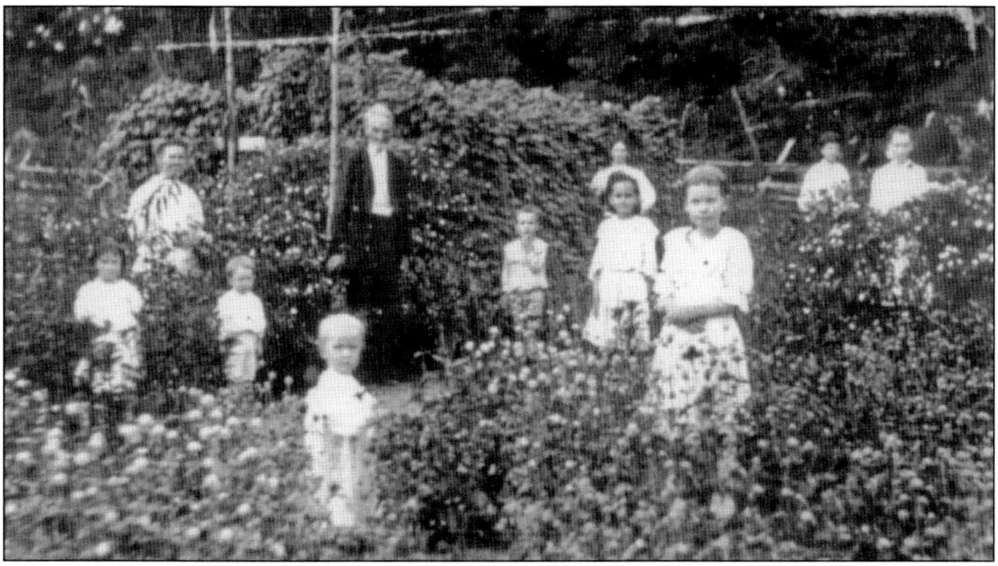

Members of John G. Martin's family enjoy his lovely flower garden in 1906. Included in the photograph are Maude Martin, Pearl Martin, Paul Martin, Colon Martin, John G. Martin, John G. Stacy, Alma Stacy, Lucile Stacy, Nettie Stacy, Mary Lou Martin, and Annie Martin. (Courtesy of the *Liberty County Herald*.)

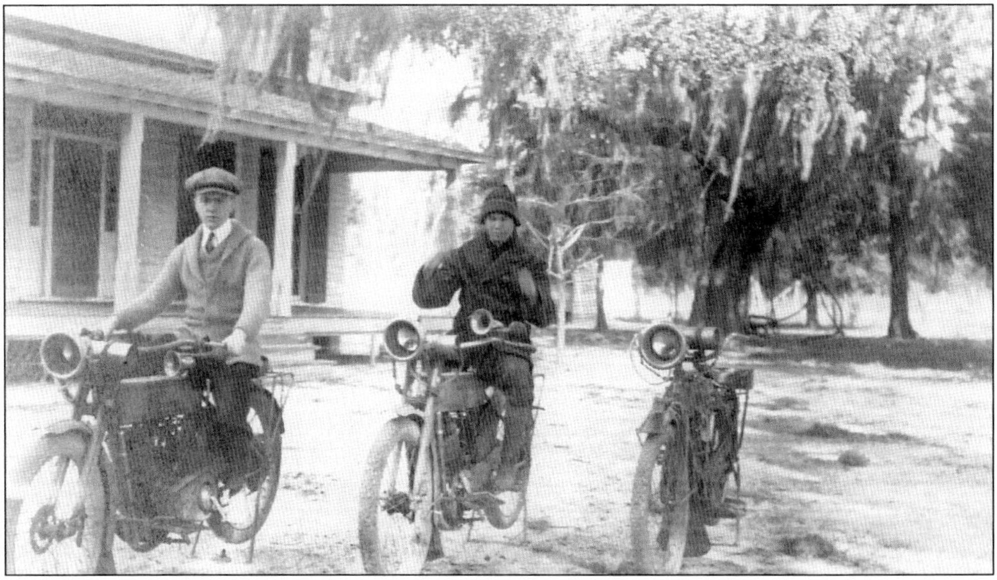

At the dawn of the 20th century, motor vehicles trickled into the Liberty County countryside. In this photograph, young men pose on their motorcycles in front of the Henry Dana Stevens house at Palmyra Plantation in the late 1910s. (Courtesy of the Springfield Legacy Foundation.)

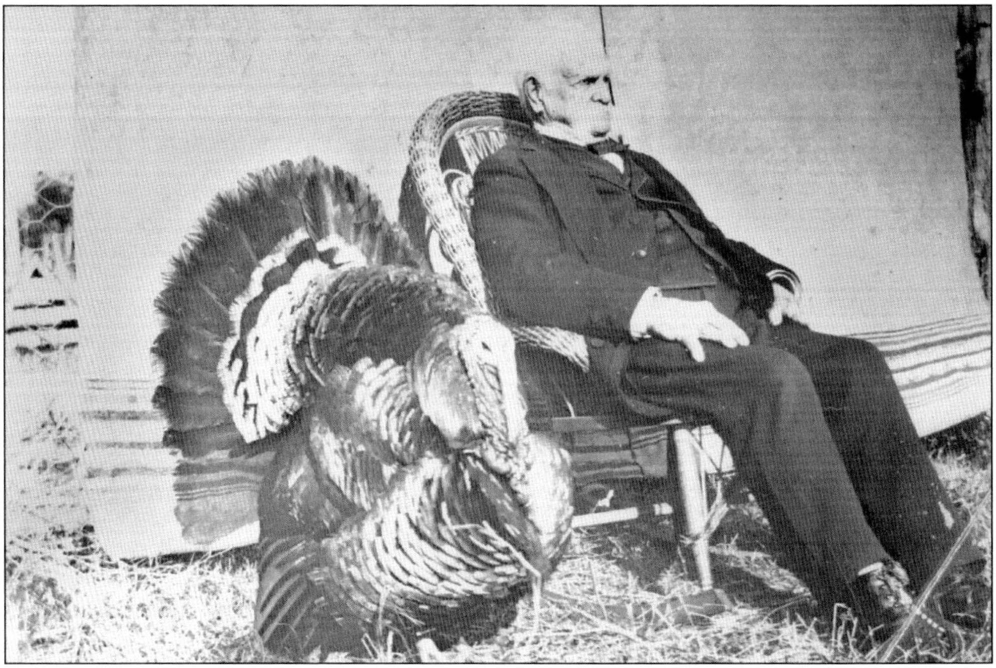

At a time when survival was paramount and luxuries were uncommon, photographs were considered events. Rather than "taken," photographs were usually "made," and large groups of people and formal portraits dominate early images. The photographic collection taken by Julia Maxwell King, therefore, offers an unusually candid view of coastal Georgia from the 1880s through the early 1900s. An example of this is the mocking portrait titled "Mr. Lewis;" one is not sure which subject is Lewis, but the resemblance suggests a joking kinship between the two. (Photograph by Julia King; courtesy of the Springfield Legacy Foundation.)

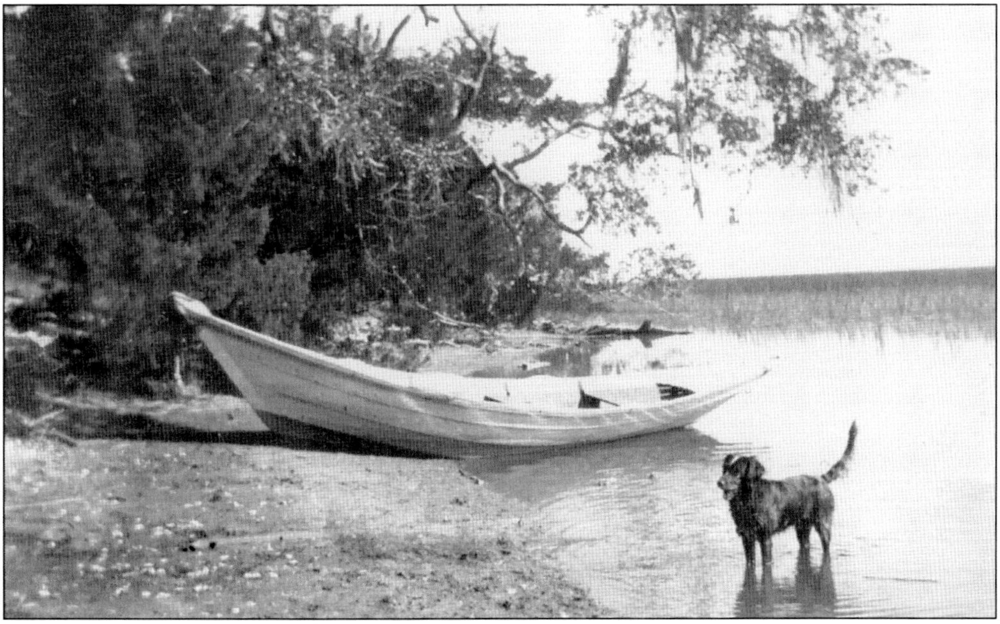

Using a larger format camera, Julia King's photographs did require preparation and use of a stabilizing tripod, but her treatment of ordinary subjects foreshadows candid and documentary photography common in the 20th century. King failed to identify many of her subjects, yet the moments she captured preserved a little-documented and erstwhile period in Liberty County's history. Her images show details of everyday life, work, and play at the end of the era of animal traction, poor roads, and purely agrarian, rural life in Liberty County. Living on the water at her father's home, Maxwellton, on the eastern side of Colonels Island, King took many photographs of life on the tidal creeks and rivers. In these two images from the late 19th century, an unidentified man and his dog set off in a double-ended dory, sometimes used as an oyster boat for ease of landing and launching from either end. (Photographs by Julia King; courtesy of the Springfield Legacy Foundation.)

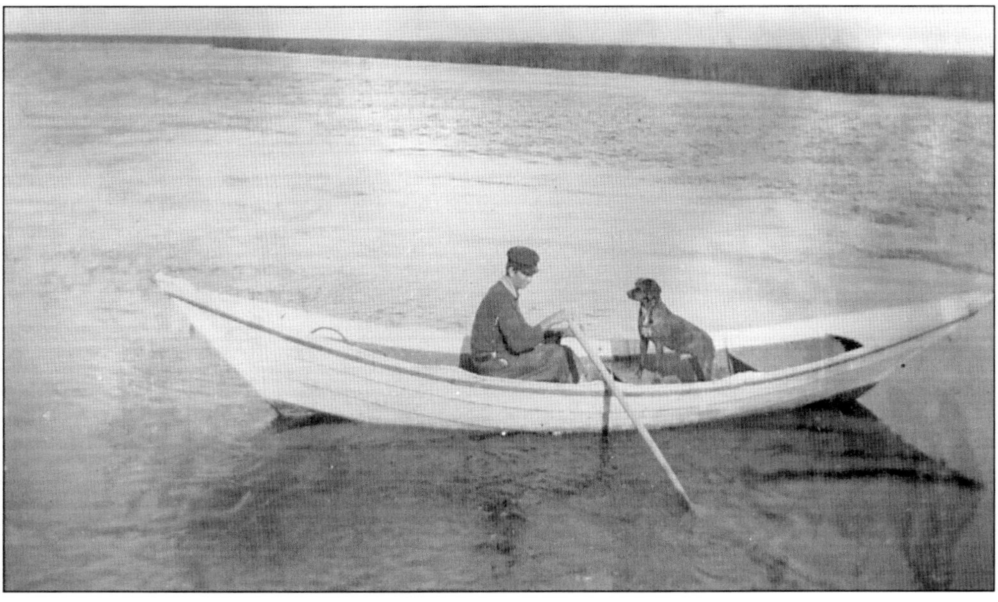

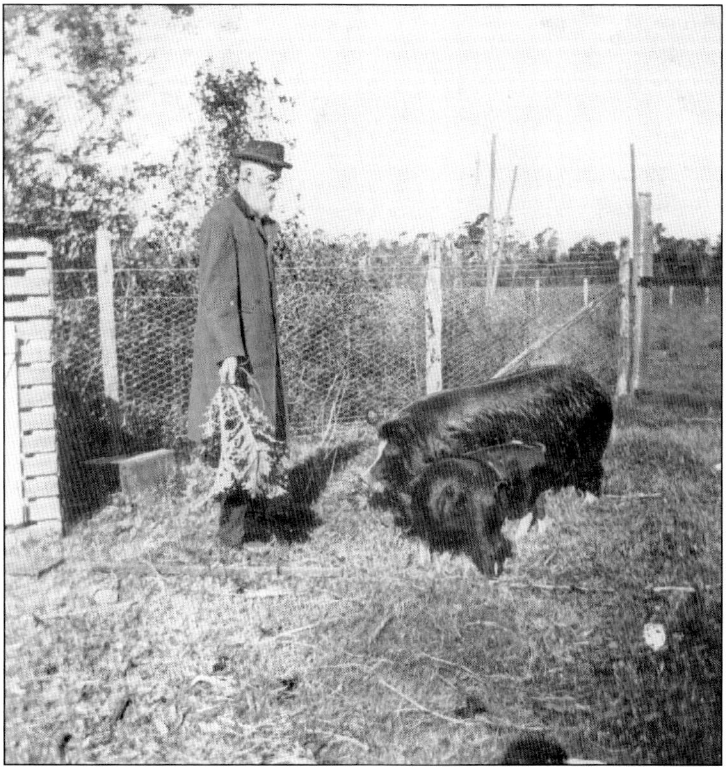

Julia King took this photograph of her father, Audley Maxwell King, feeding greens to his hogs at his Colonels Island home, Maxwellton. (Photograph by Julia King; courtesy of the Springfield Legacy Foundation.)

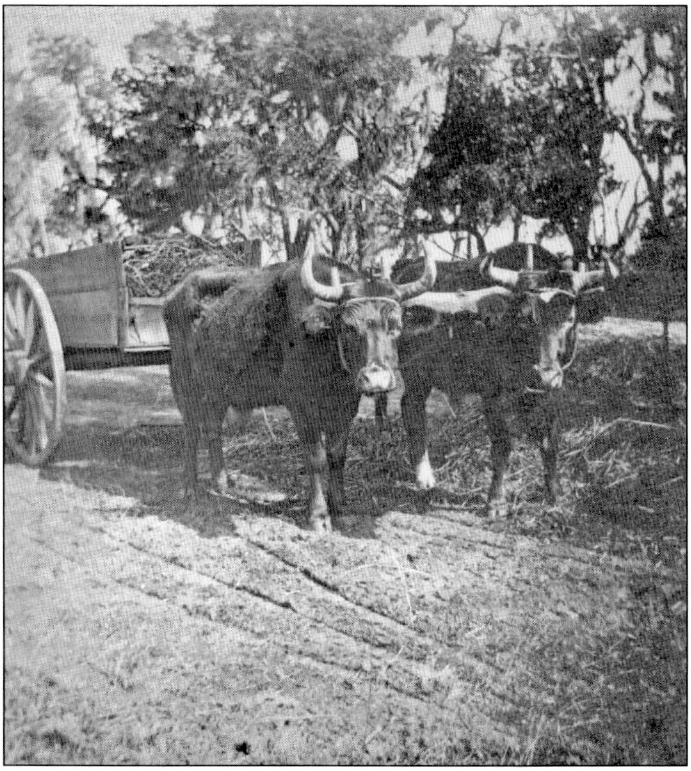

Because of the swampy terrain of coastal Georgia, many farmers used oxen, which, because of their cloven hooves, had better traction than horses and mules in the mud. Oxen and mules were considered smarter than horses and could be trained to follow voice commands. In this photograph from around 1900 is a team of oxen drawing an oxcart. Oxen were used in Liberty County into the 20th century. In portions of McIntosh County, oxen removed timber from the path of Interstate 95 in the early 1970s. (Photograph by Julia King; courtesy of the Springfield Legacy Foundation.)

In the absence of good overland roads, water transportation was common through the first part of the 20th century. This photograph shows sailing cargo ships in St. Catherine's Sound in the 1890s. (Photograph by Julia King; courtesy of the Springfield Legacy Foundation.)

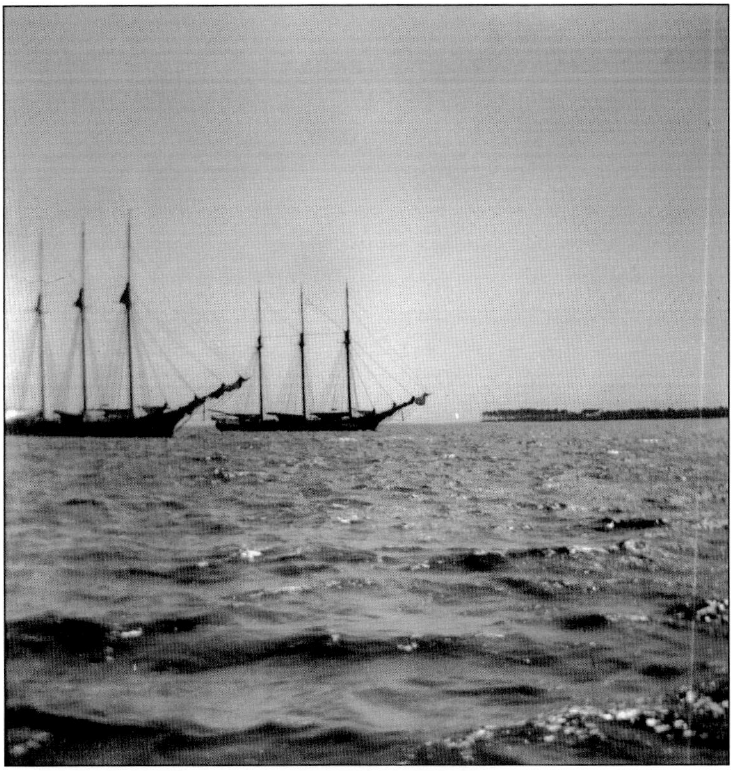

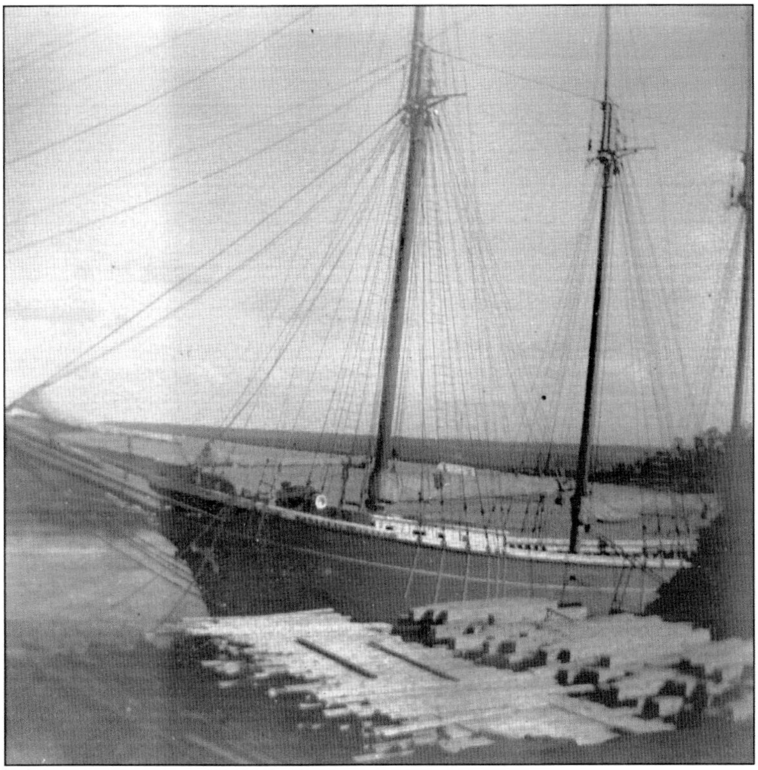

Sunbury, long overshadowed by ports at Savannah and Brunswick, continued to receive ships transporting goods. Here a ship lies at the Sunbury wharf in the 1890s as it is loaded with lumber cut in Liberty County. (Photograph by Julia King; courtesy of the Springfield Legacy Foundation.)

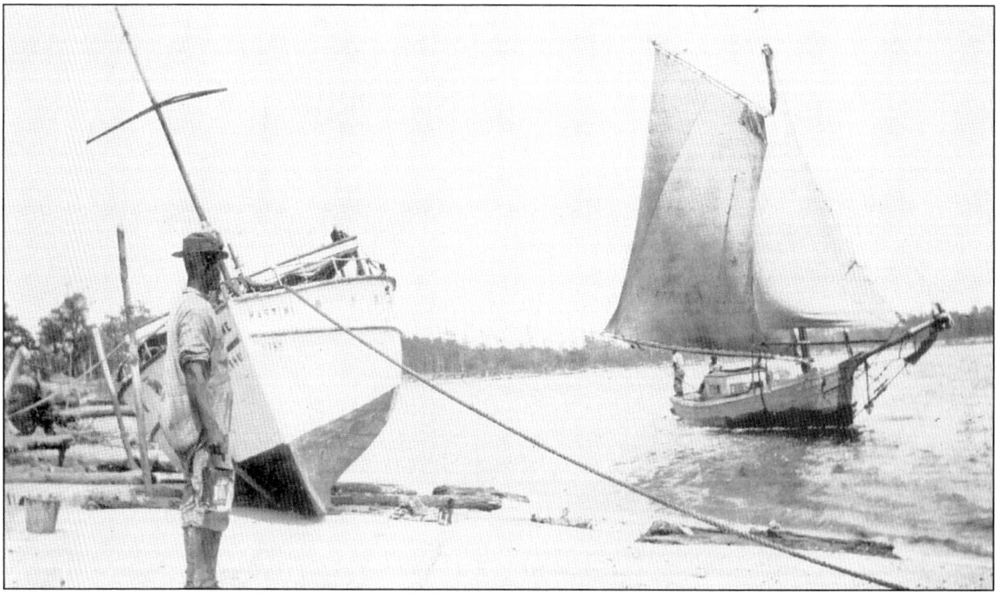

An unidentified man watches a small sailboat skirt the shoreline in the late 1800s. He was repainting the bottom of the vessel on the left to protect the sailboat from water damage. Using the huge tides as a tool, mariners often took their boats to a sandbar and waited for the outgoing tide to beach them. They had a few hours to do work before the tide came back in. Note the logs wedged under the waterside of the boat to keep it from rolling over. (Photograph by Julia King; courtesy of the Springfield Legacy Foundation.)

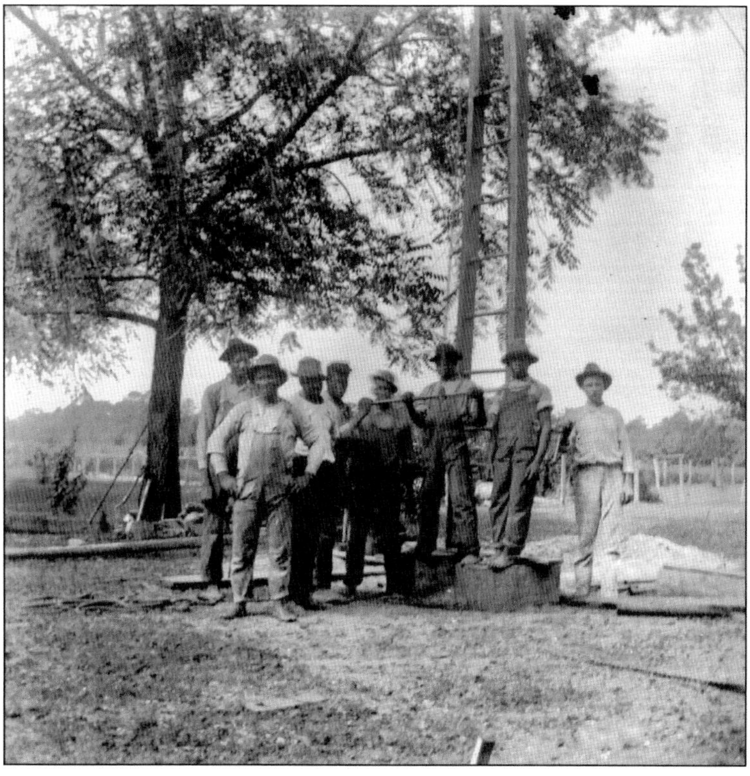

An unidentified group of men poses for a photograph in the late 1800s. They are holding a ladder possibly used to shake nuts out of pecan trees. (Photograph by Julia King; courtesy of the Springfield Legacy Foundation.)

The steamer pictured here in the 1890s carried mail and packages between Savannah, Brunswick, and points in between. (Photograph by Julia King; courtesy of the Springfield Legacy Foundation.)

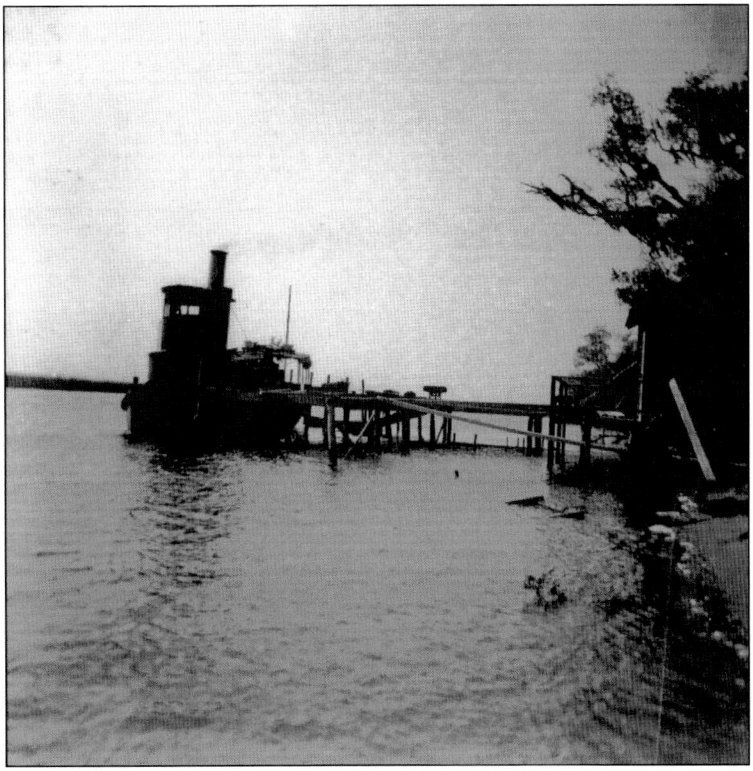

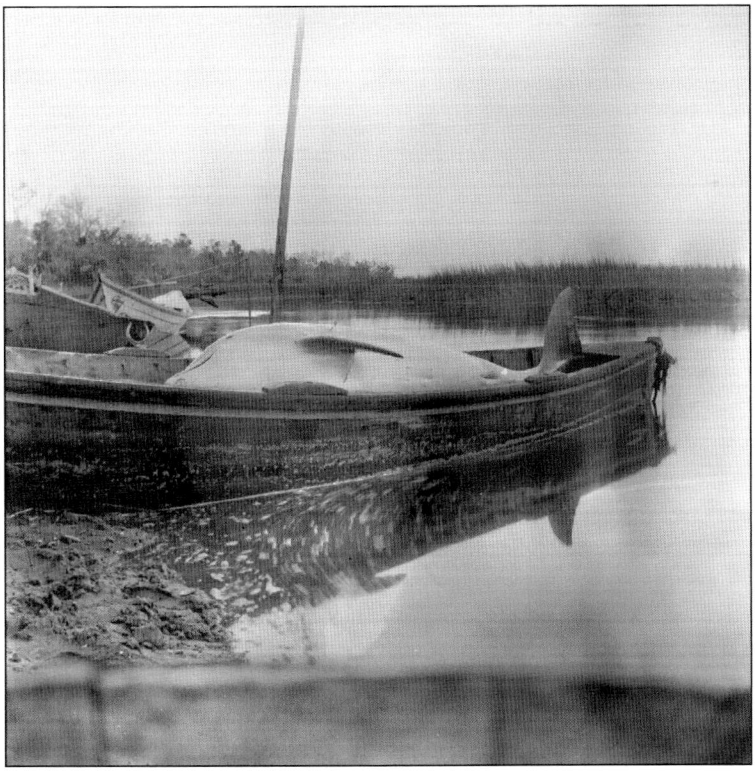

Julia King captured this unusual image of a dead bottlenose dolphin in a boat. Dolphins, common in coastal Liberty County waters, were not hunted for food or sport. (Photograph by Julia King; courtesy of the Springfield Legacy Foundation.)

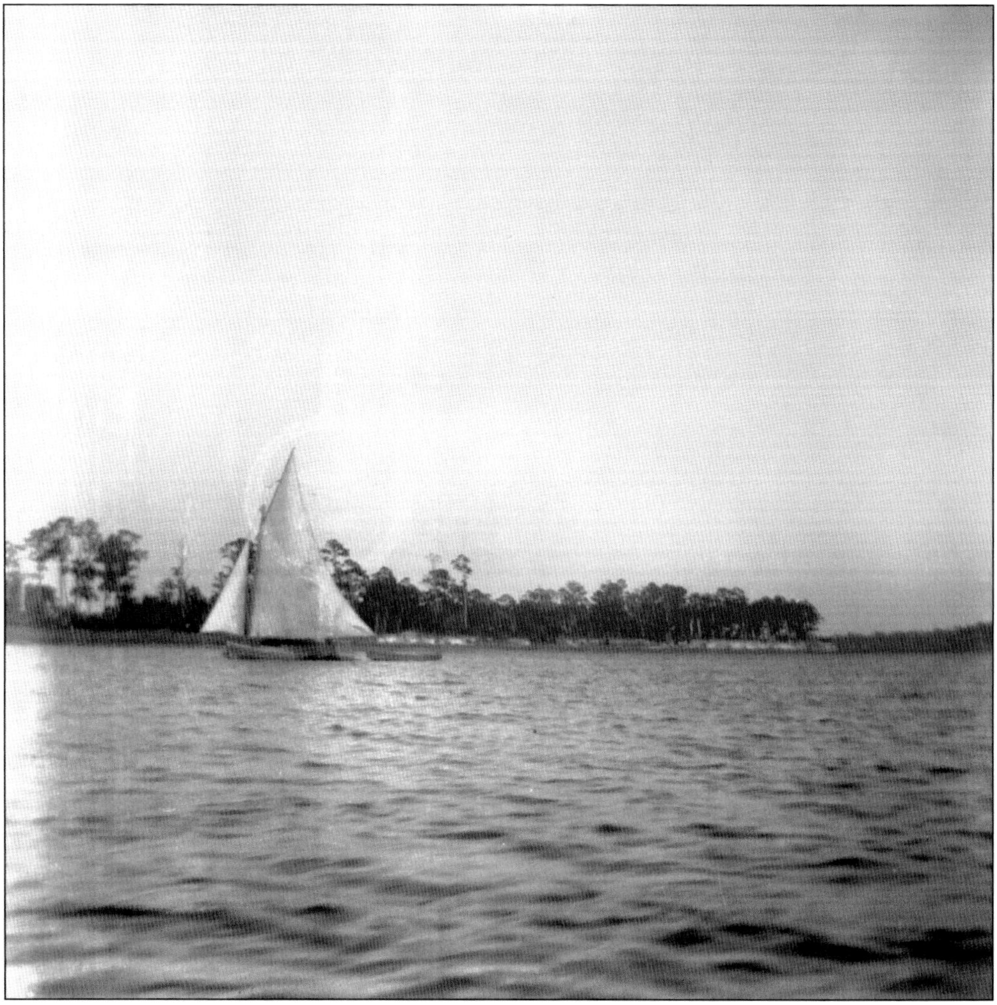

Until modern roads were constructed in the 1920s, the easiest way to travel along the coast was by water. Vessels of every description carried people, goods, and mail through the labyrinth of tidal channels. Often communities that were nearby on land were not as closely affiliated as those that were accessible by water. (Photograph by Julia King; courtesy of the Springfield Legacy Foundation.)

Farmers needed machinery to refine raw agricultural products into usable goods. In addition to sawmills, turpentine stills, cotton gins, and gristmills, various types of iron boilers were found throughout coastal Georgia. Used for boiling hogs, cane syrup, and salt, boilers were made of and came in a variety of sizes. Here an unidentified man sits near an unusually small boiler of unknown purpose. (Photograph by Julia King; courtesy of the Springfield Legacy Foundation.)

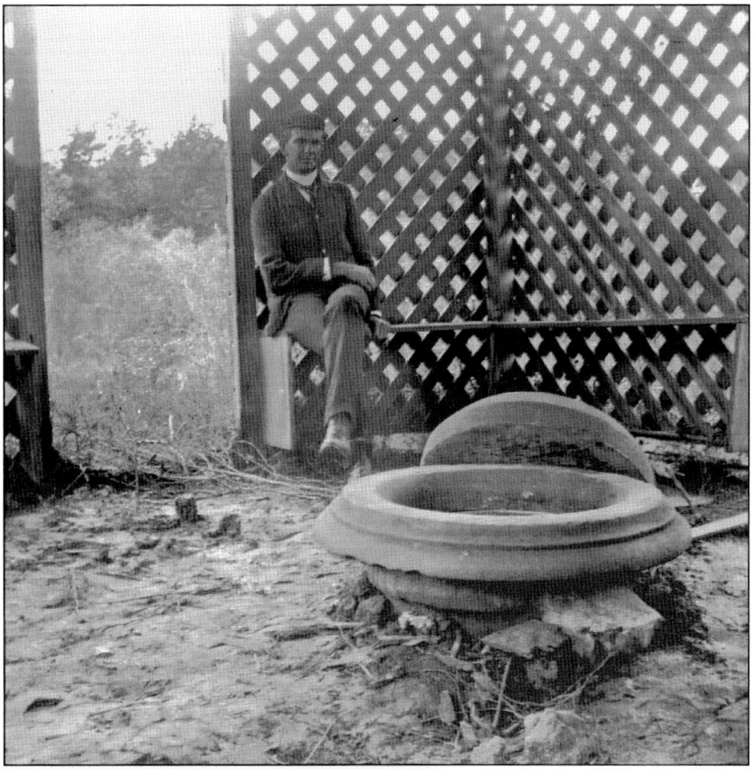

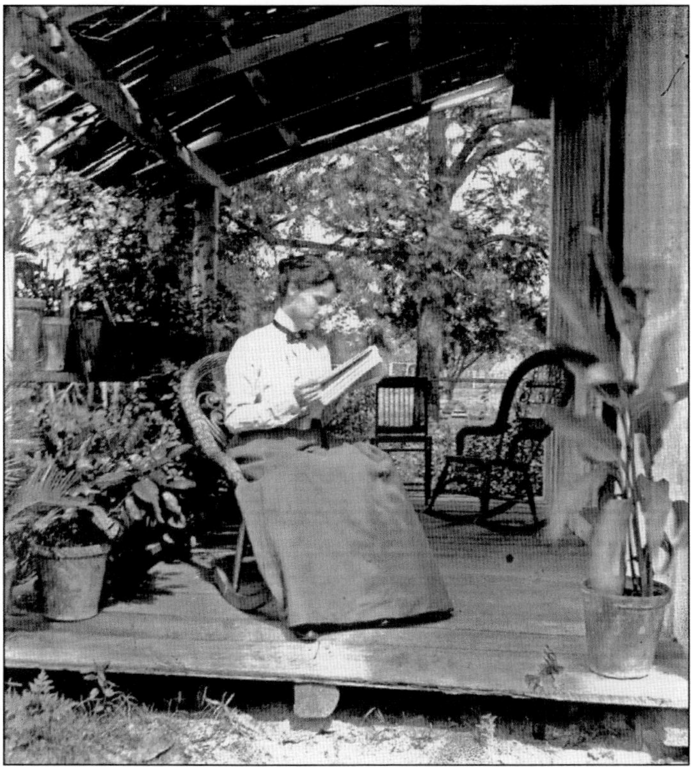

A woman of letters, Julia King never married. She enjoyed a life of relative leisure and spent much of her time researching history and remaining current with intellectual friends such as Henry W. Grady, editor of the *Atlanta Constitution* and leader of the New South movement. Here she sits reading on the porch of her summerhouse at Maxwellton in the late 1890s. Inside her room were books, musical instruments, and scientific devices. (Courtesy of the Springfield Legacy Foundation.)

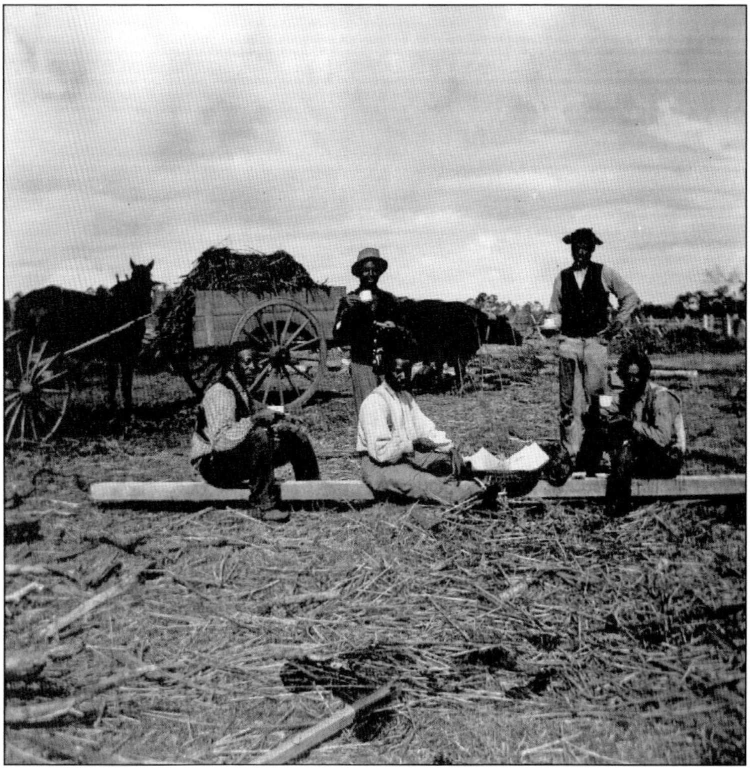

A group of unidentified African American farm workers takes a coffee break in the field in the late 1890s. They appear to be gathering sugarcane using mules and oxen, which are used to transport the harvest to a refining point. (Photograph by Julia King; courtesy of the Springfield Legacy Foundation.)

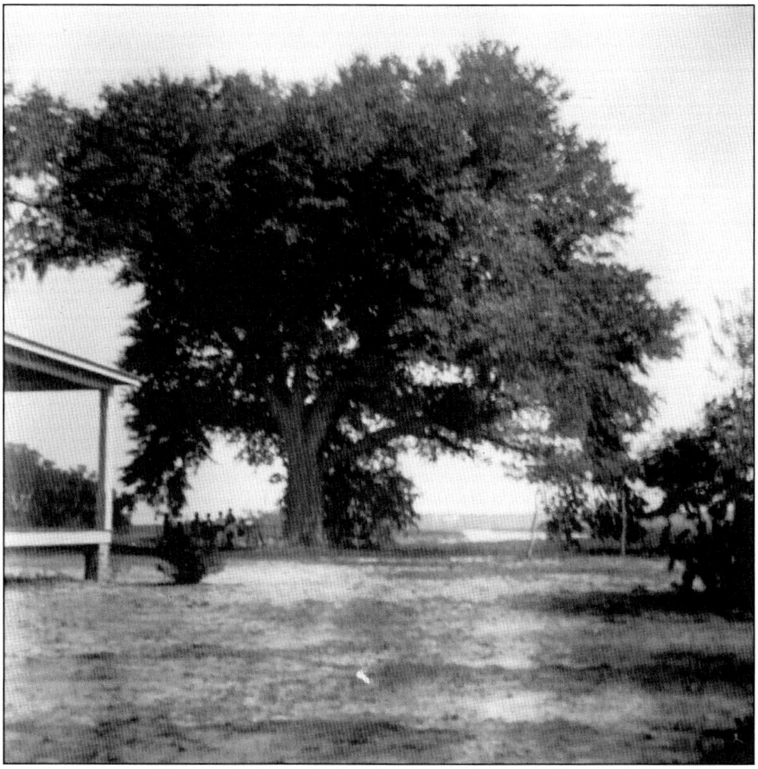

Here a group enjoys a picnic under the magnificent live oak tree in front of the house at Palmyra Plantation. The marsh and creek can be seen beyond the group. (Photograph by Julia King; courtesy of the Springfield Legacy Foundation.)

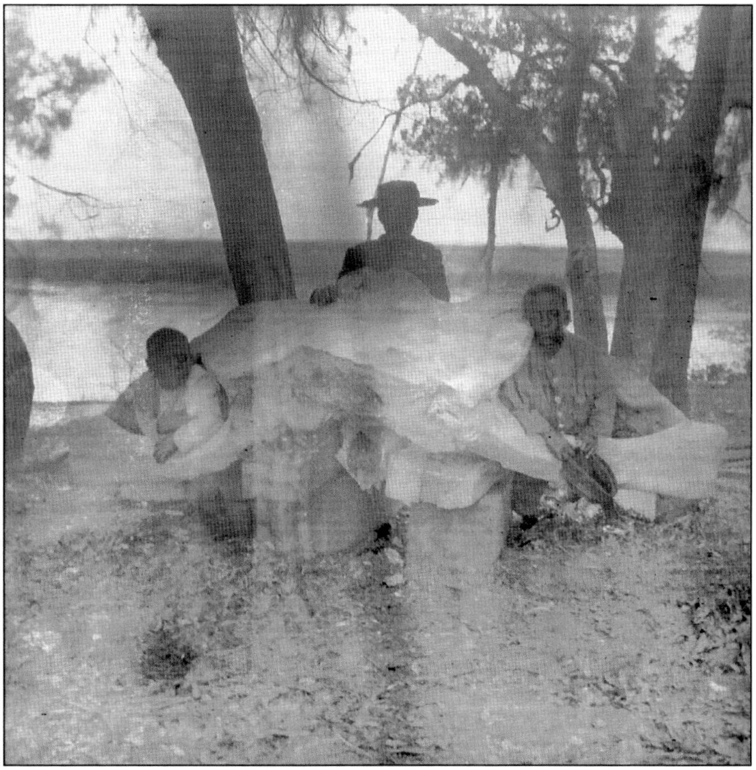

This photograph provides the only known image of a fossilized mastodon pelvis discovered on Colonels Island in the late 1800s. Three young, unidentified African American boys pose with the enormous fossil. (Photograph by Julia King; courtesy of the Springfield Legacy Foundation.)

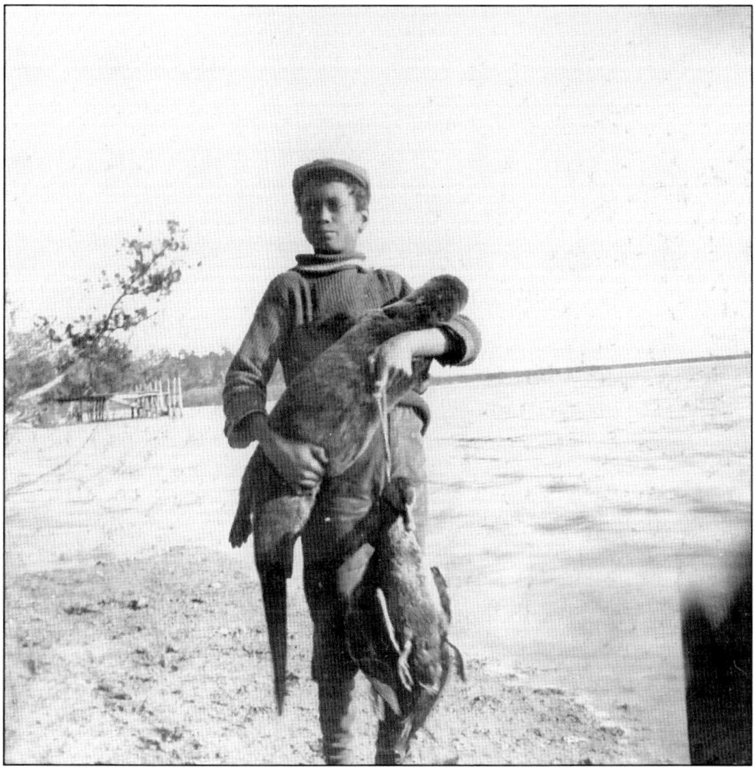

An unidentified boy holds a dead river otter. Along with mink, otters are common mammals in Liberty County's vast salt marsh. (Photograph by Julia King; courtesy of the Springfield Legacy Foundation.)

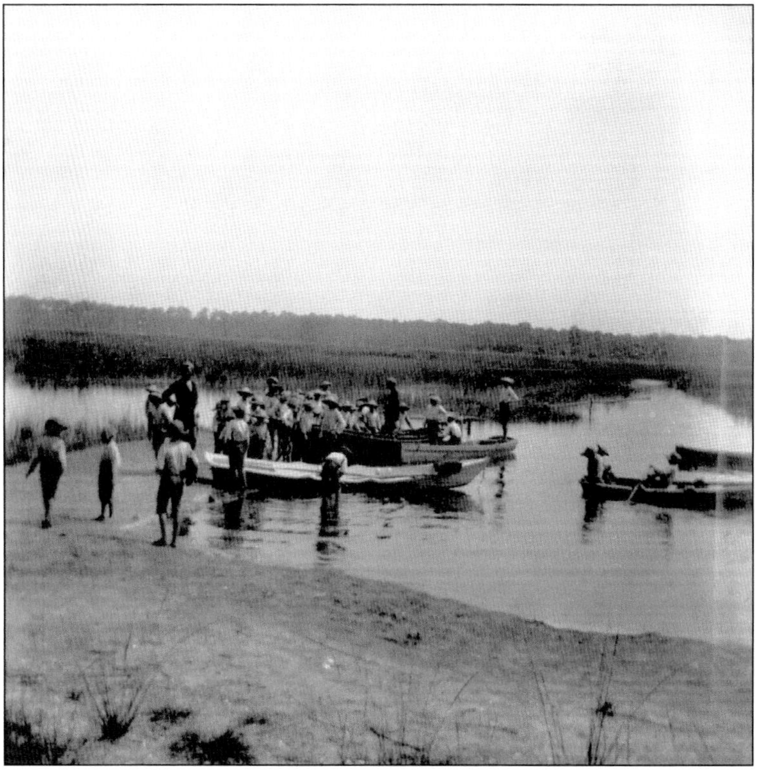

African American children arrive at a landing on Colonels Island in the late 1800s. After Reconstruction, African Americans living in Harris Neck in McIntosh County often traveled to St. Catherine's Island to attend church. Residents of the Seabrook-Trade Hill community west of Sunbury had strong ties—by water—with Pin Point community near Savannah. (Photograph by Julia King; courtesy of the Springfield Legacy Foundation.)

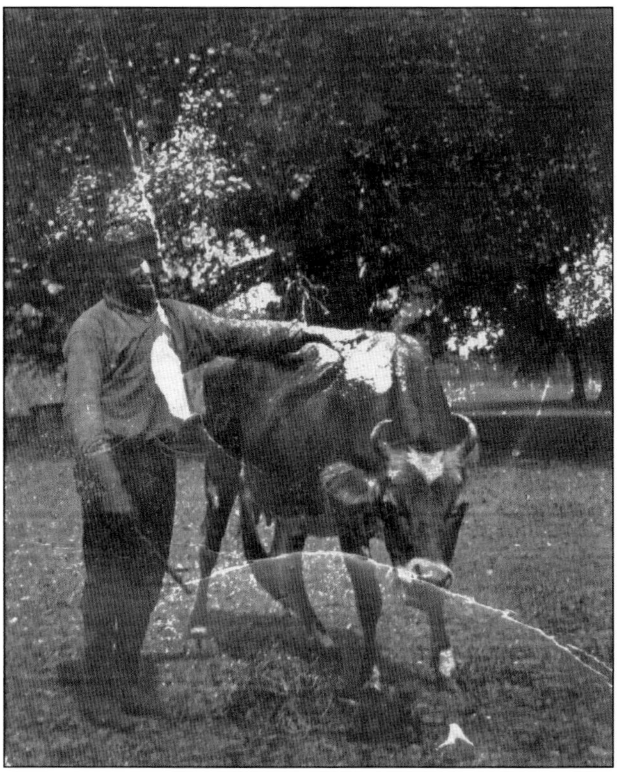

In addition to working steers and oxen, cows were kept for milk and meat. In this photograph, an unidentified man shows off his cow. (Photograph by Julia King; courtesy of the Springfield Legacy Foundation.)

Later in life, Julia King began writing a history of Liberty County, a work she never finished. Many of her descriptive letters and notes now reside at the Midway Museum. Here Julia stands in a yucca garden. (Courtesy of the Springfield Legacy Foundation.)

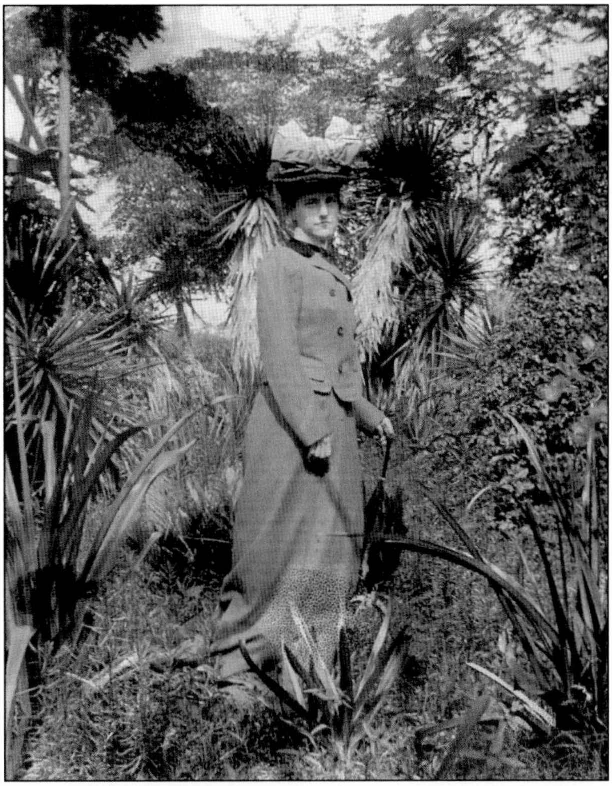

The reuse of buildings and their components was common in pre-World War II rural, coastal Georgia. Bricks and lumber from burned buildings were scavenged, and sometimes entire buildings were moved using logs and draft animals. An unusual bit of recycling was found in Julia King's house, which was constructed of remains of a British ship wrecked near Maxwellton on Colonels Island. Notice the unusual balustrade above the porch made of the ship's railing. (Courtesy of the Springfield Legacy Foundation.)

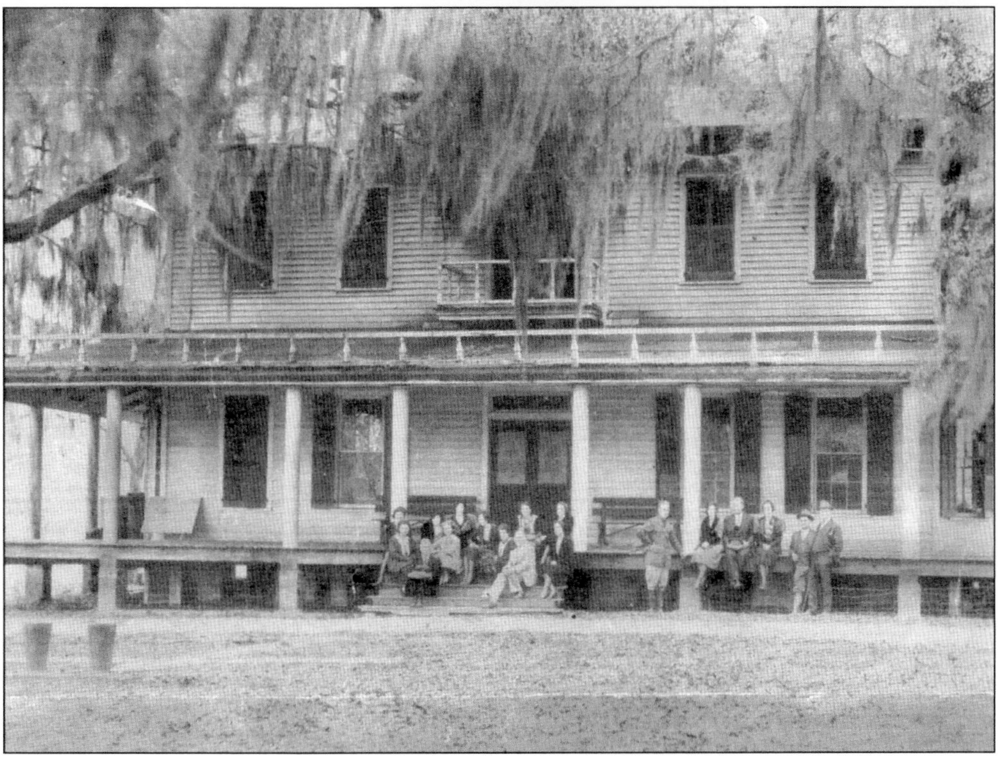

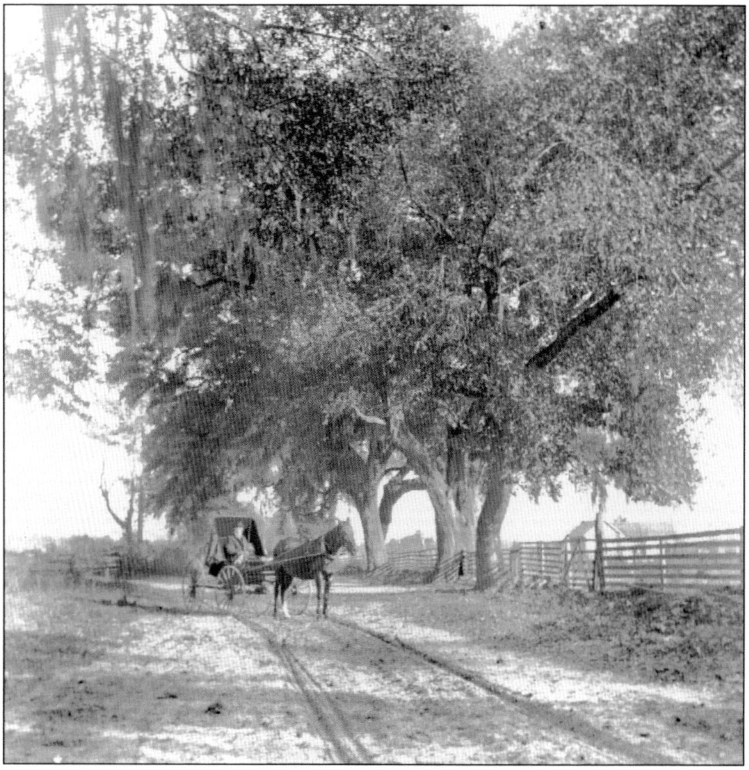

In the 1890s, Julia King took a road trip from her home at Maxwellton on Colonels Island to Midway and Riceboro. Taking her camera, she captured a rare series of images of the landscape and structures. In this photograph is her horse-drawn buggy driven by an unknown companion as they set out from Maxwellton. (Photograph by Julia King; courtesy of the Springfield Legacy Foundation.)

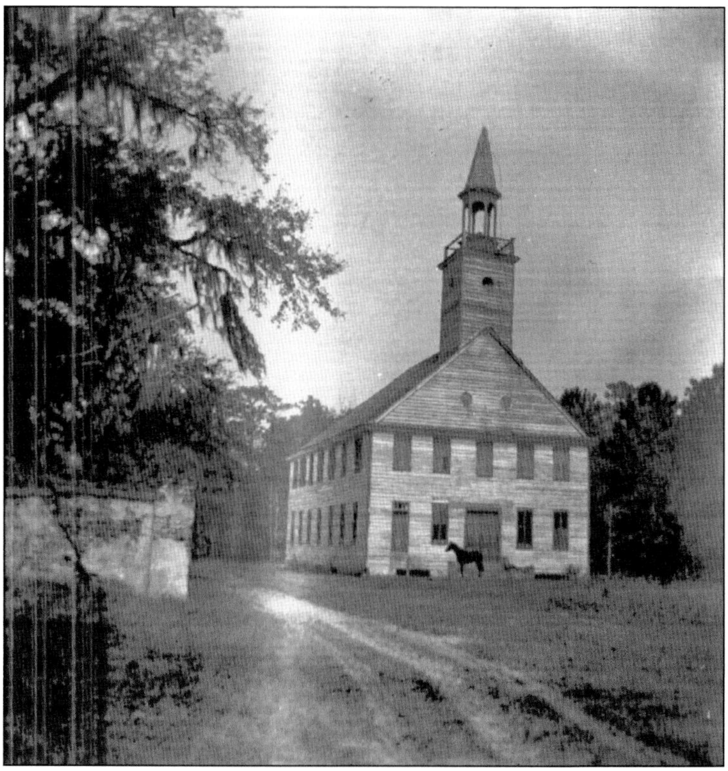

Until the Midway Congregational Church was built at Golden's Grove in 1872, African American communicants of the Midway Church held services in the mother church after the Civil War. This photograph, taken in the 1890s, shows the Midway Church as it was nearly 20 years after it ceased regular services. The Barrington Ferry Road, later to become U.S. Route 17, is seen as a barely used dirt track running between the church and cemetery. (Photograph by Julia King; courtesy of the Springfield Legacy Foundation.)

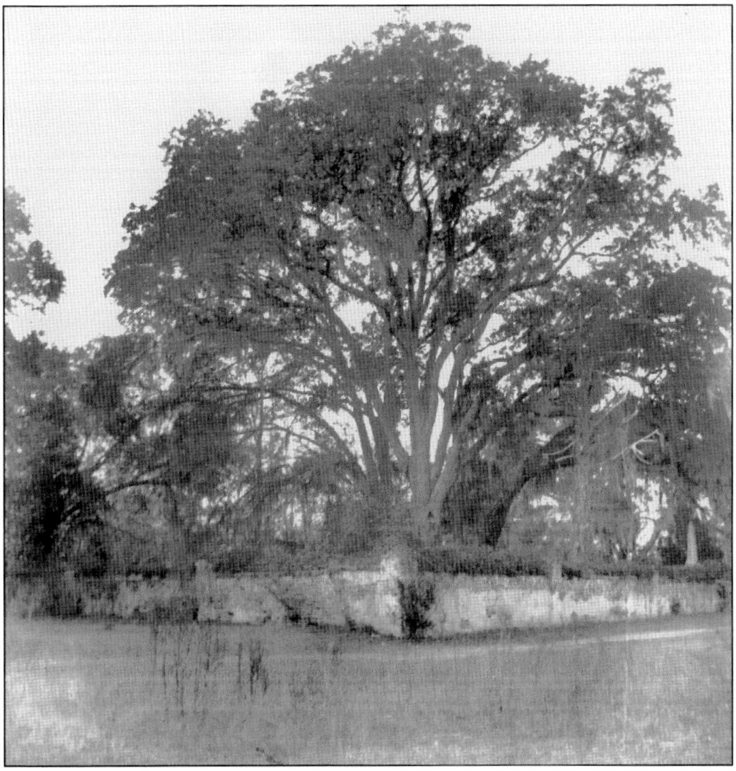

These photographs were taken at Midway Cemetery possibly after the Sea Island Hurricane of 1893. The top photograph was taken facing northwest from the Sunbury Road in front of the Midway Church. The bottom photograph was taken inside the cemetery and shows the overgrown walls and state of neglect. (Photograph by Julia King; courtesy of the Springfield Legacy Foundation.)

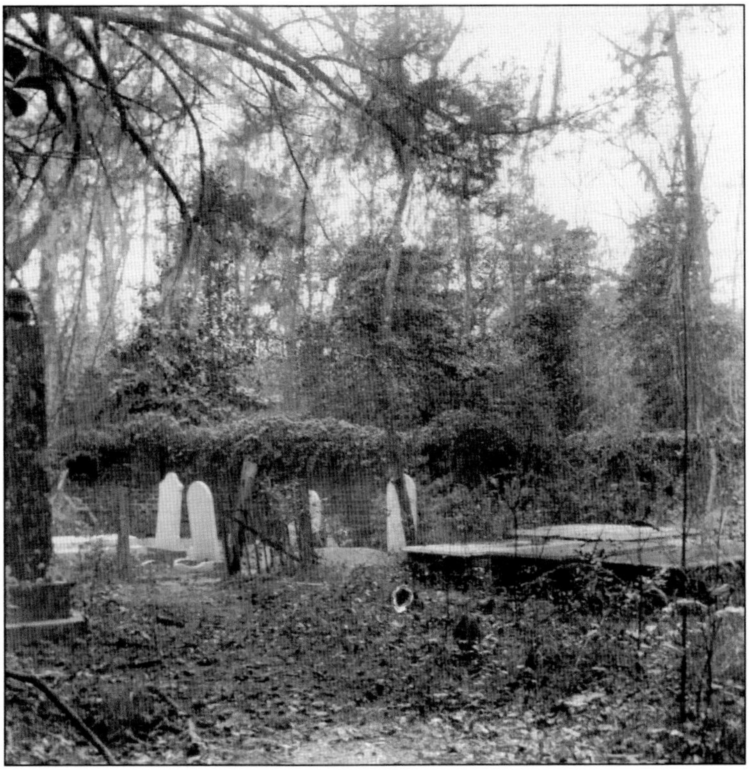

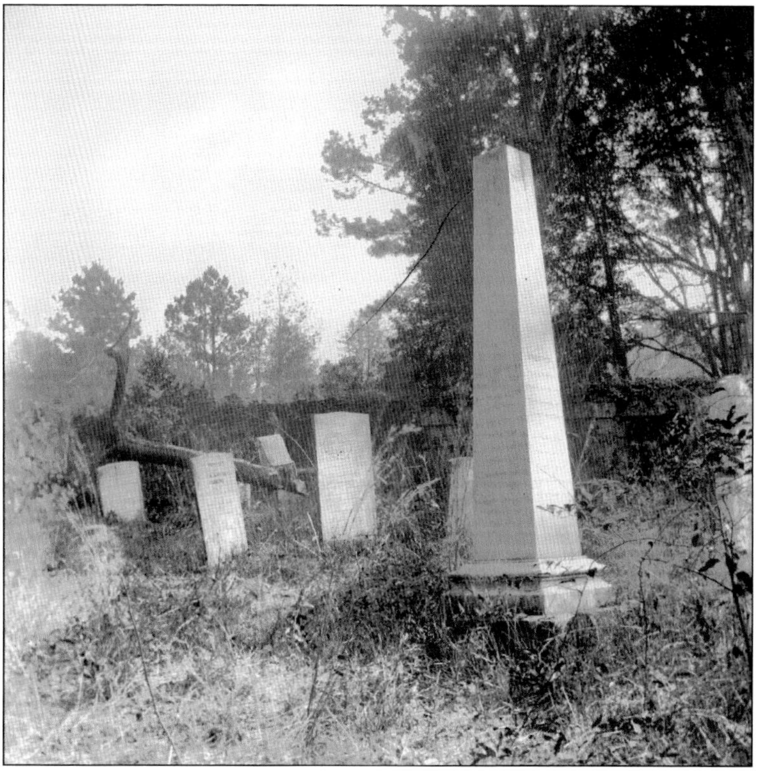

Another angle inside the Midway Cemetery shows fallen limbs and monuments in disrepair. Abandoned since 1872, the cemetery became the responsibility of the Midway Society, reorganized in 1887, and the board of selectmen. (Photograph by Julia King; courtesy of the Springfield Legacy Foundation.)

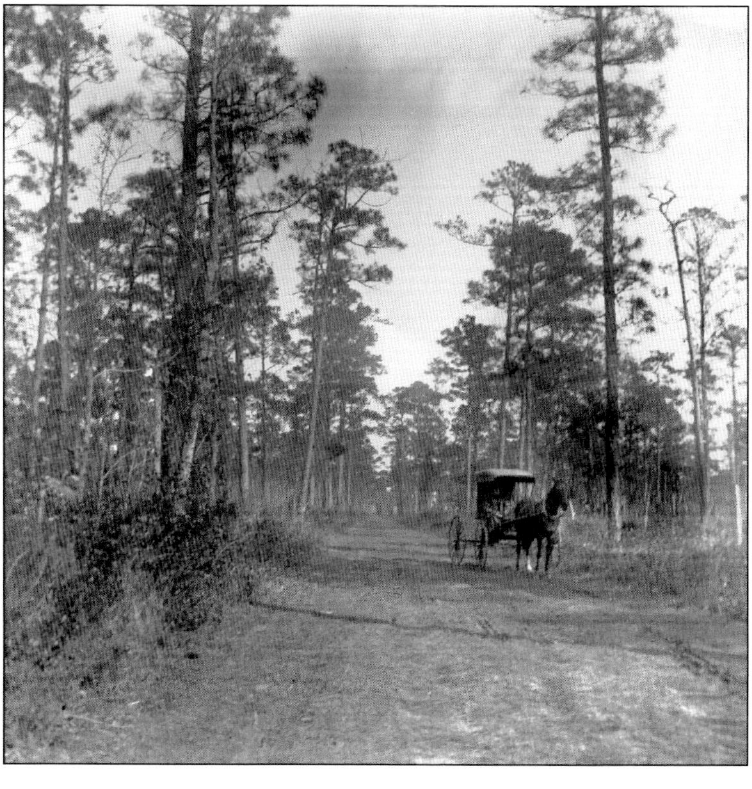

On the road again, Julia King photographed her buggy as it stood in the middle of a road lined with pine forests. This may have been taken on the Barrington Ferry Road north of Riceboro. (Photograph by Julia King; courtesy of the Springfield Legacy Foundation.)

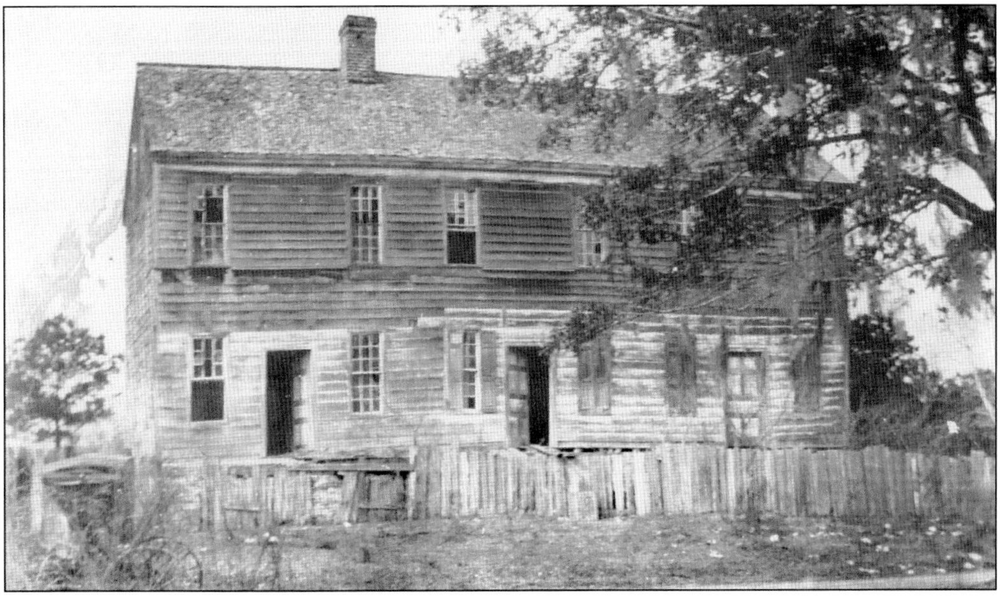

At the end of her road trip, Julia King photographed what remained of an old inn at Riceboro. The county seat from 1797 until 1837, Riceboro was the center of wealth in Liberty County prior to the Civil War. Located on the Barrington Ferry Road, land travelers passed through Riceboro when moving between Savannah and Darien. With the collapse of large-scale rice cultivation, the town withered through the end of the 19th century. (Photograph by Julia King; courtesy of the Springfield Legacy Foundation.)

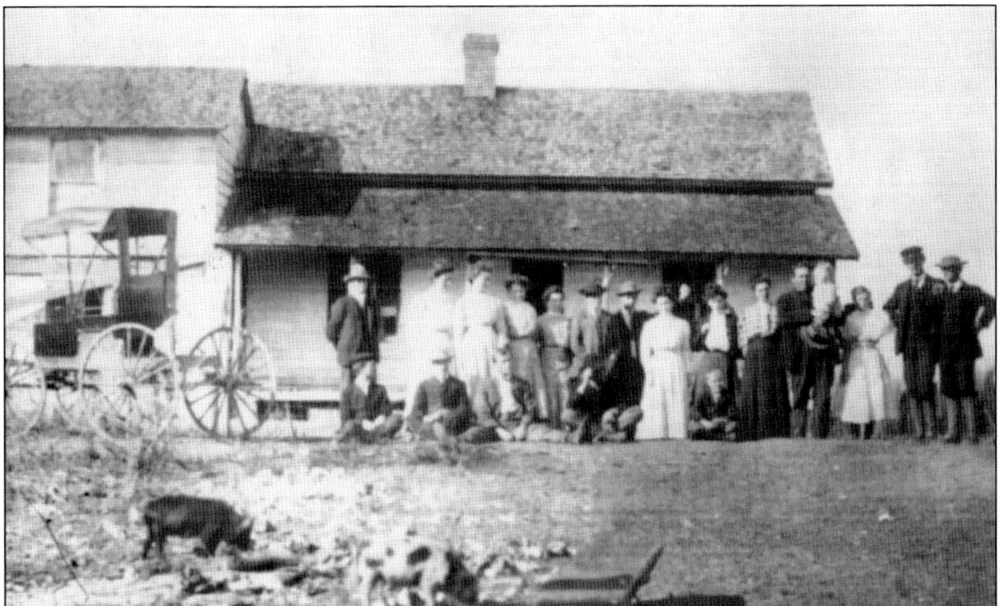

Around 1900, countians enjoyed visiting others' homes, having picnics, and going on extended camping trips—or maroons. This photograph shows a group gathered on a maroon at Sunbury on January 1, 1908. Members include Henry Rahn, Tom Rahn, Lonnie Stafford, Edward Stafford, Bird Daniel, Stella Stafford, John Stafford, Leroy Way, Susie McLean, and Ellie Mae Stacy. (Courtesy of the *Liberty County Herald*.)

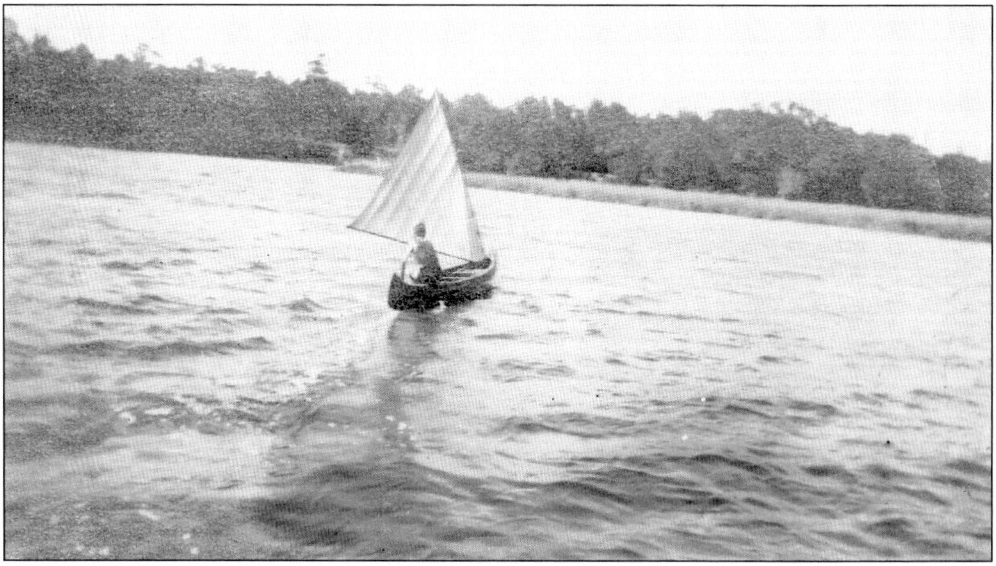

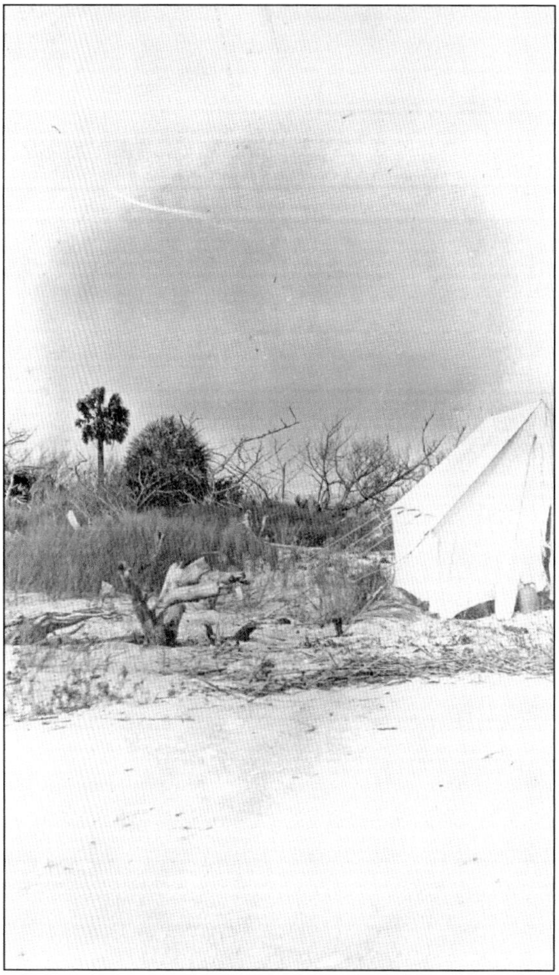

In the first years of the 20th century, Liberty countians loved going on maroons—or romanticized camping trips—to places such as Sunbury or the barrier islands. Liberty County native Francis Robert Goulding wrote an enormously popular book for boys, *The Young Marooners*, in 1852. Generations of young people sought to recreate the adventures in the novel and its sequels, set along the Florida coast, in their own backyards. This series of extraordinary photographs documents one such maroon on Raccoon Key north of Ossabaw Island in 1913. Setting out in a northeaster, the boys rigged a sail to a canoe (top photograph). Once settled on the beach, they pitched a tent (bottom photograph). (Courtesy of the Springfield Legacy Foundation.)

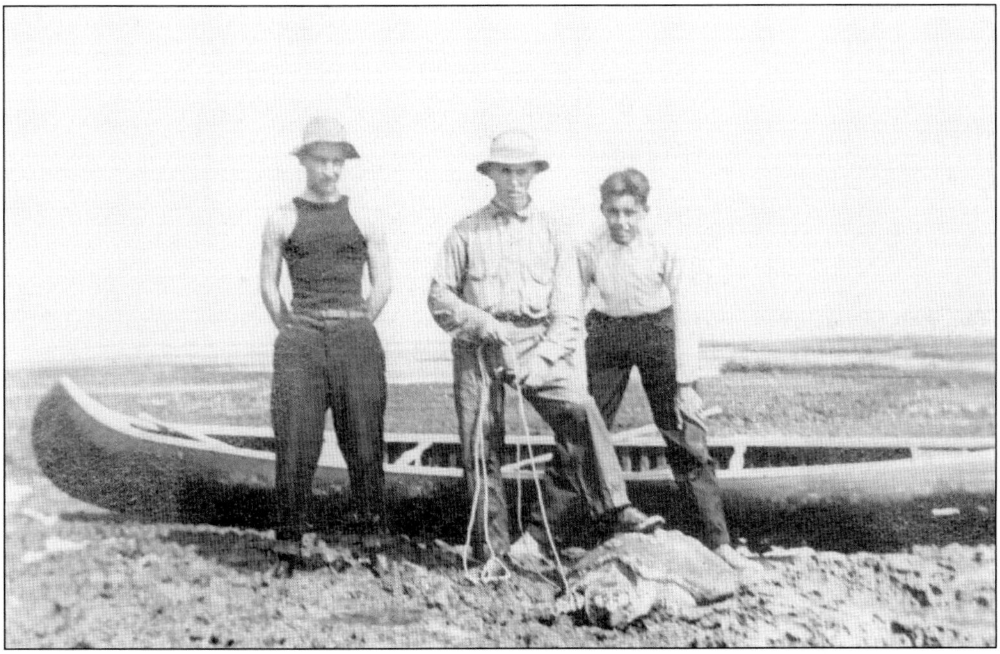

To pull their canoes, the boys foolishly lassoed a loggerhead sea turtle, seen on the ground in front of the group. The animal immediately dived into the water in an attempt to escape, dragging the canoe and its occupants on a wild ride. Eventually the turtle tired and was subdued. (Courtesy of the Springfield Legacy Foundation.)

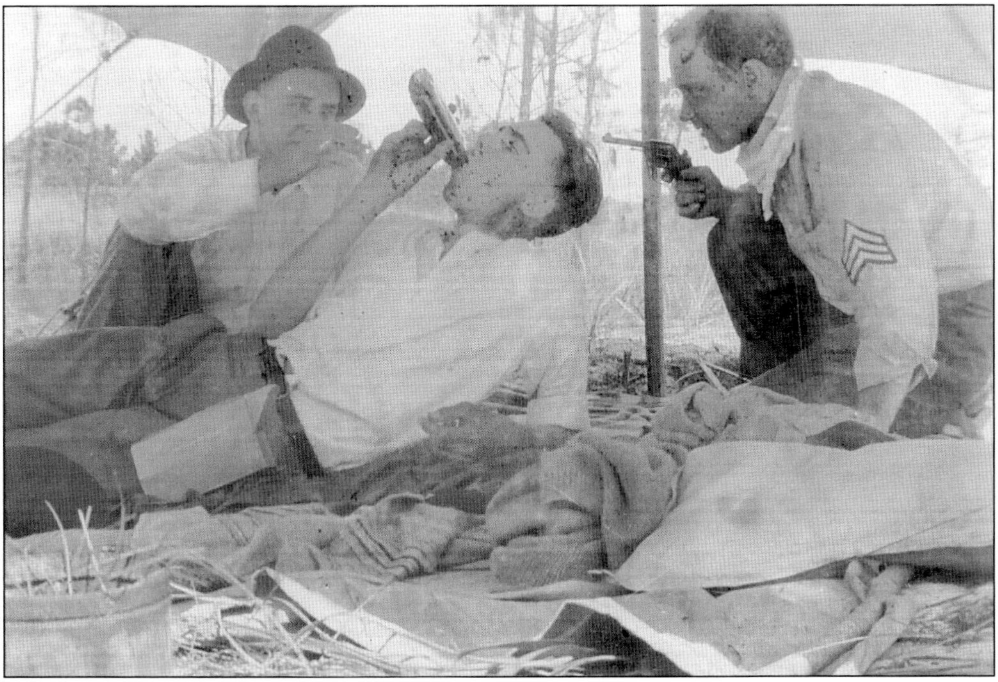

Continuing on their maroon, the boys joked around with a flask and a gun. The purpose of these excursions was to escape and experiment with mildly dangerous things. (Courtesy of the Springfield Legacy Foundation.)

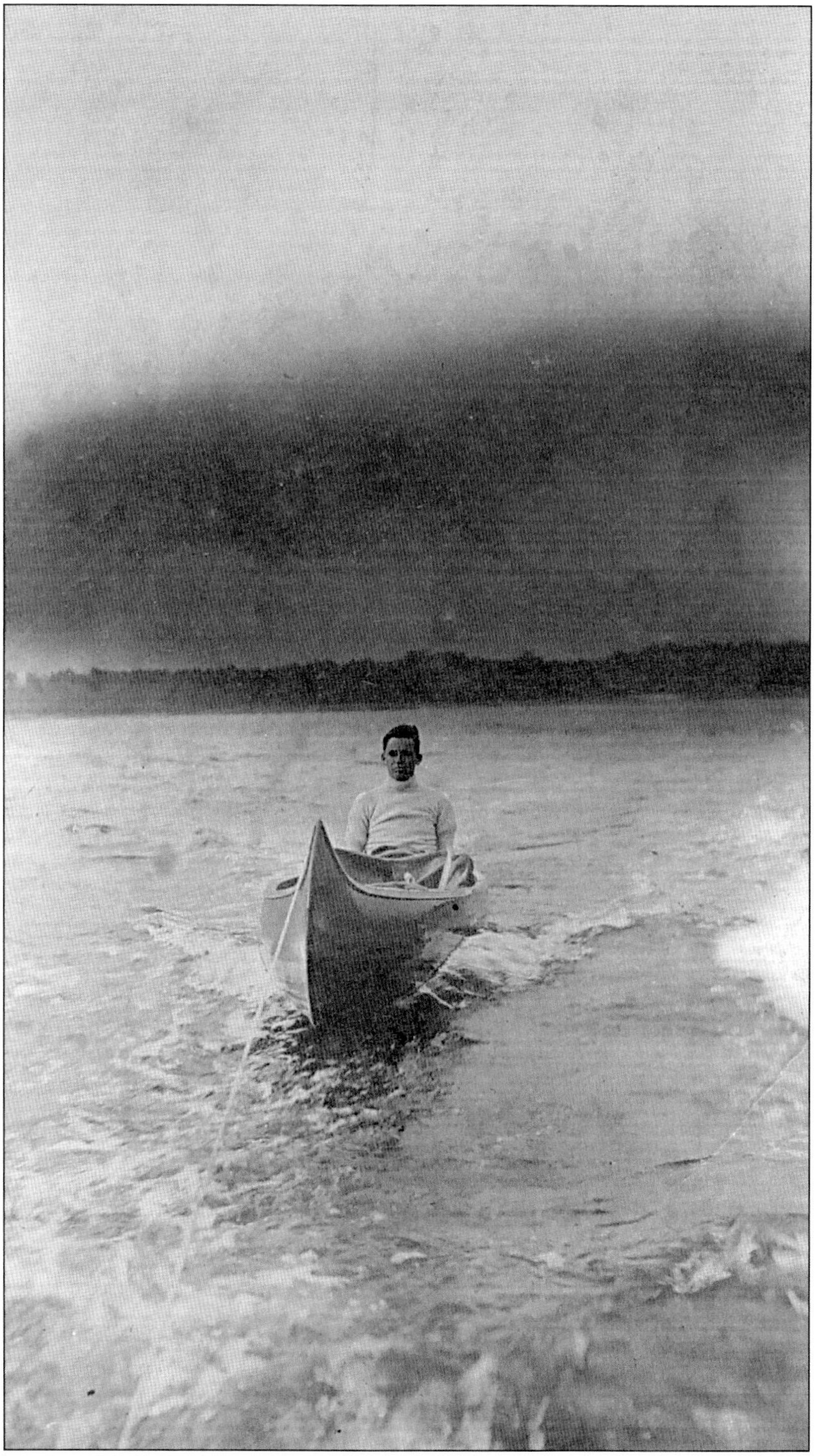

In this photograph John P. Stevens was towed home from the maroon. In the background, the sky is black with smoke from a fire on Green Island south of Skidaway Island. (Courtesy of the Springfield Legacy Foundation.)

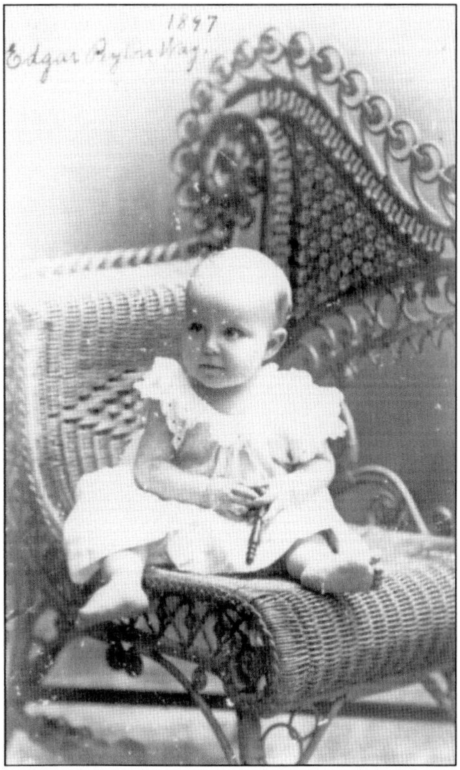

The top portrait was made of Edgar Peyton Way on his first birthday in 1897. Nineteen years later, a 20-year-old Edgar Peyton Way (bottom) served in Troop B of the Georgia Calvary stationed at Fort Bliss, Texas, when this photograph was taken in December 1916. Many young men from Liberty County joined the military before and during World War I. (Courtesy of the *Liberty County Herald*.)

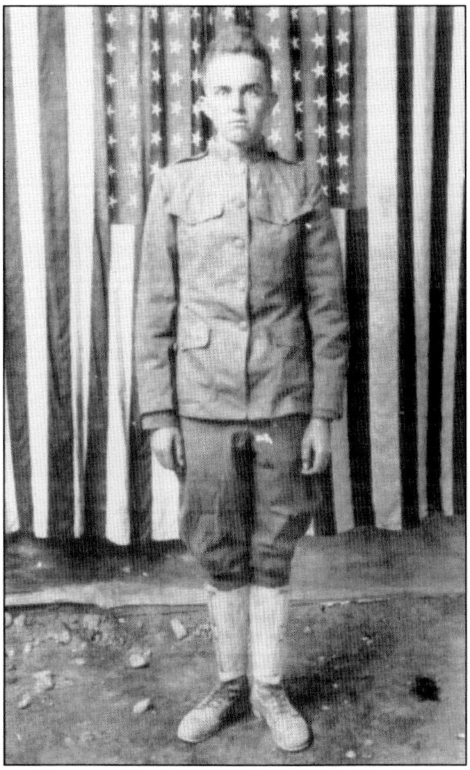

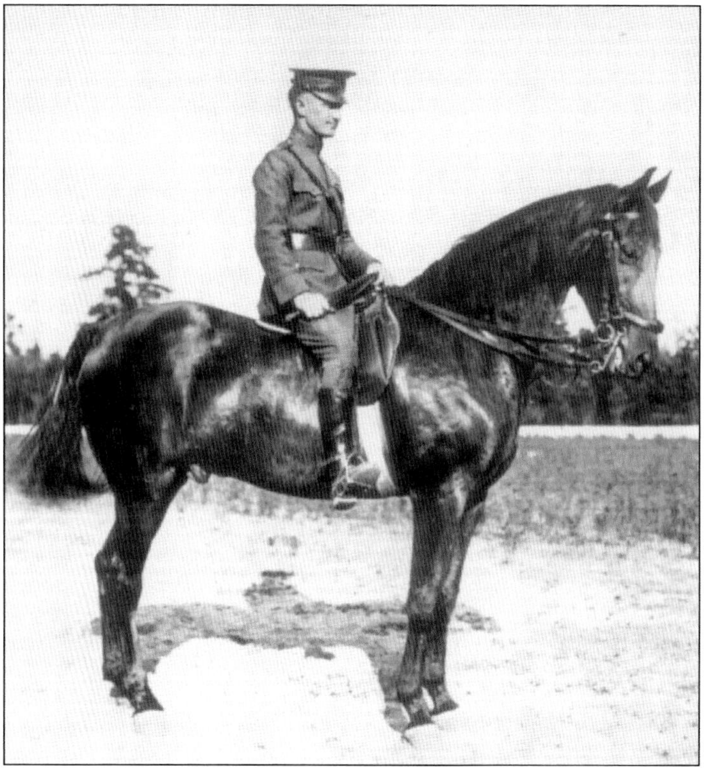

First Lt. Charles Jones Martin Jr. sits astride his army mount. The photograph was made around 1922 when Martin was a member of the local troop. (Courtesy of the *Liberty County Herald.*)

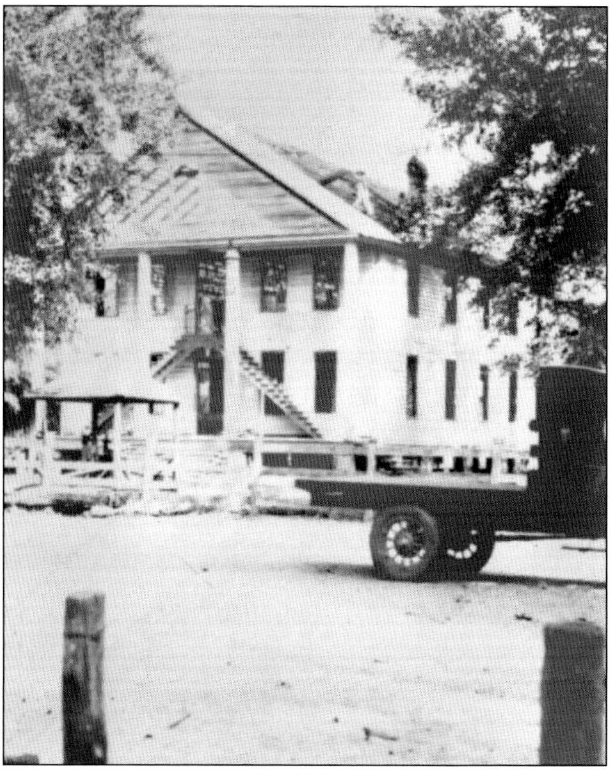

The old Liberty County Courthouse served as the focal point for local government from 1837, when Hinesville became the county seat, until 1926 when a new courthouse was built. It was a common practice for citizens to observe court proceeding whether or not they had personal court business. Many would bring a packed lunch, or dinner—as it was called—and slake their thirst at the hand pump located in the foreground of this 1923 photograph. (Courtesy of the *Liberty County Herald.*)

Three

THE LAST YEARS OF COUNTRY LIFE

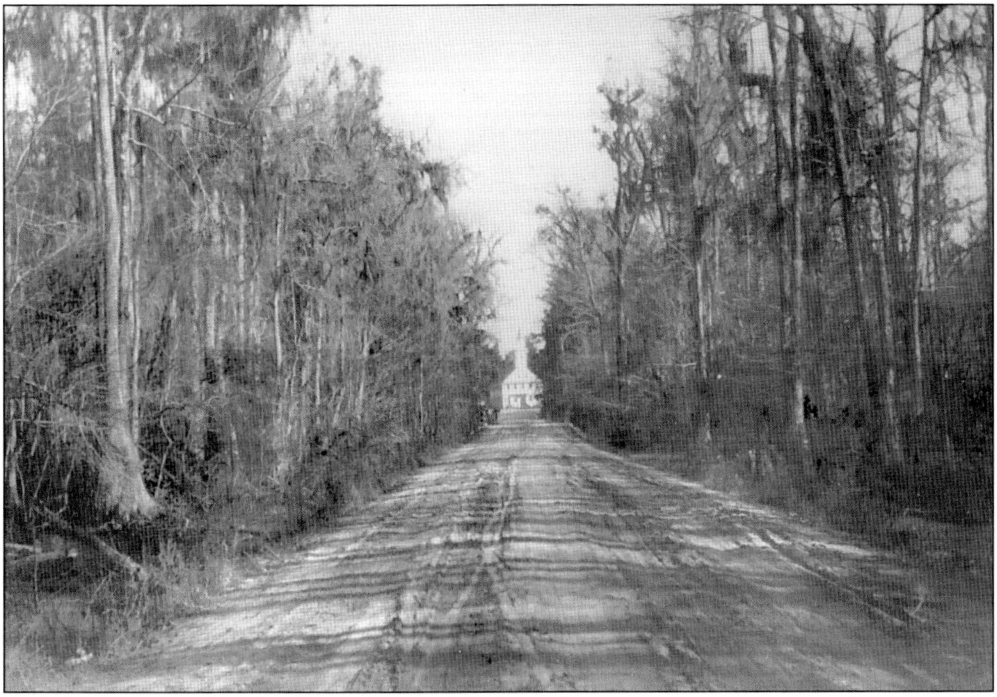

Prior to the creation of the Dixie Highway, later known as U.S. Route 17, travelers driving from Savannah to Darien along the old Barrington Ferry Road braved a muddy track through endless swamps. This view of the Midway Church from the south on Barrington Ferry Road prior to 1920 gives a sense of the traveling conditions. Through the end of the 1930s, Liberty remained a rural, farming community. Hinesville was still a small courthouse town in 1900, but the county remained largely rural and isolated. In the 1930s telephones were available at railroad depots, and subscriber lines began to work across the county. There was no electricity. Most citizens lived on farms that supplied their basic needs. Jobs were tied directly to farms and forests, and food crops, lumber, tobacco, and naval stores were the most important commodities produced in Liberty County. Sawmills launched two new towns in Willie and Allenhurst. With the arrival of the Great Depression, markets for agricultural products declined along with the national economy. Able to survive on their farms and feed themselves from the bounty of rivers and forests, people in the country still struggled to pay their taxes and provide shoes and clothing for their families. (Courtesy of the Springfield Legacy Foundation.)

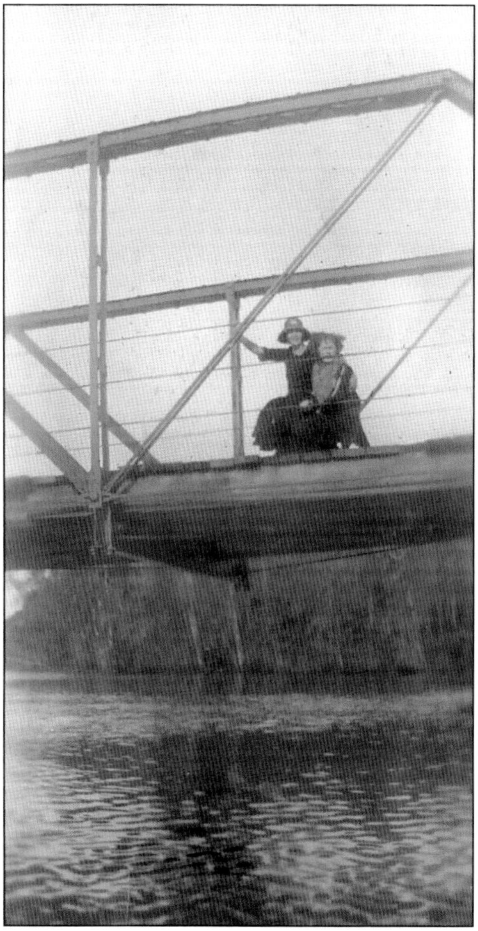

In this photograph two girls pose on a modern steel bridge over Bridge Creek bridge in the 1930s. (Courtesy of the Springfield Legacy Foundation.)

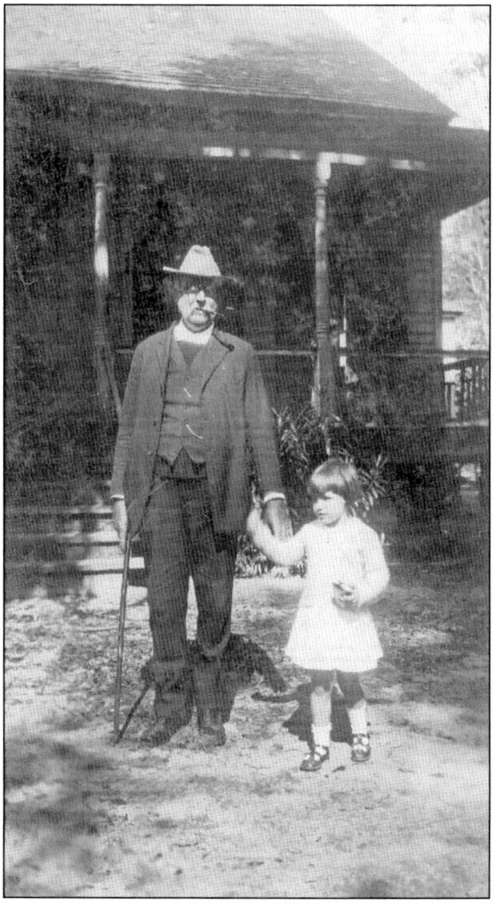

William Maxwell Stevens stands with his young granddaughter Martha Randolph Stevens at Springfield Plantation in the 1920s. Farmers like Stevens depended on short-term credit to pay expenses between harvests. Having held title to the property since 1755, the family nearly lost the land when a cotton lien was called in 1925 after a poor harvest. W. M. Stevens's son John borrowed money from his wife's family to pay off the lien and keep Springfield in the family. (Courtesy of the Springfield Legacy Foundation.)

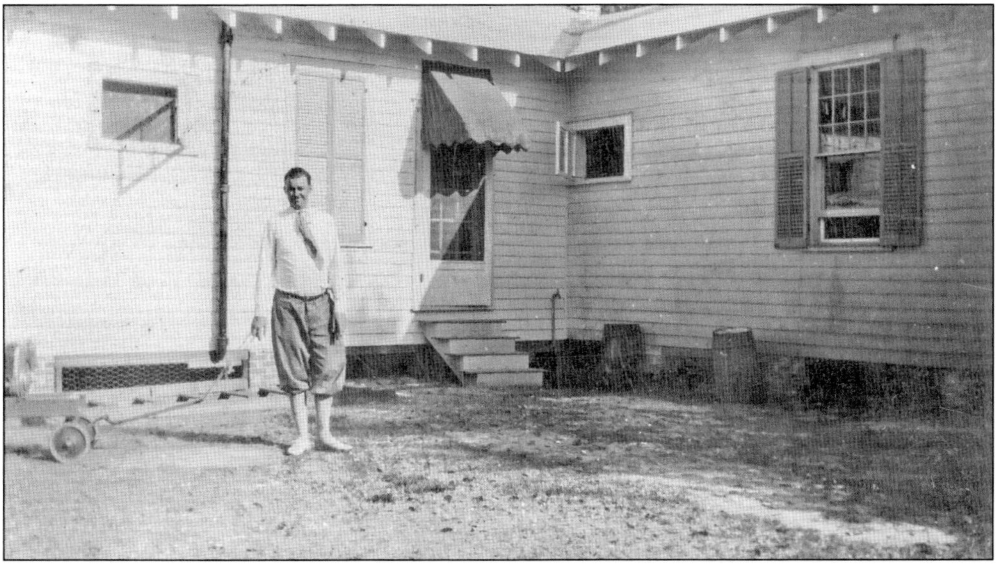

John Porter Stevens is at his newly built home at the Springfield Plantation around 1926. He is towing a small portable electric generator. He also established a Delco battery house to generate electricity. It worked by storing electrically charged water in large glass jars. Rural electrification was not available in the area until the 1950s. (Courtesy of the Springfield Legacy Foundation.)

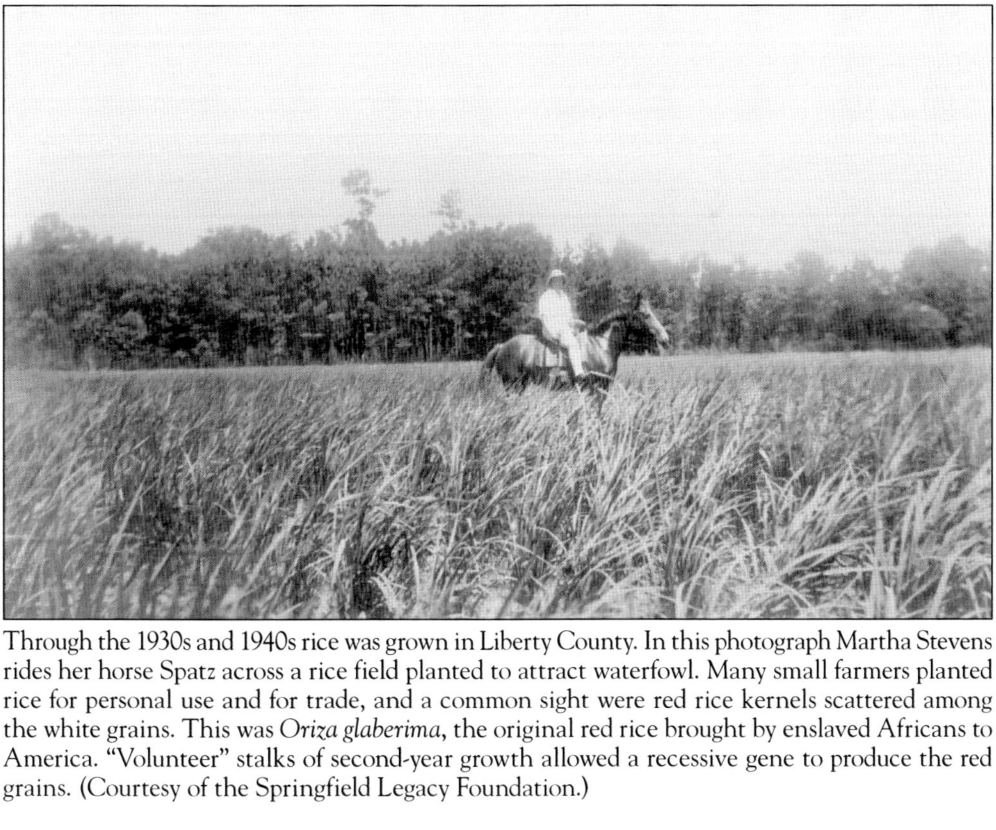

Through the 1930s and 1940s rice was grown in Liberty County. In this photograph Martha Stevens rides her horse Spatz across a rice field planted to attract waterfowl. Many small farmers planted rice for personal use and for trade, and a common sight were red rice kernels scattered among the white grains. This was *Oriza glaberima*, the original red rice brought by enslaved Africans to America. "Volunteer" stalks of second-year growth allowed a recessive gene to produce the red grains. (Courtesy of the Springfield Legacy Foundation.)

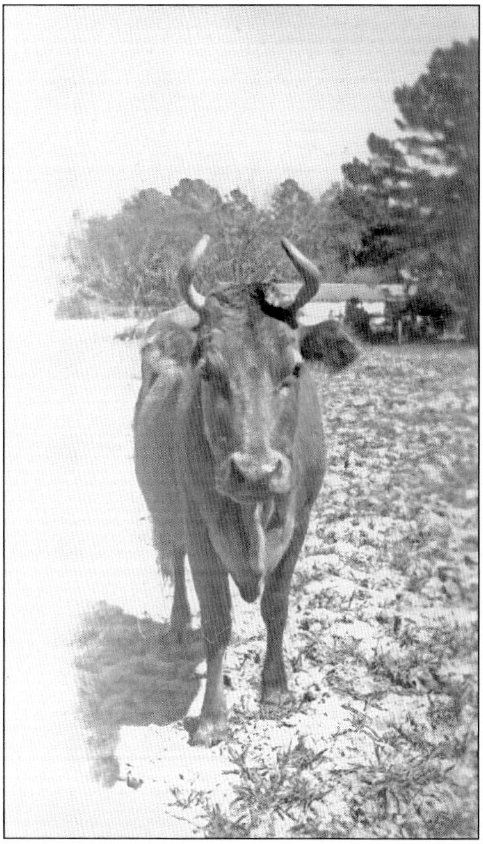

Well into the 20th century, cattle continued to roam freely in Liberty County. In the 1930s, an exotic-looking cow stares at a photographer. (Courtesy of the Springfield Legacy Foundation.)

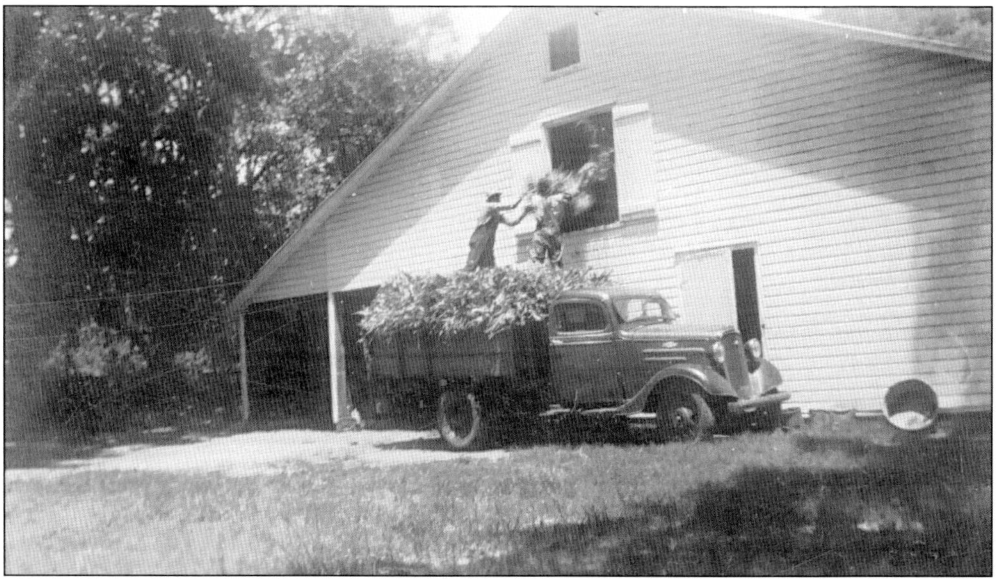

Men unload hay into the hayloft of this new barn constructed in 1930 at Palmyra Plantation. Large fields covered much of Liberty County creating vast horizons of gently rolling land. In the late 1930s, many farmers converted annual cropland to pine forests as paper mills were constructed in Brunswick and Savannah. (Courtesy of the Springfield Legacy Foundation.)

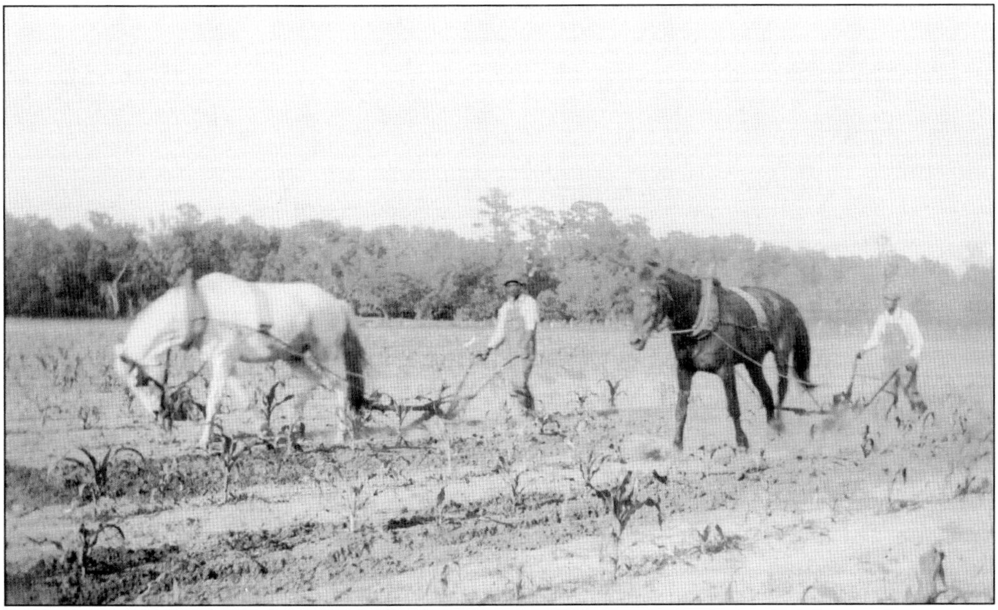

While tractors were available, animal traction was still more commonly used on Liberty County farms. In this photograph, two unidentified men work a field with a team of mules in the early 1930s. (Courtesy of the Springfield Legacy Foundation.)

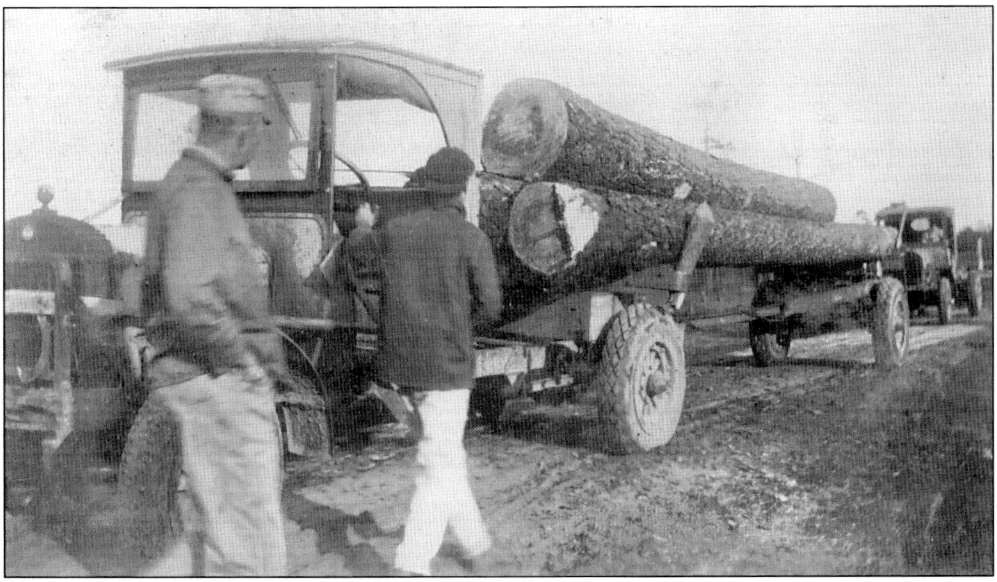

An early 1930s log truck hauls large pine trees to a lumber mill. These trees were harvested from old fields abandoned 60 to 70 years earlier during the Civil War. (Courtesy of the Springfield Legacy Foundation.)

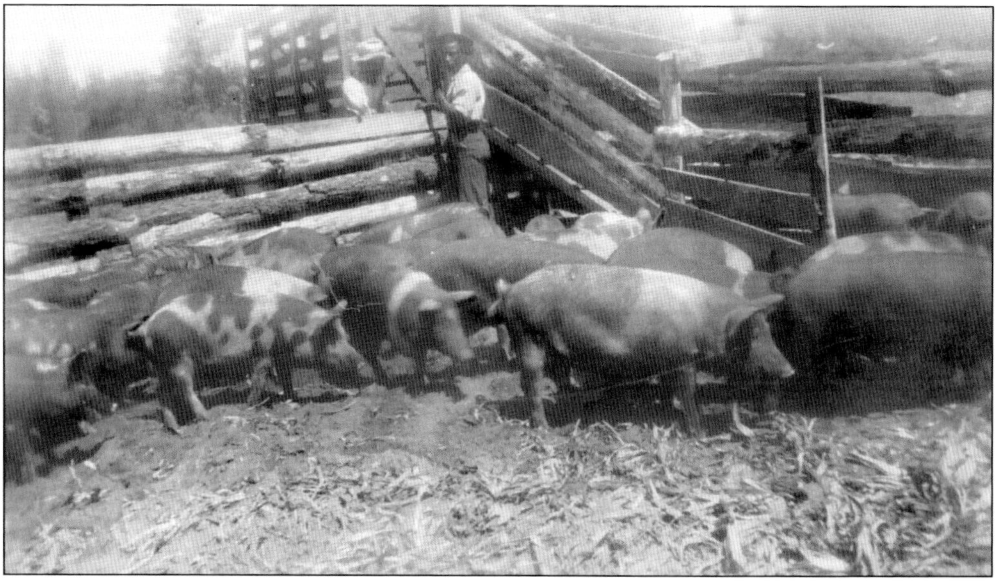

In 1934, African Americans owned 560 farms in Liberty County totaling over 23,000 acres. Similar to their white counterparts, black farmers grew small plots of rice, corn, sugar cane, and vegetables to feed their families and worked outside jobs for extra money. In this photograph from the early 1930s, men feed hogs on a farm. (Courtesy of the Springfield Legacy Foundation.)

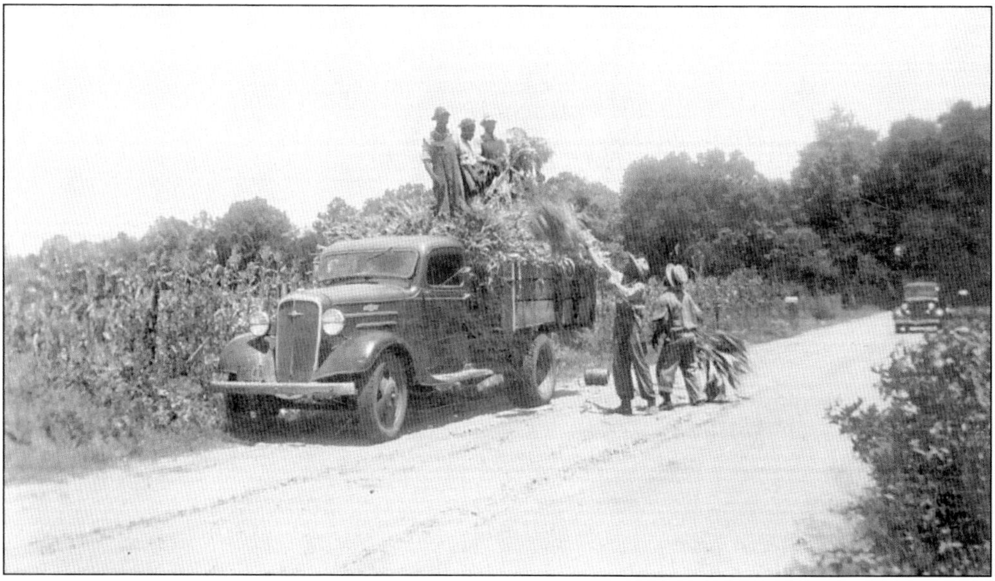

Throughout the 19th and early 20th centuries, corn was a dominant crop in Liberty County. Used for livestock feed, grits, and meal, nearly 20,000 acres of corn were planted in the mid-1930s. Another use for corn was the illegal-yet-lucrative manufacture of corn whiskey, also known as moonshine. In this photograph, men harvest corn—for legal uses—in the 1930s. (Courtesy of the Springfield Legacy Foundation.)

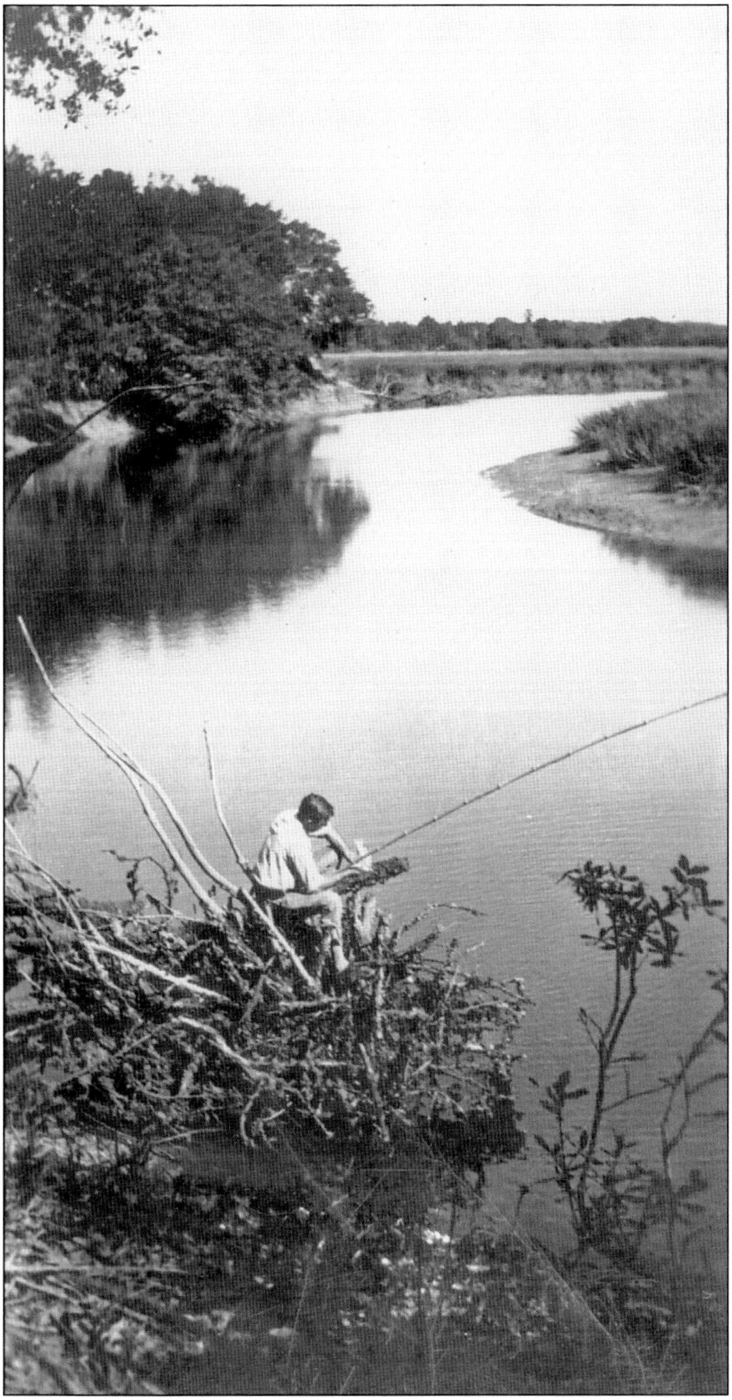

Coastal residents of Liberty County were extremely fortunate compared to residents of the interior of the Deep South. Fish, shrimp, oysters, mussels, and waterfowl teemed in tidal creeks and provided essential nutrients such as iodine and protein as well as additional income. In the mid-1930s, an unidentified man fishes in a Liberty County saltwater creek in this photograph. (Courtesy of the Springfield Legacy Foundation.)

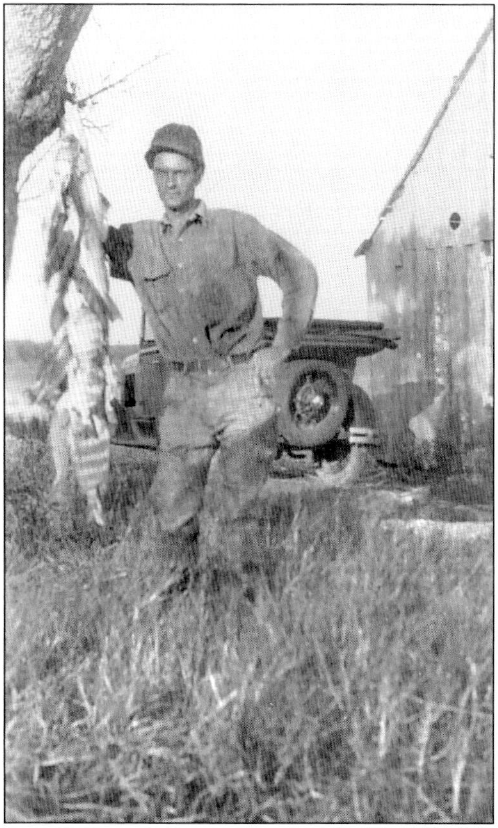

John Toby Woods is shown here with newly caught fish in the early 1930s. A fisherman and hunter, Woods became caretaker of St. Catherine's Island in 1929. His son, John Toby Woods Jr., who grew up on the island, became superintendent of St. Catherine's Island after his father retired. Royce Hayes succeeded John Toby Woods Jr. as superintendent, but members of the Woods family continued to work on the island into the 21st century. (Courtesy of the Springfield Legacy Foundation.)

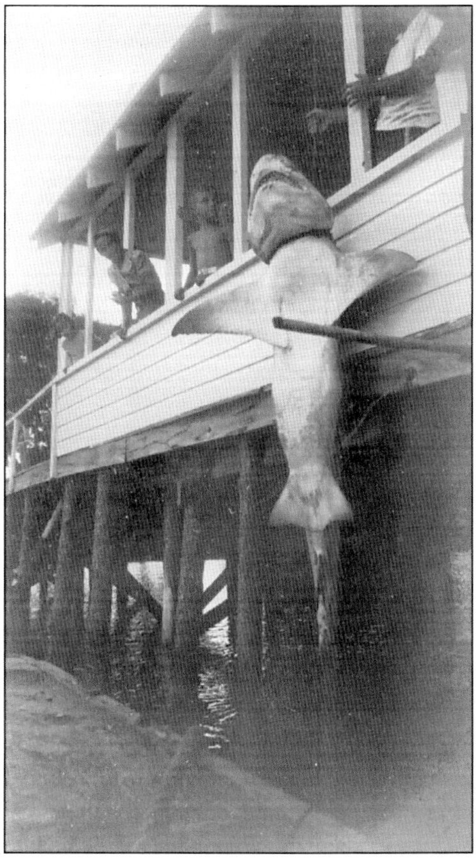

With plentiful specimens of large sharks in the coastal waters of Liberty County, the most adventurous anglers went in search of this dangerous game. Shark tournaments were popular events. (Courtesy of the Springfield Legacy Foundation.)

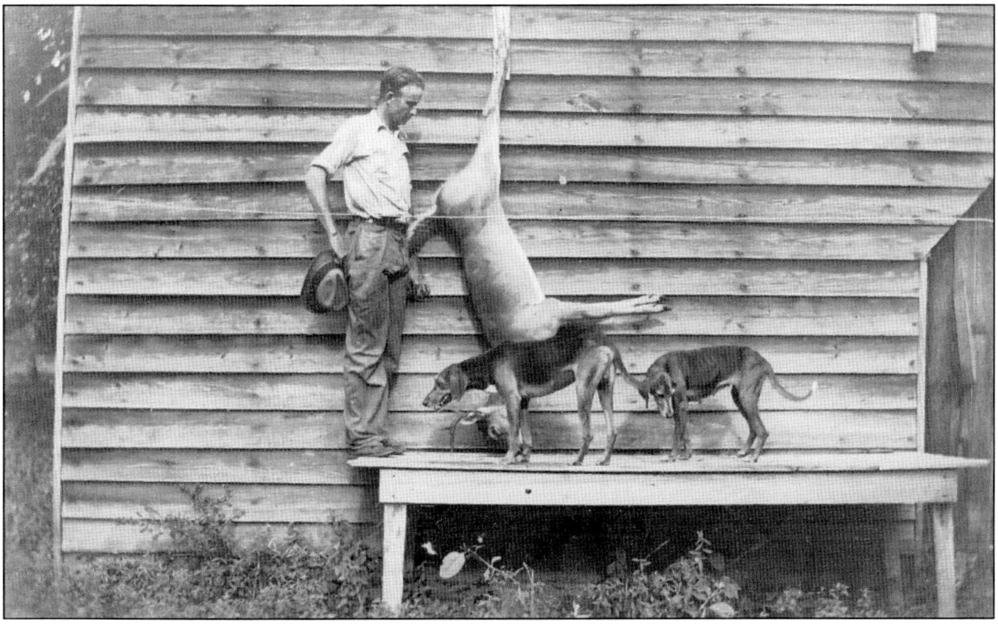

Another common food source was the whitetail deer. Venison, along with raccoon, opossum, and rabbits, was popular game, and their population control was essential to lessening crop damage. In this photograph Dana Stevens stands with a dead deer and his hounds in early 1930s. Through loss of habitat from cotton cultivation, the whitetail deer was extinct by the 1950s in Georgia. (Courtesy of the Springfield Legacy Foundation.)

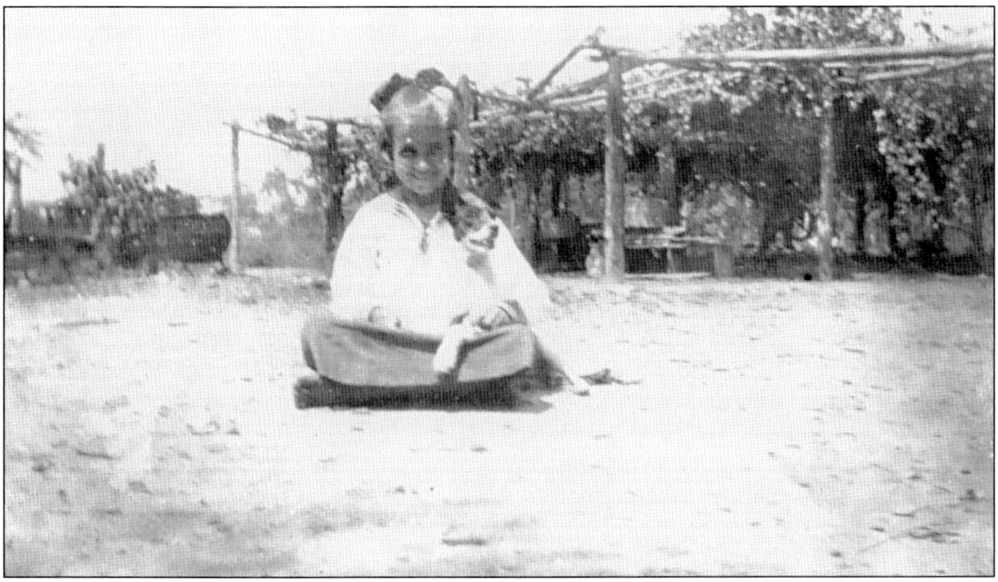

Nearly every farm in Liberty County had a grape arbor. In this photograph a little girl sits with her dog in the early 1900s with the family's grape arbor in the background. Arbors were rectangular or round and usually constructed of spare bits of wood—preferably cedar. Locals grew scuppernongs and muscadines, which are very tart but make jellies. (Courtesy of the Springfield Legacy Foundation.)

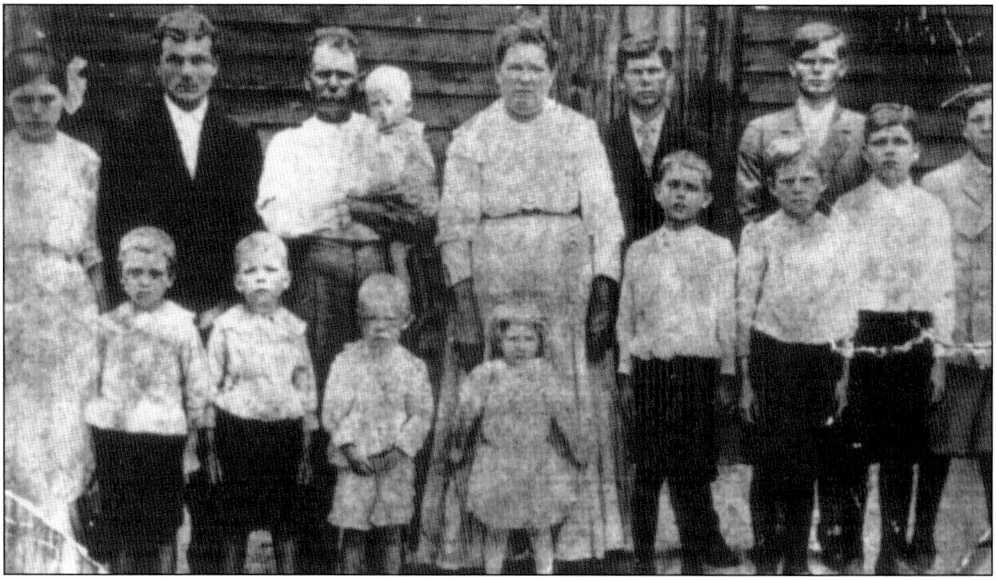

The Willie Bacon family, photographed in 1911 in the top picture with 13 of their children, lived in the vicinity of Bethany Church, an area later consumed by Fort Stewart. The family farmed and operated a sawmill, cotton gin, and general store. In 1931 the bottom photograph was taken, 20 years after the picture above and shows all 14 children of the Willie Bacon family. James S. Bacon identified his father, Shelley Bacon, second row, second from left, who later operated a barbershop on Main Street in Hinesville. The only other family members identified are, on the second row, Charlie Bacon, third from left, who was a partner in Bacon's Cleaners in Hinesville, and Harley Bacon, fourth from left, former superintendant of schools. On the first row, sixth from left, is Wilton Bacon, who was also a partner in Bacon's Cleaners. (Courtesy of the *Liberty County Herald.*)

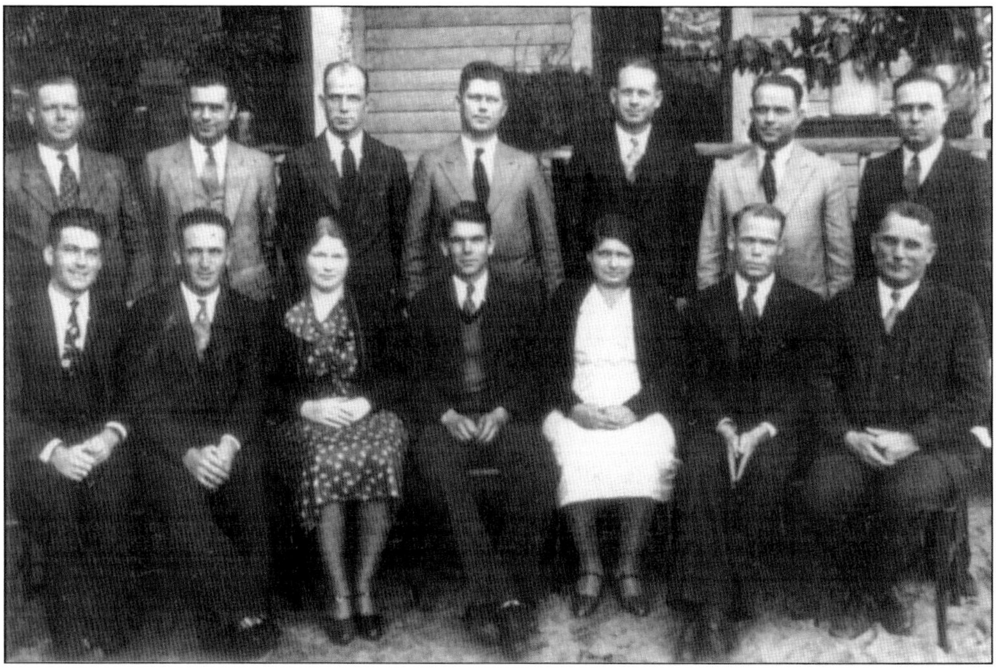

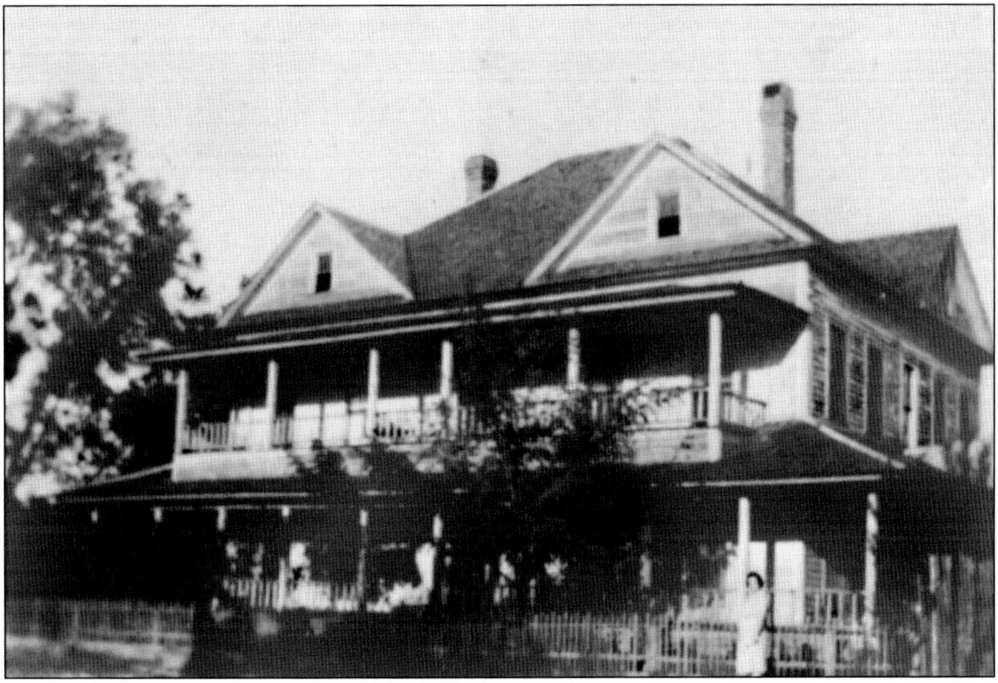

The Willie Bacon home was one of the largest homes built in Liberty County. Pictured here in the early 20th century, the house had 10 fireplaces. (Courtesy of the *Liberty County Herald.*)

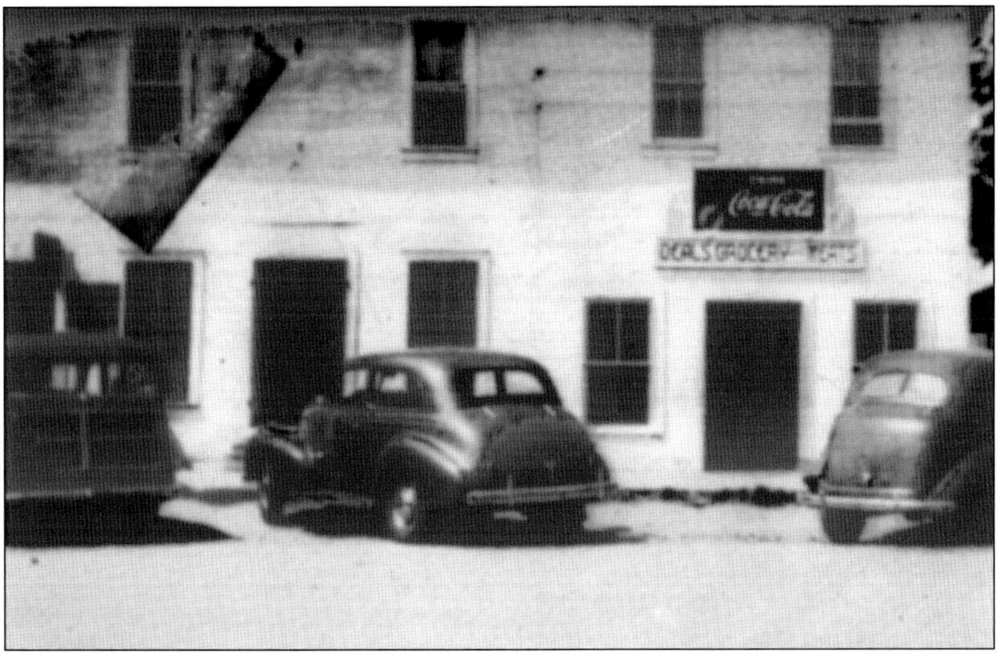

A view of Hinesville's Main Street in 1940 shows Deal's Grocery. The location was later occupied by Georgia Power. In 1939, Hinesville was still a small town serving a rural county. The business district had two gas stations, two cafes, a drugstore, three general stores, three grocery stores, a bank, a telephone exchange, a medical office building, and a post office. (Courtesy of the *Liberty County Herald.*)

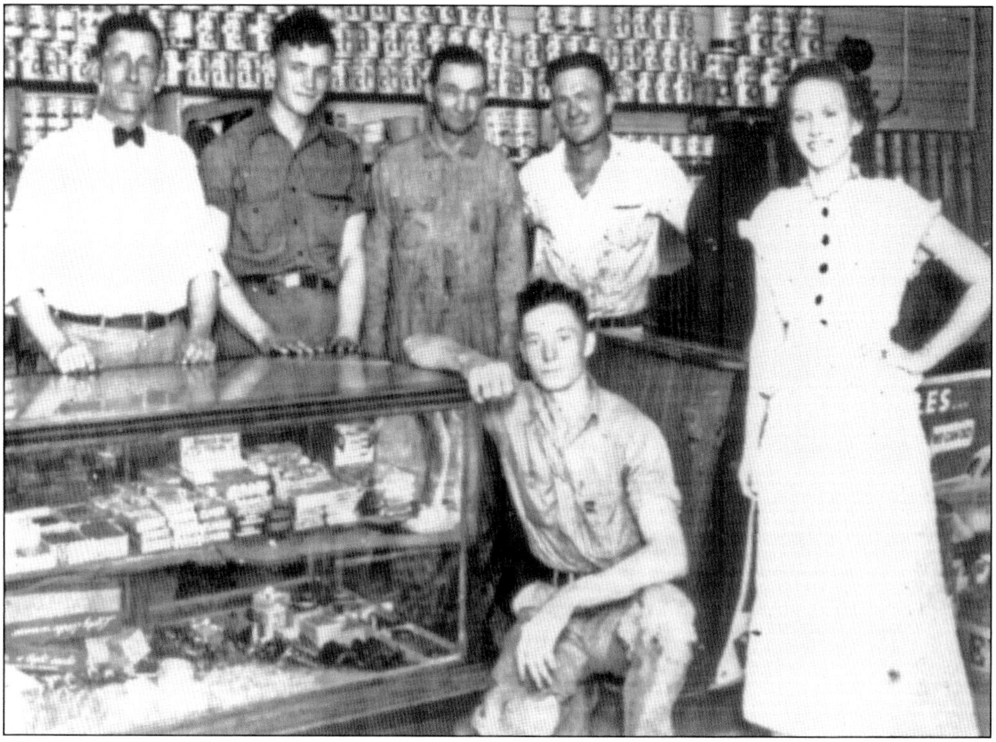

This picture was taken at the Atlantic Service Station in Hinesville on April 19, 1937. In the photograph are, from left to right, Enoch Bagley, J. B. Bradley, Ben Bradley, Cecil Dasher, Helen Bagley and kneeling, Lee Young. (Courtesy of the *Liberty County Herald*.)

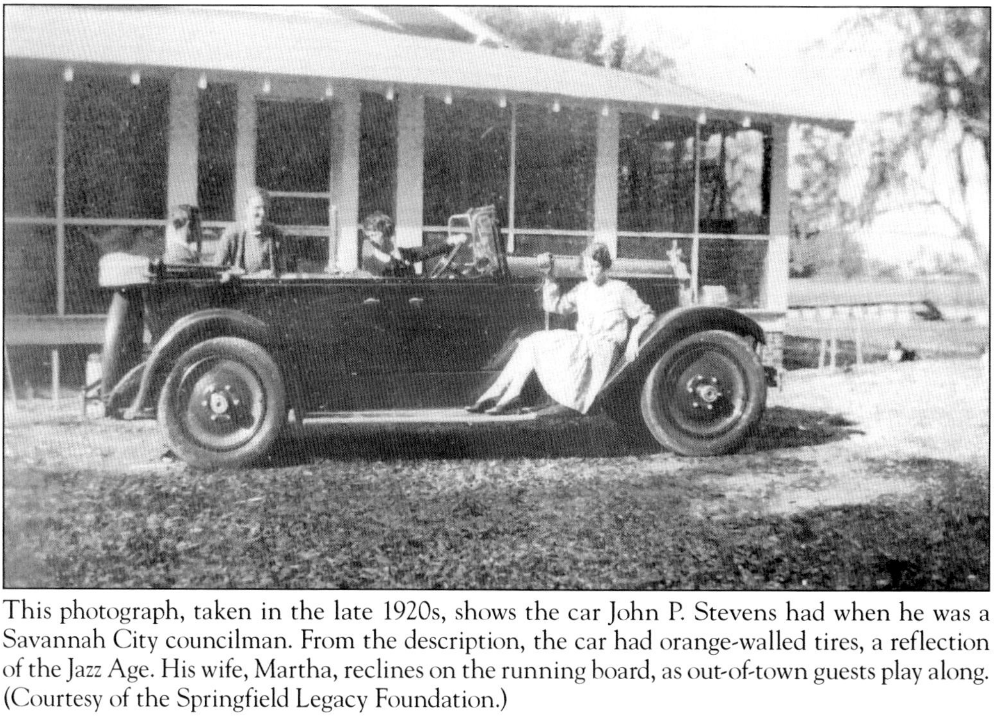

This photograph, taken in the late 1920s, shows the car John P. Stevens had when he was a Savannah City councilman. From the description, the car had orange-walled tires, a reflection of the Jazz Age. His wife, Martha, reclines on the running board, as out-of-town guests play along. (Courtesy of the Springfield Legacy Foundation.)

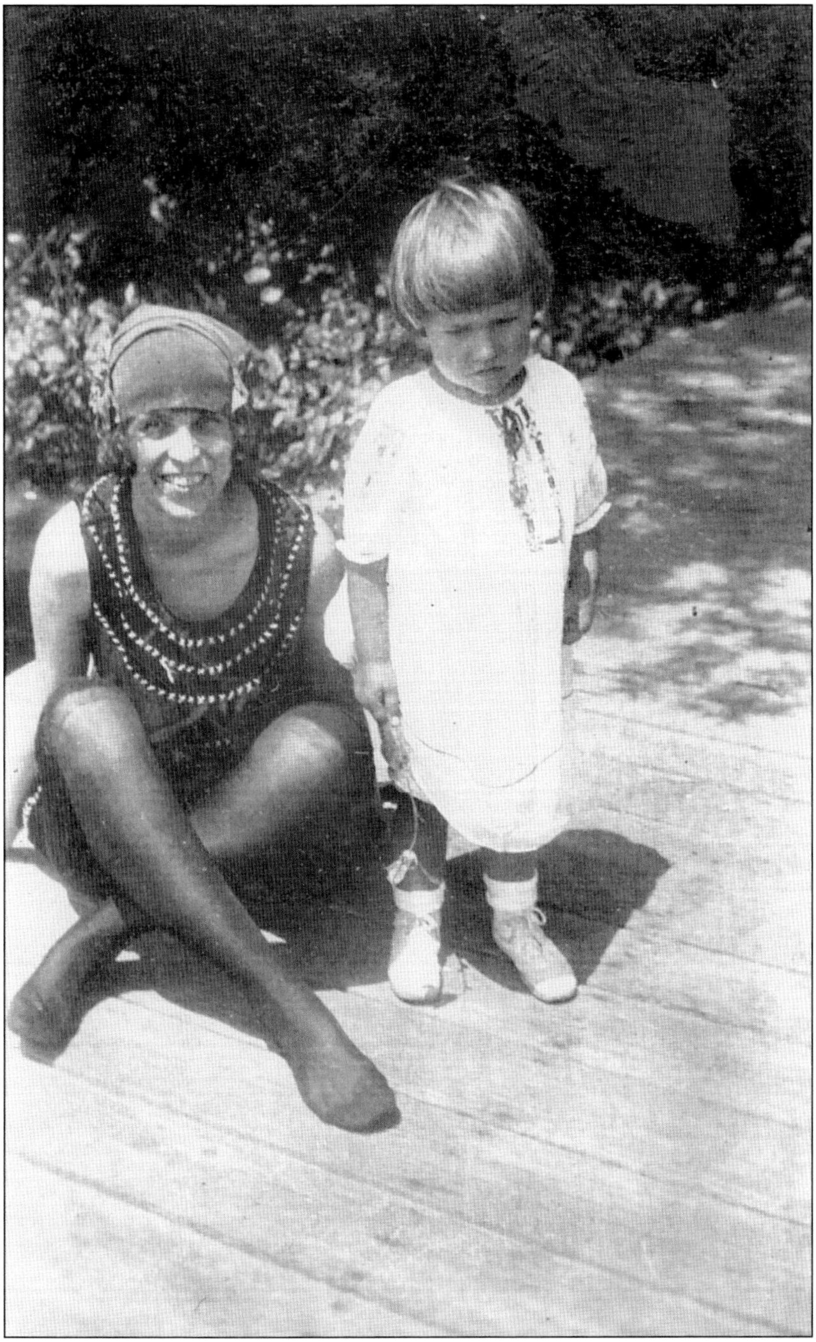

Martha Randolph Stevens (left) and her daughter, Martha Randolph Stevens (right), prepare for a day on the water in the 1920s. The little girl was born with developmental problems, possibly the result of a high-forceps delivery. She drowned in 1936 at the age of 14. In 1947, her father, John P. Stevens, gave land to the African American citizens of Liberty County for a coastal park and named the park after his daughter. The Martha Randolph Stevens Park, also known as the Landing, was the first public park for African Americans in segregated Liberty County. (Courtesy of the Springfield Legacy Foundation.)

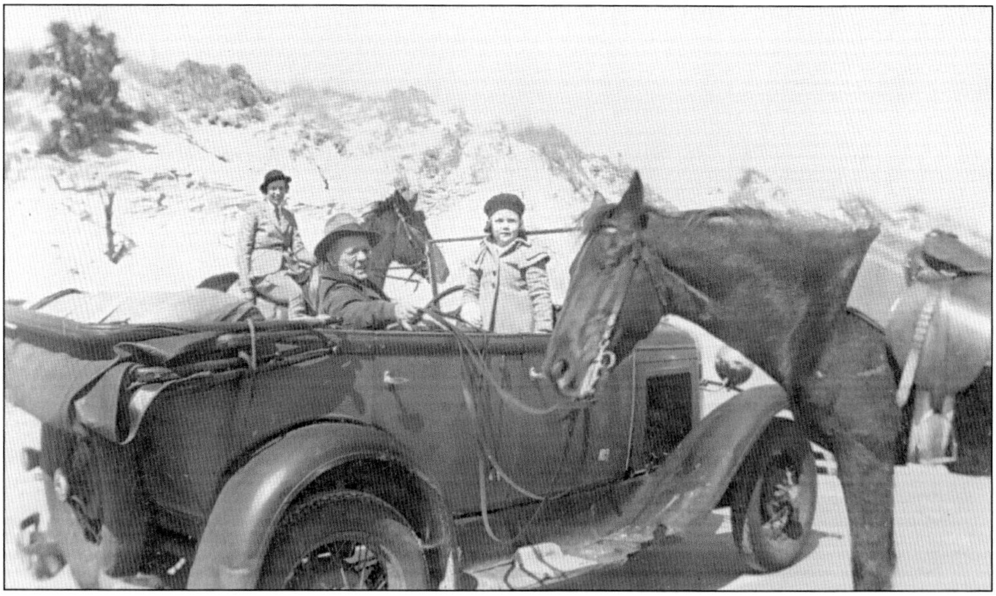

In the late 1920s, Clem Keys, a former philosophy professor and aviation pioneer, purchased St. Catherine's Island and restored the slave cabins and Button Gwinnett House. In this photograph, he is seated in the automobile as he entertains guests, Martha Stevens (on horse) and her daughter Laura (standing on right), on the beach at St. Catherine's Island in 1937. (Courtesy of the Springfield Legacy Foundation.)

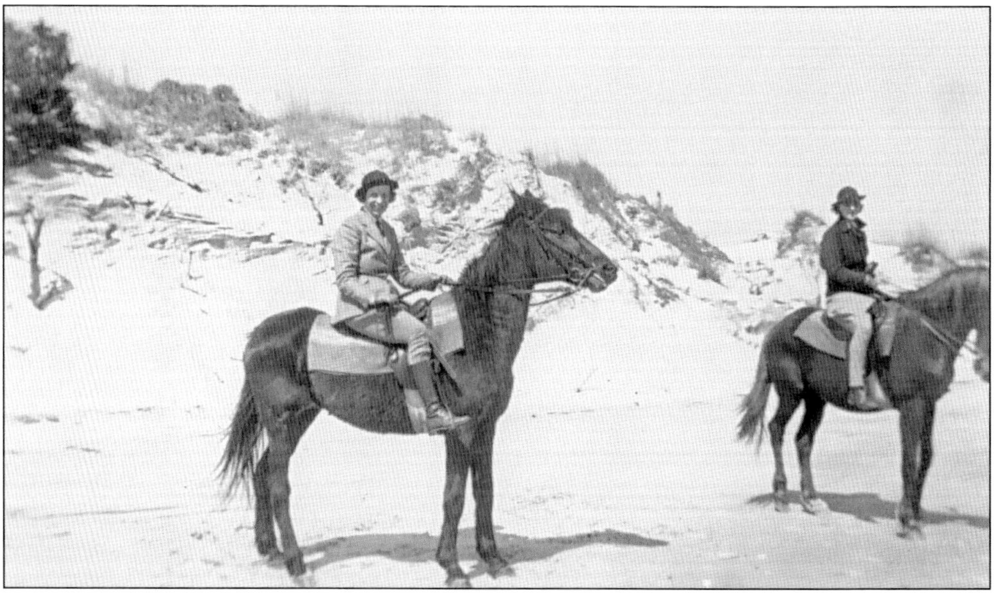

Northerners bought many of Georgia's barrier islands during the late 19th and early 20th centuries. Owners and their guests island hopped—or visited each other up and down the coast. In this photograph, Martha Stevens (left) is hosted by India Keys (right) as they ride horses on St. Catherine's beach. (Courtesy of the Springfield Legacy Foundation.)

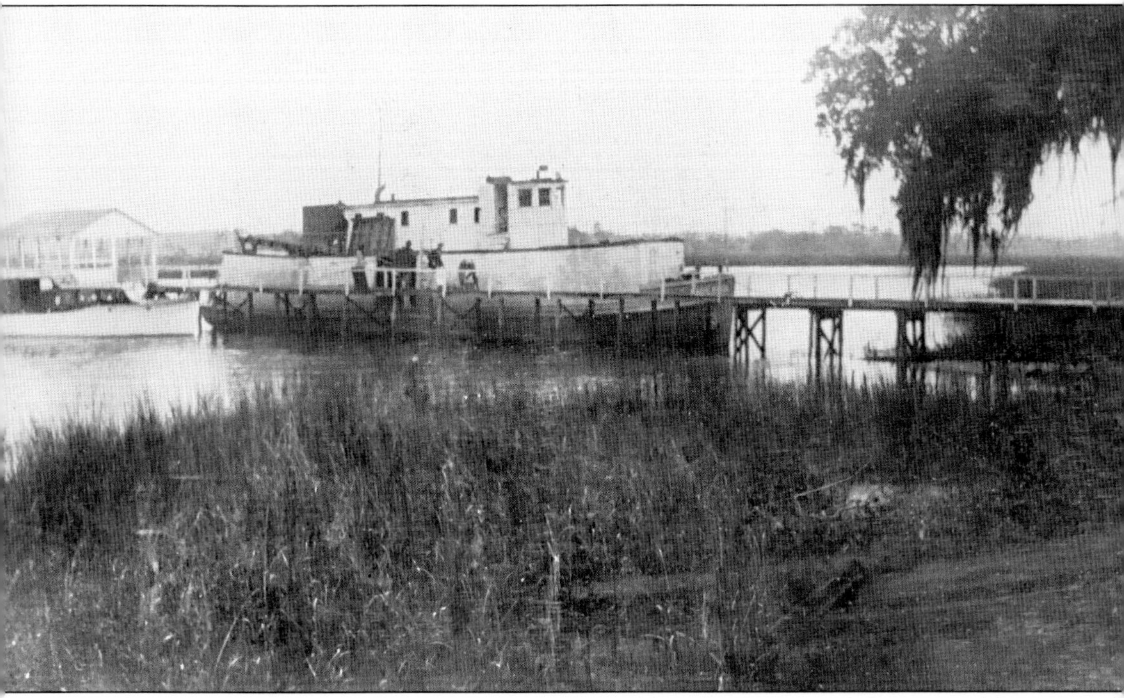

The stock market crash of 1929 devastated Clem Keys. Although Keys eventually regained his fortune as the father of commercial aviation and established Trans World Airlines—TWA—he did not hold onto St. Catherine's Island. In addition to relinquishing the island to the Rauers family, the Keys sold all of their possessions. This photograph shows a steamer bringing all of the Keys furniture and horses to Springfield Plantation in 1938. (Courtesy of the Springfield Legacy Foundation.)

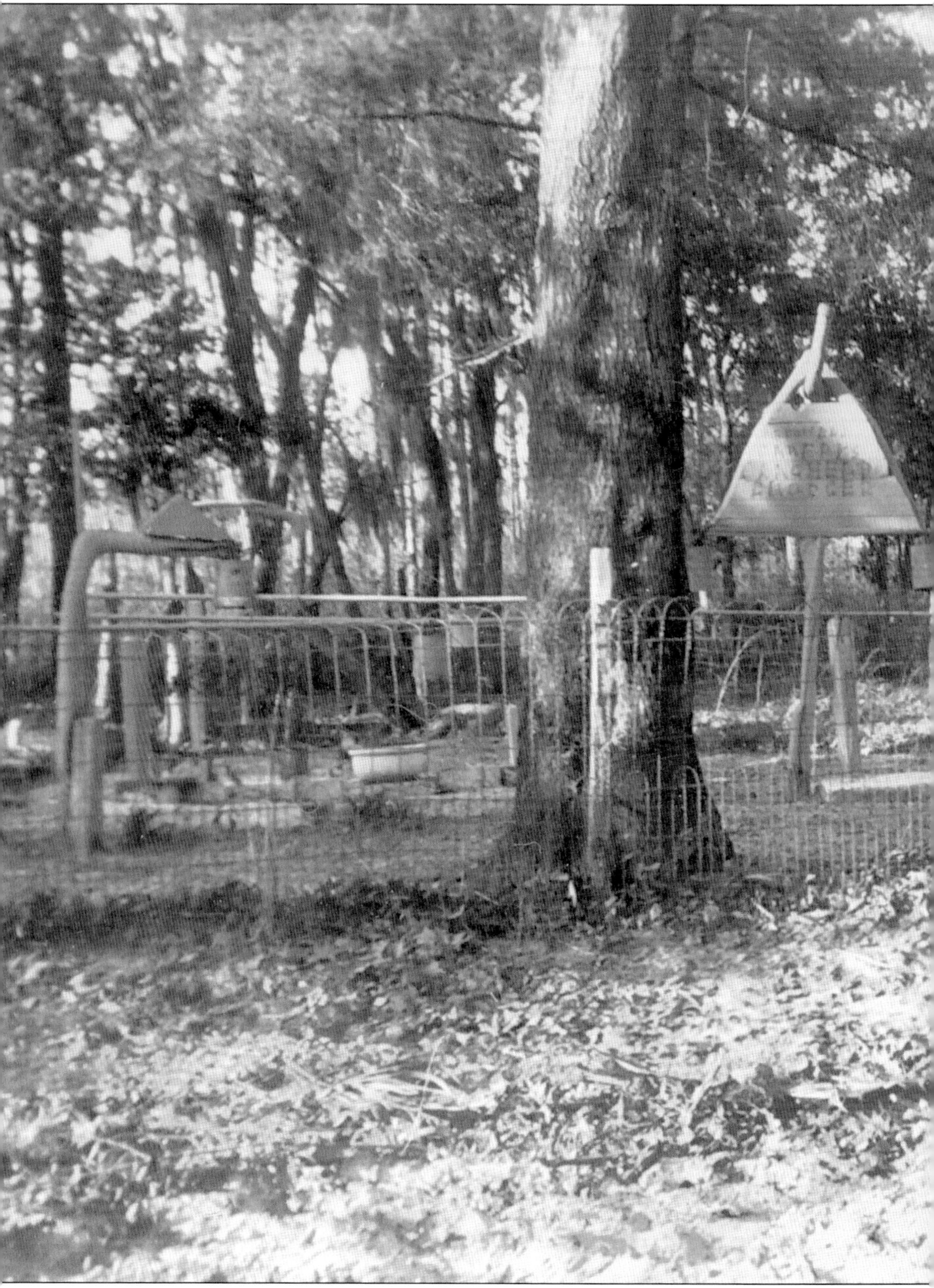

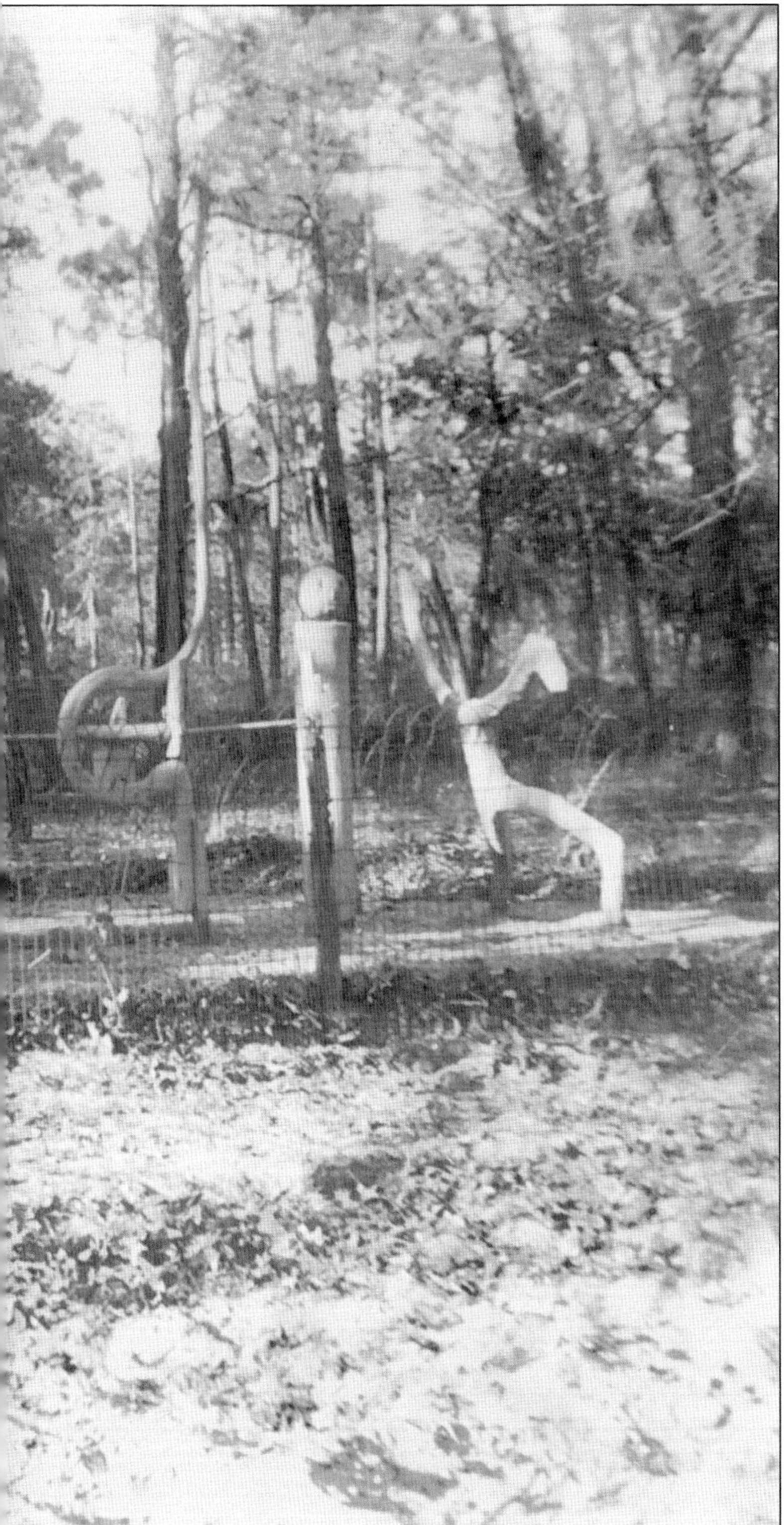

On an international level, one of the most famous sites in Liberty County was located at Sunbury Baptist Church in the Trade Hill community. This photograph from the 1930s shows the Bowens' family plot at Sunbury Baptist Church cemetery. In the late 1930s, the Savannah Writers' Project through the Works Progress Administration—WPA—undertook a survey of African culture in coastal Georgia. Mary Granger, project coordinator, worked with photographers Muriel and Malcolm Bell to produce *Drums and Shadows*, an anthropological sampling of the African American culture found in the rice-growing region of Georgia. Among the places visited was the Sunbury Baptist cemetery where Cyrus Bowens created a series of grave sculptures reminiscent of West African artistic traditions. (Courtesy of the Springfield Legacy Foundation.)

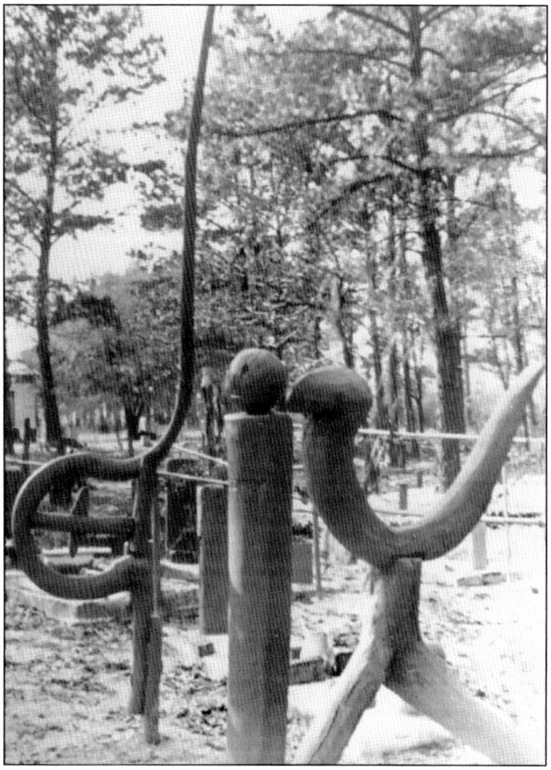

Collecting driftwood, bottles, and other found materials Cyrus Bowens decorated graves in his family plot. The top photograph shows a more detailed view of some of the driftwood pieces as they stood in the cemetery in the 1930s. Another item in the Bowens' plot, and a common sight in yards throughout the South, was a bottle tree seen in the bottom photograph. Intimately aware of the presence of spirits, African Americans set up bottle trees to catch bad spirits. Certain colors such as white, blue, and metallic gold and silver were considered favorable, and many African Americans in Liberty County applied what was known as haint-blue paint to their houses to ward off bad spirits. (Courtesy of the Seabrook Village Foundation.)

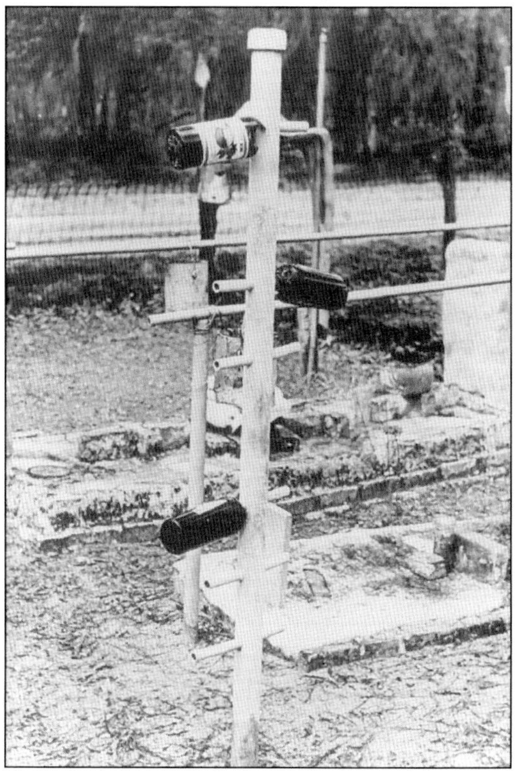

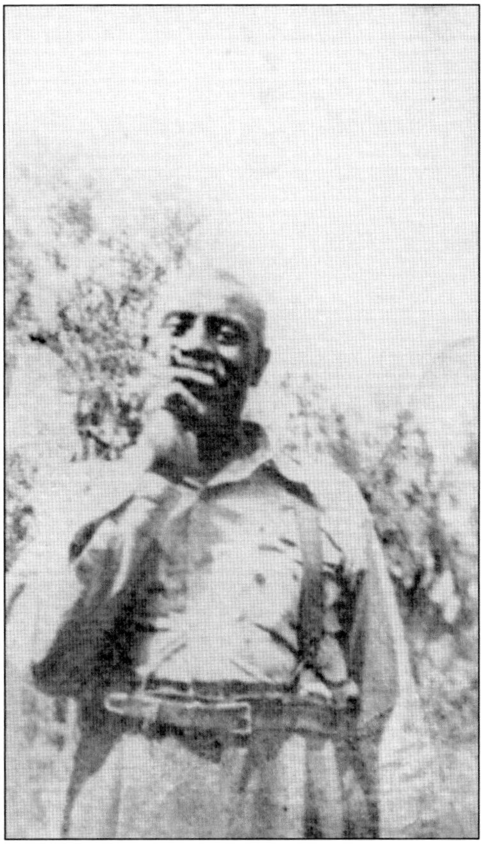

Although Cyrus Bowens was alive during the WPA visit, the team did not interview the artist (top). Given the similarities of Bowens' artwork to decorative and cultural traditions in West Africa, he probably drew from his heritage. Bowens took his vision to the grave and left generations of scholars pondering the meaning of his work. The final work in his collection was the marker he selected for his own grave: a dolphin skull, painted silver, and mounted on a plain white cross (bottom). Over the years, pieces disappeared from the Bowens plot, and several items including the dolphin skull were stolen in the 1980s. The thief then left the items at Fort Morris Historic Site, which later donated the artifacts to Seabrook Village. (Courtesy of the Seabrook Village Foundation.)

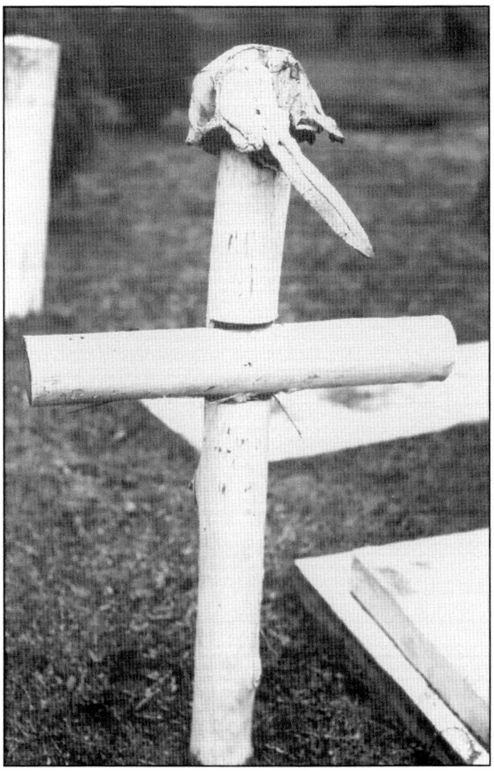

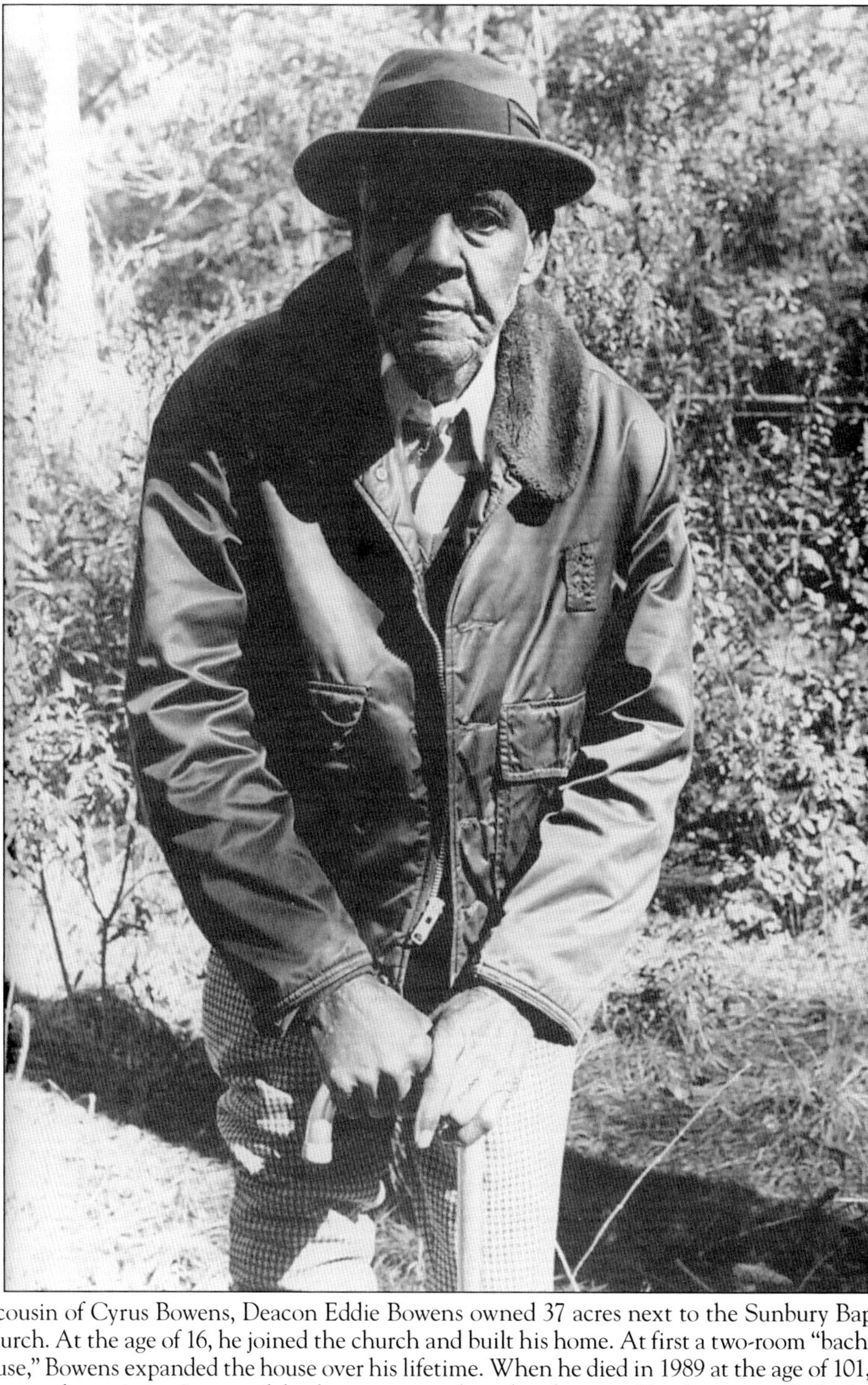

A cousin of Cyrus Bowens, Deacon Eddie Bowens owned 37 acres next to the Sunbury Baptist Church. At the age of 16, he joined the church and built his home. At first a two-room "bachelor house," Bowens expanded the house over his lifetime. When he died in 1989 at the age of 101, his house and remaining 9 acres of the farm were purchased and restored by the nonprofit Seabrook Village Foundation as a museum. The Bowens Farm was placed on the National Register of Historic Places in 2002. (Courtesy of the Seabrook Village Foundation.)

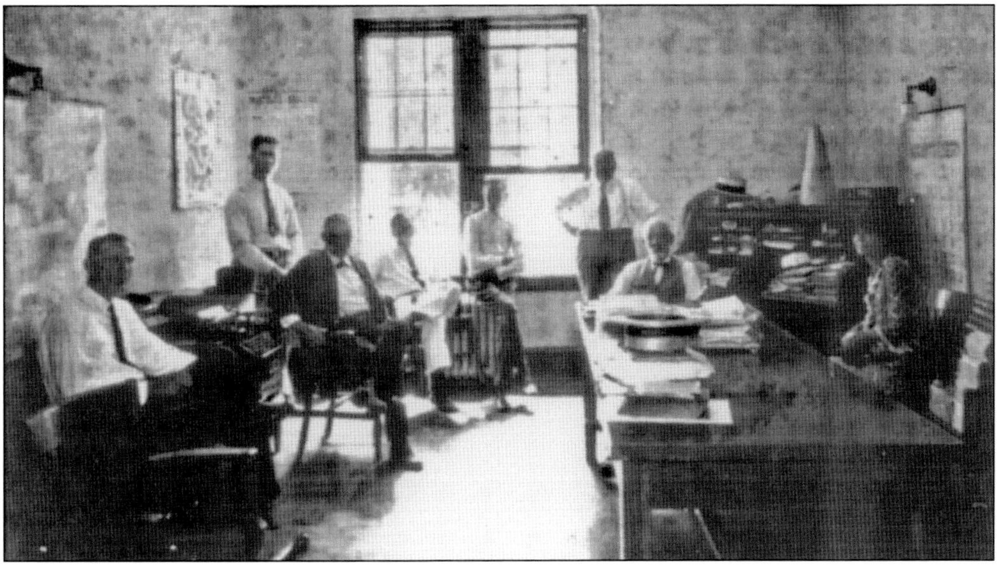

This photograph was made in July 1926 during a regular session of the Liberty County Board of Education in the Liberty County Courthouse. From left to right are (seated) H. F. Long of the Gum Branch-Walthourville District, E. L. Crowley of the Fleming District, J. G. Ryon of the Hinesville District, unidentified, W. A. Jones of the Riceboro-Dorchester District, and Edna Fennell, first home demonstration agent for Liberty County. Standing are Harley A. Bacon (left)—superintendent—and W. P. Gooden (right) of the Willie-Taylors Creek District. (Courtesy of the *Liberty County Herald*.)

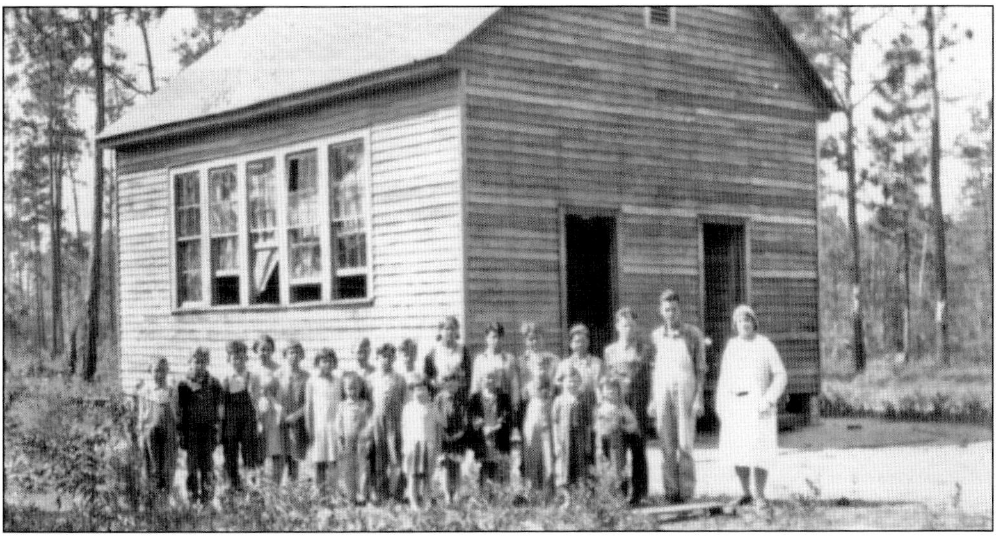

Until the 1930s and 1940s, most children in Liberty County received their education in one-room and two-room schoolhouses in rural communities. These country schools offered first through seventh grades and emphasized the antiquated three r's of elementary education: reading, 'riting, and 'rithmetic, taught to the tune of a hick'ry stick. As local schools remained segregated until the 1970s, white and black children attended similar yet separate schools. Pictured above in the 1930s is the Providence School near Gum Branch, which operated until consolidation in the 1940s. Theo Hodges Wilkinson (far right) served as teacher for all seven grades. (Courtesy of the *Liberty County Herald*.)

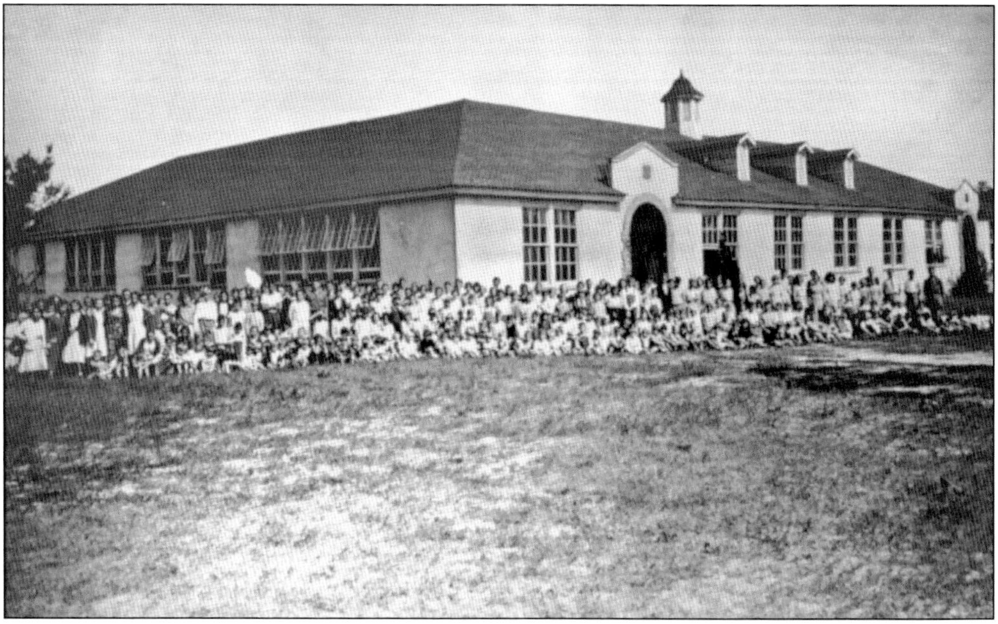

In a rare 1930s photograph, faculty and students pose outside Bradwell Institute in Hinesville. Replacing the original school building, this structure was first occupied in 1925 near the site of the board of education offices built in the early 21st century on Washington Avenue. Bradwell Institute offered first through eleventh grades for white students. Through the 1930s, African American children could pay to attend the private Dorchester Academy through twelfth grade. (Courtesy of the *Liberty County Herald.*)

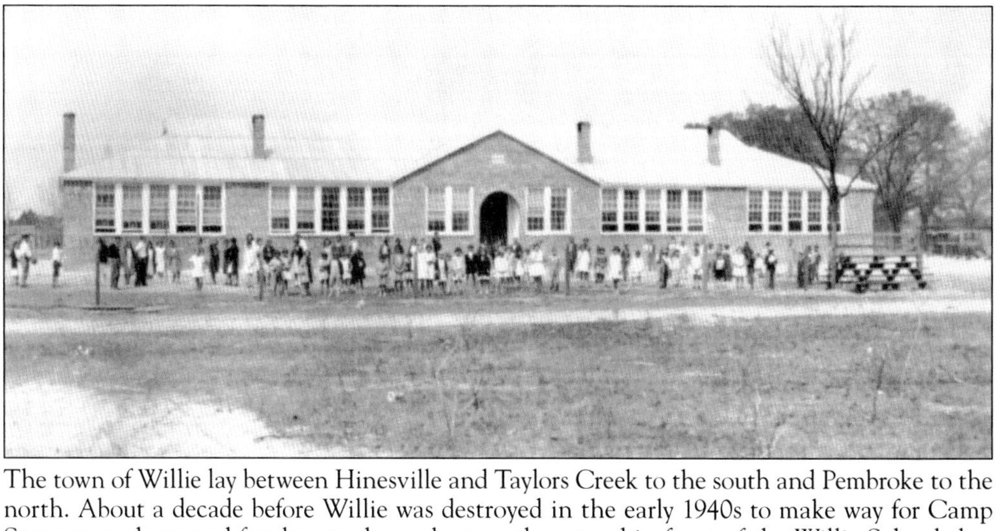

The town of Willie lay between Hinesville and Taylors Creek to the south and Pembroke to the north. About a decade before Willie was destroyed in the early 1940s to make way for Camp Stewart, students and faculty are shown here as they stand in front of the Willie School that consolidated students from white country schools in Salem, Soules Chapel, Harmony, Thomas Hill, and Corinth. Constructed in 1925, the building began use in 1930. (Courtesy of the *Liberty County Herald.*)

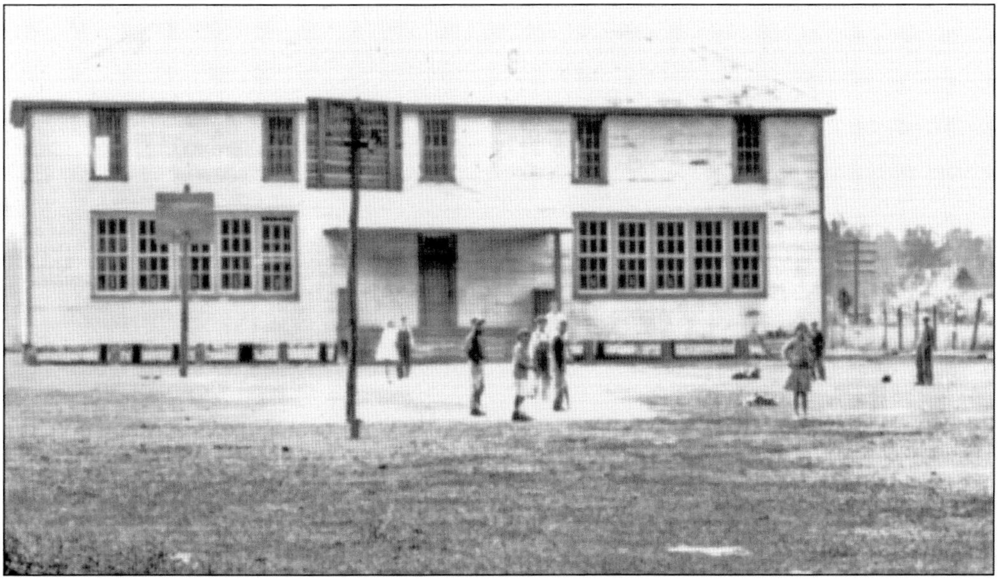

Before the 1940s, several communities like Willie existed on the north side of Liberty County. The largest of these hamlets was Taylors Creek. The old Taylors Creek School, pictured here, was replaced with a brick structure in 1930. All grades were taught in the same building. A basketball court is in the center of the schoolyard, and poles to the left carry telephone lines. (Courtesy of the *Liberty County Herald.*)

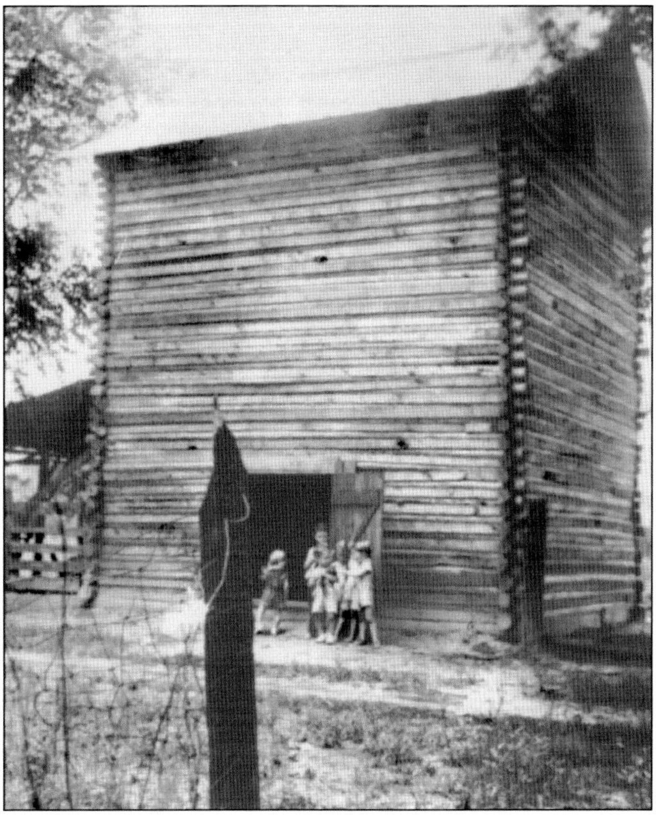

This tobacco barn stood at Taylors Creek in 1935 and was located on a farm operated by the late Liberty County sheriff William E. "Bill" Phillips. Standing in front of the barn are, from left to right, Earl Phillips, Betty Phillips, Gene Martin, and Marilyn Martin. (Courtesy of the *Liberty County Herald.*)

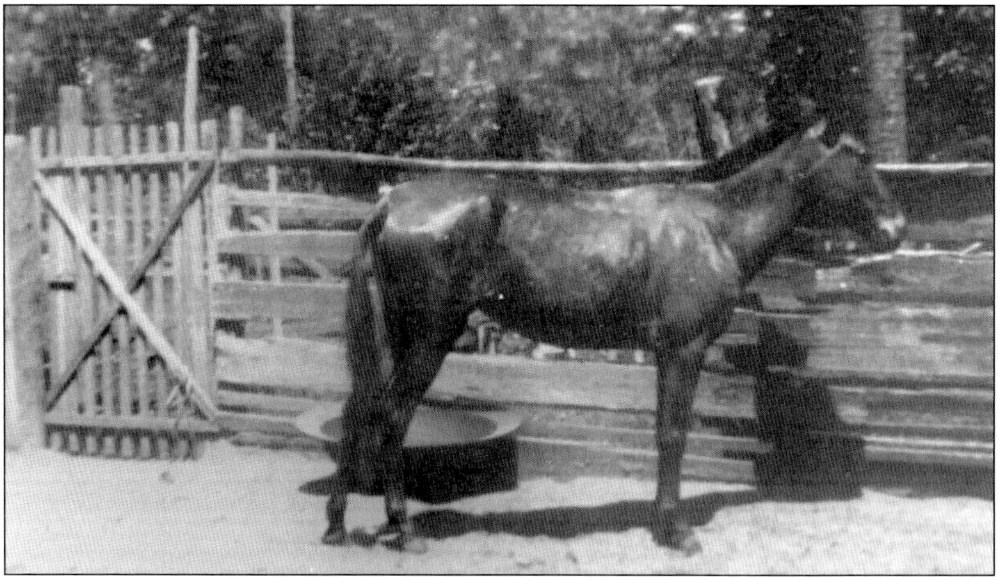

The Taylors Creek area featured good farmland for tobacco, cotton, corn, and other crops. Mules were a common sight throughout the South until tractors became more affordable. The animal in the top photograph belonged to Edward Minus, a Taylors Creek farmer. Simply called the Bad Red Mule, Minus's steed evidently proved difficult to break. A cross between a horse and a donkey, mules are considered smarter yet more tractable than horses. Southern mule drovers believed that a mule would work faithfully for 10 years for the opportunity to kick its master once. The phrase "stubborn as a mule" meant that a mule had its own mind, and, while working faithfully, an animal had individual quirks that were unchangeable. Much like oxen, mules would stop working if they felt exhausted, lying down in their traces and refusing to continue. On the contrary, horses could be driven to death. Mules worked as singles and in teams. The bottom photograph shows an unidentified Taylors Creek farmer in the 1930s preparing to work his cornfield with a mule team. The animals have their ears cocked back waiting for the driver's voice commands. (Both, courtesy of U.S. Army Photographs.)

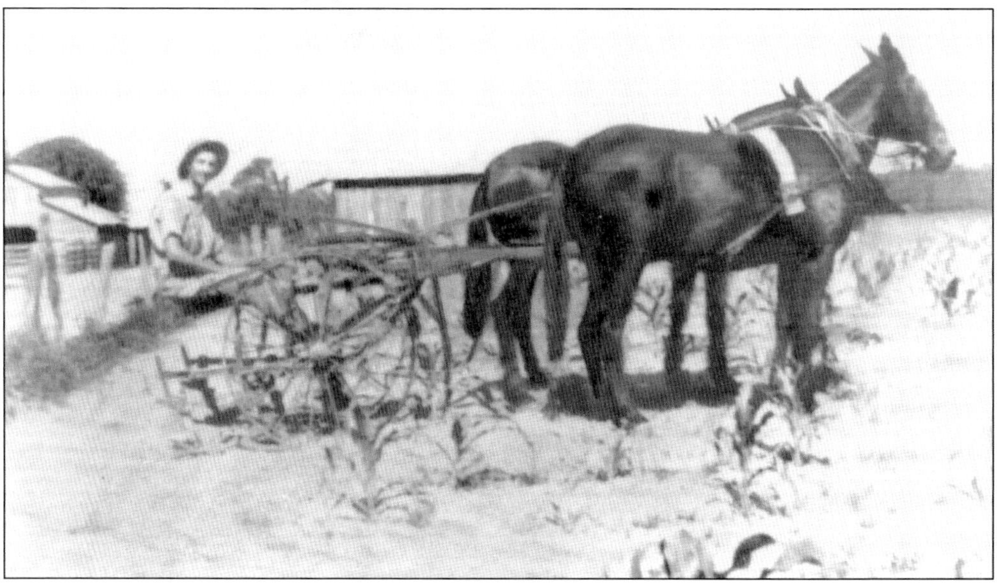

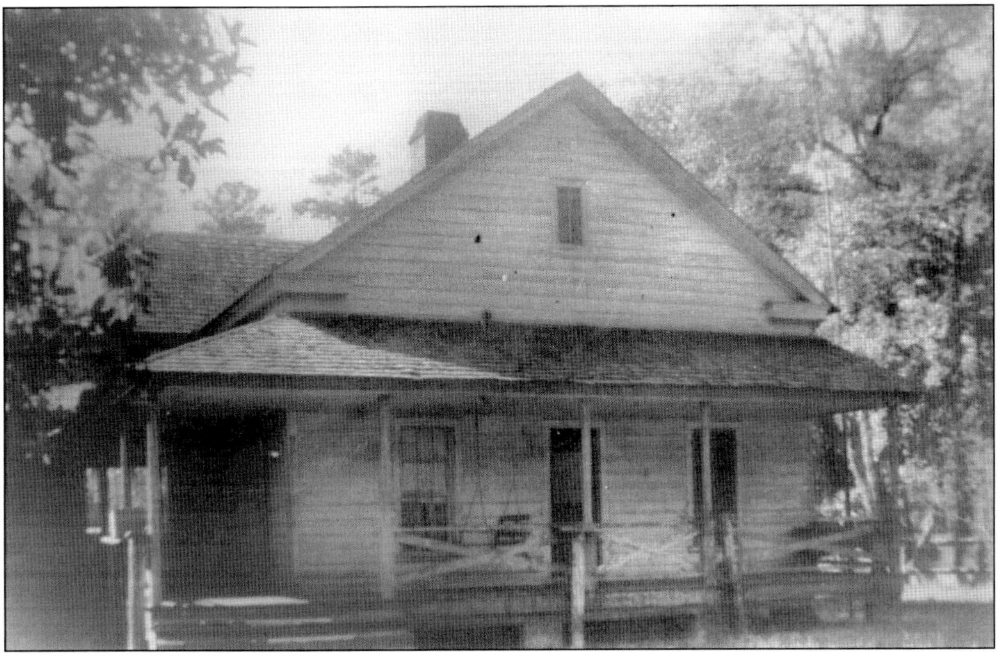

Taylors Creek was settled around 1760 and grew after the American Revolution. By 1859, the village had a post office. Serving as a center of commerce for people living on surrounding farms, in 1879, the town of 80 also had four general stores and four sawmills. Pictured here is the home of W. E. Minus in the village of Taylors Creek in the late 1930s. (Courtesy of U.S. Army Photographs.)

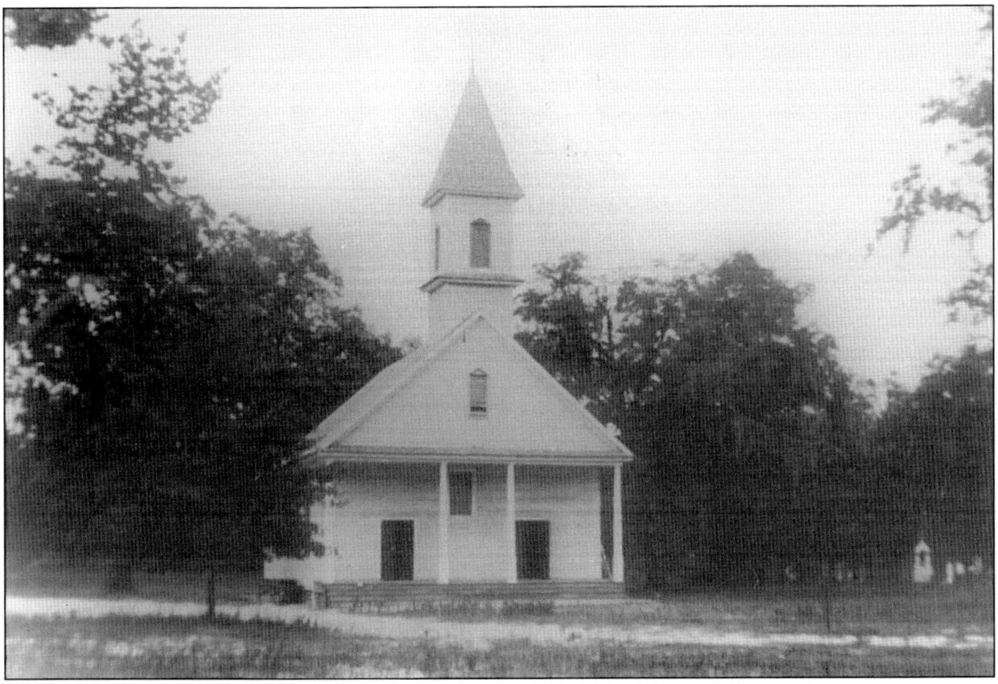

The Taylors Creek Methodist Church stood next to the cemetery at the village center until the early 1940s. In the 1920s, E. M. Elder was a pastor at Taylors Creek Methodist Church and at the Hinesville Methodist Church. (Courtesy of U.S. Army Photographs.)

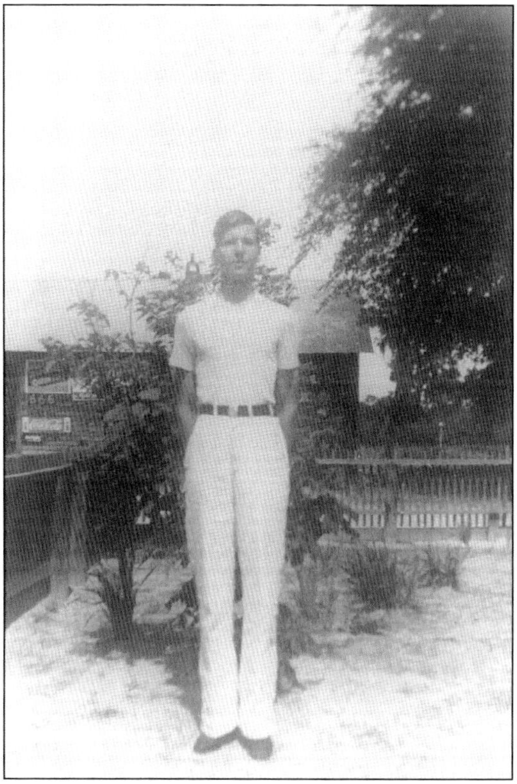

William C. Elder stands in the front yard of his house, across a dirt road from the Taylors Creek cemetery. D. J. Martin's country store is in the background. Located at the center of the village, the Elder house lay within 100 yards of the Pink Porter Store, the Edward Martin Store, Taylors Creek School, and Taylors Creek Methodist Church. (Courtesy of U.S. Army Photographs.)

The teenaged Wilbur M. Elder stands looking at his nine-year-old brother Jack W. Elder with his arm around their cousin, Larry Minus, who was about three years old when this photograph was taken in the late 1930s. The boys are in the backyard of the home of Edward E. Minus in Taylors Creek. Wilbur Elder later joined the Marine Corps and served in World War II, the Korean War, and the Vietnam War, finally retiring as Lt. Col. Wilbur Elder. (Courtesy of U.S. Army Photographs.)

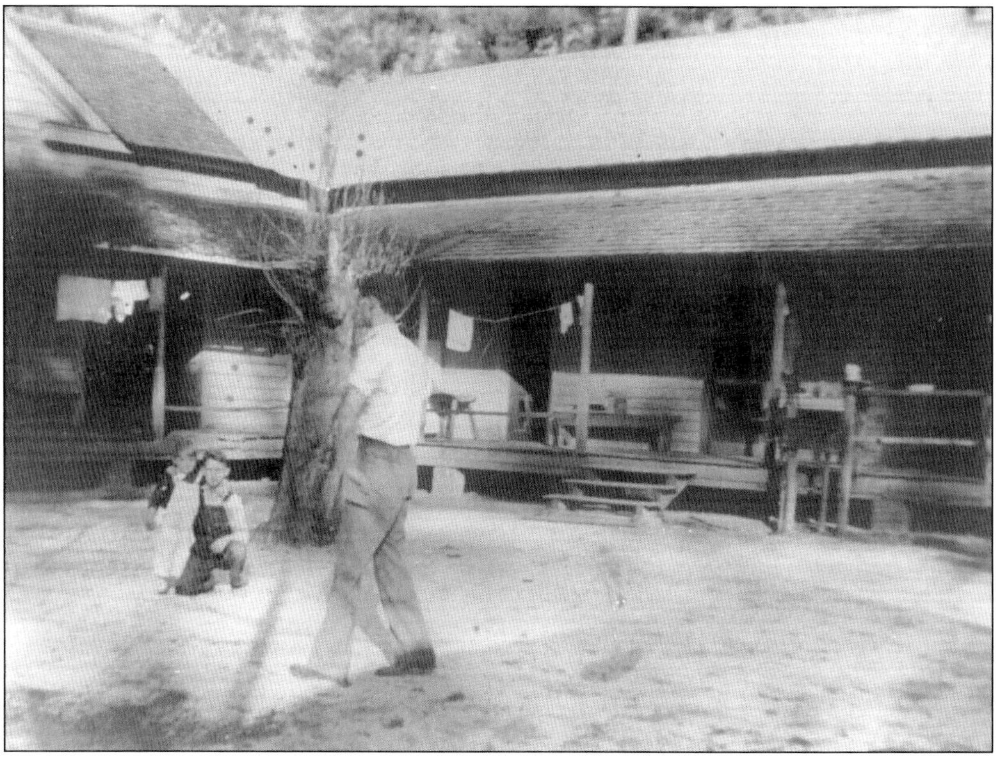

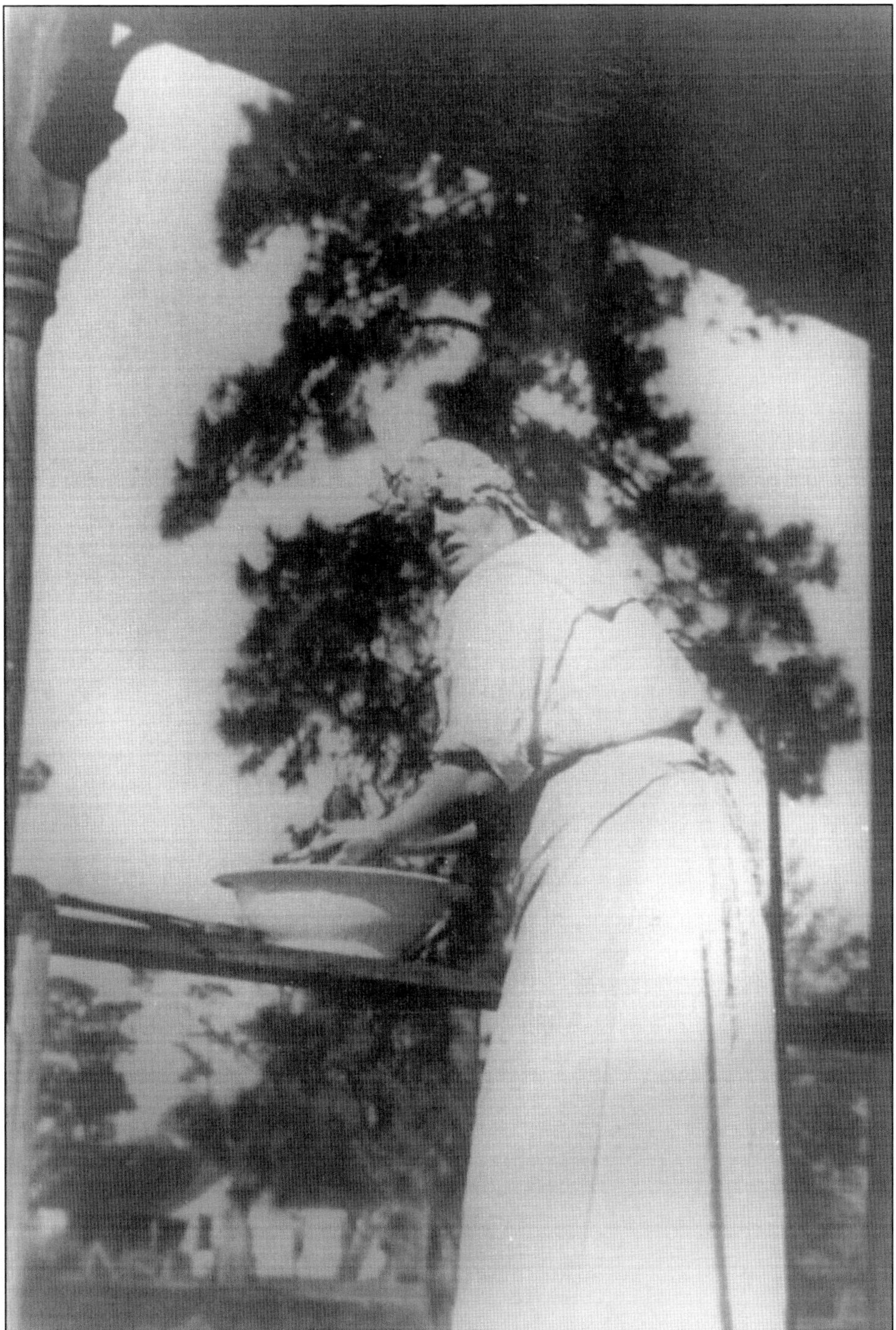

Bonnie Reynolds Elder—mother of William Cullen Elder, Wilbur M. Elder, and Jack W. Elder—stands at a washbowl on her porch in Taylors Creek in the 1920s. As an adult, Jack Elder served in the U.S. Navy in World War II and then joined the U.S. Geological Service, surveying most of the United States and the South Pole. (Courtesy of U.S. Army Photographs.)

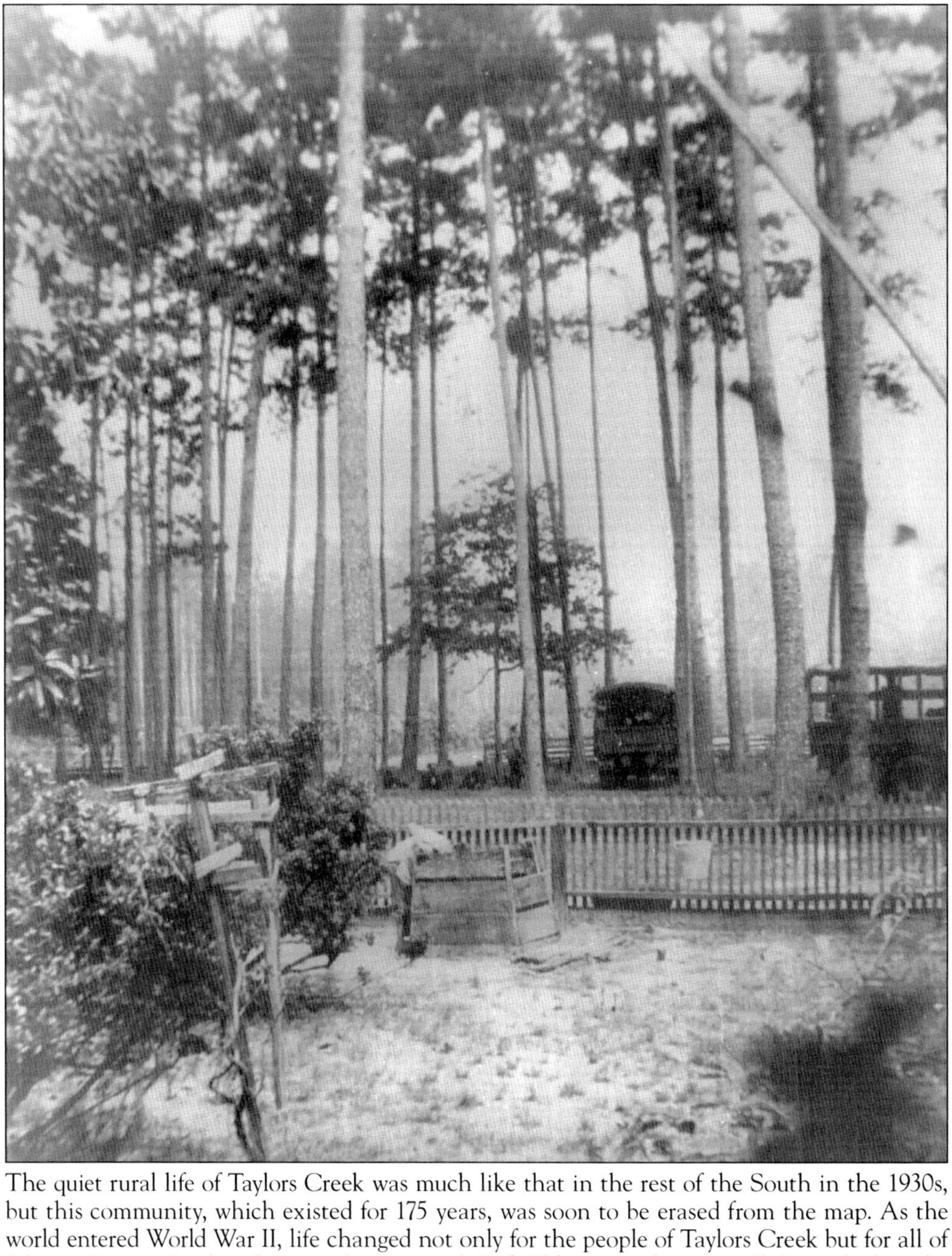

The quiet rural life of Taylors Creek was much like that in the rest of the South in the 1930s, but this community, which existed for 175 years, was soon to be erased from the map. As the world entered World War II, life changed not only for the people of Taylors Creek but for all of Liberty County. In this photograph, an impish Jack Elder peers down a well. Drenched in the sunshine of a lazy day, he appears oblivious to the large military trucks in the trees behind him, foreshadowing the changes to come. In 1941, around the time this photograph was taken, the U.S. Army established a land acquisition office at Camp Stewart, adjacent to Hinesville. The office purchased land to create what became the largest military installation east of the Mississippi River. Soon, the town of Taylors Creek along with villages such as Willie were leveled and relegated to memory. In hindsight, someone wrote on the back of this photograph, "Taylors Creek dying and Fort Stewart being born." (Courtesy of U.S. Army Photographs.)

Four

Camp Stewart

A solitary soldier stands guard at Camp Stewart in 1941. In September 1940, work commenced on establishing an army training facility near Hinesville. Named Camp Stewart after Liberty County's Revolutionary hero Brig. Gen. Daniel Stewart, the base eventually encompassed over 300,000 acres of Liberty, Bryan, Tattnall, and Evans counties. From January 10, 1941, until July 24, 1946, the base was Camp Stewart Anti-Aircraft Artillery—AAA—Training Center. The AAA Training Center was disbanded from 1946 to 1950, and Camp Stewart served as a National Guard installation. In 1950, the AAA Training Center was reestablished at Camp Stewart and expanded from 1954 to 1956 to the Camp Stewart AAA and Tank Training Center. On March 21, 1956, the base became Fort Stewart. Until World War II, Hinesville was a small town and county seat to a rural community. With the incursion of thousands of new people, Hinesville became known as "Boom Town" with new businesses, legal and otherwise, springing up to serve the needs of the military. With the advent of World War II, the South shifted from agricultural to industrial jobs and from country living to city dwelling. (Photograph by Robert Steinen; courtesy of the U.S. Army.)

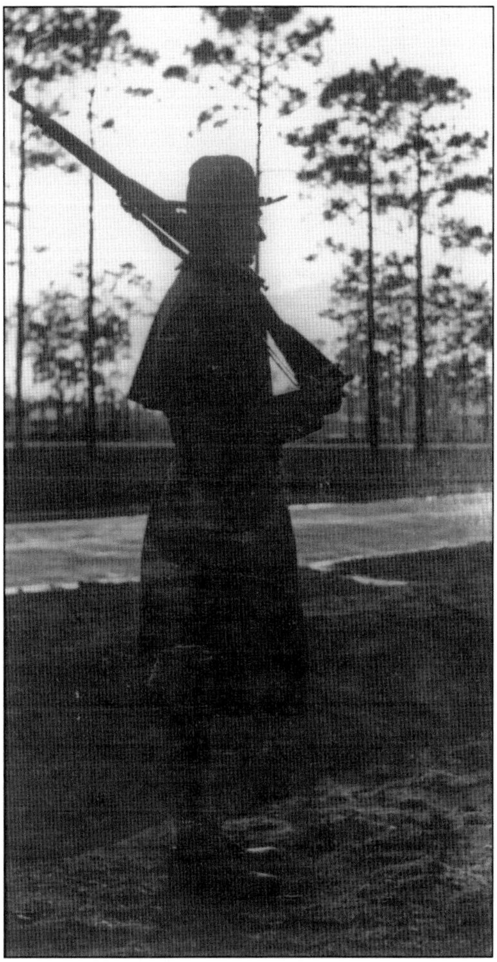

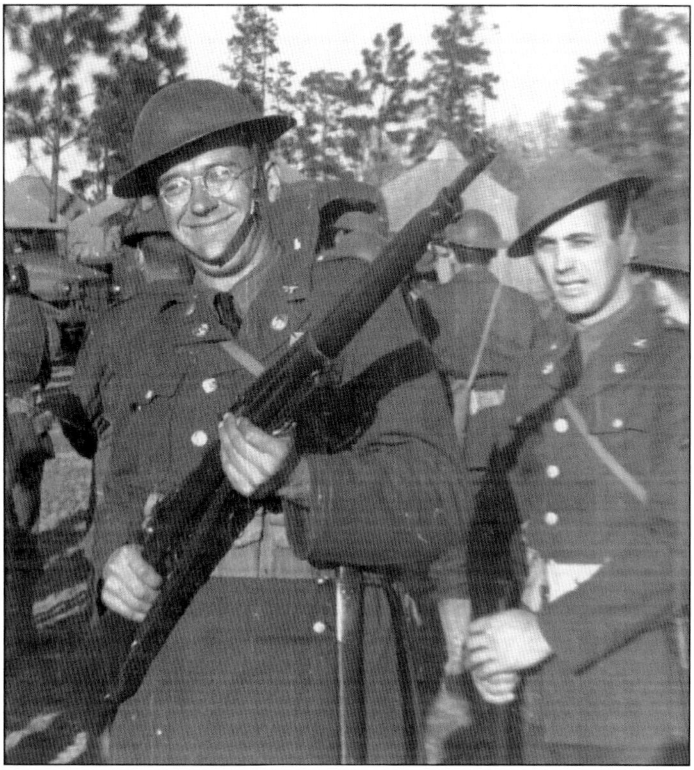

Among the first soldiers to arrive at Camp Stewart in 1941 were Gnas (left) and Torrey (right) wearing uniforms reminiscent of doughboy uniforms from World War I. Known as a "silk stocking" outfit, the 207th Coast Artillery was largely composed of well-heeled men from New York City. With more resources than the average soldier, the members of this company had still and motion picture cameras to capture everyday life at Camp Stewart. (Photograph by Robert Steinen; courtesy of U.S. Army Photographs.)

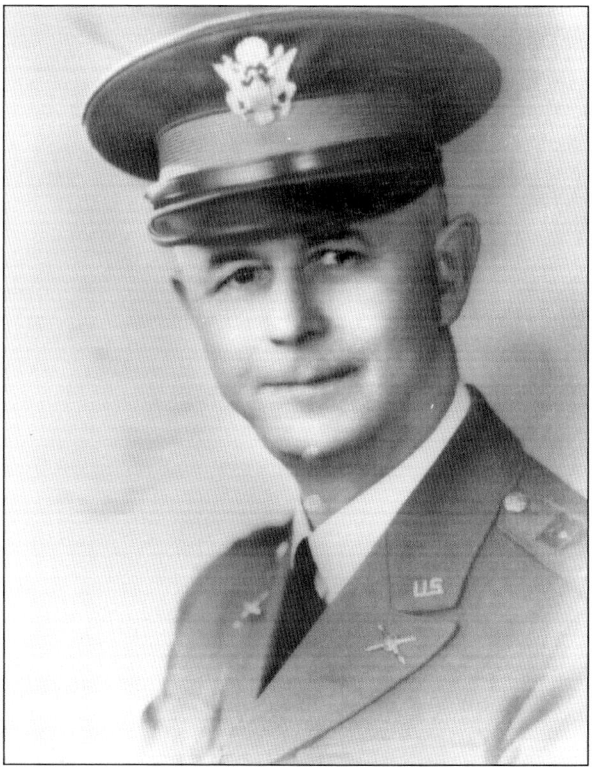

The first commanding officer of Camp Stewart was Brig. Gen. Richard R. Cox, pictured here. He served at Camp Stewart from September 1940 through March 1941 and supervised the construction of the earliest command and support buildings and initial acquisition of land for the installation. (Courtesy of U.S. Army Photographs.)

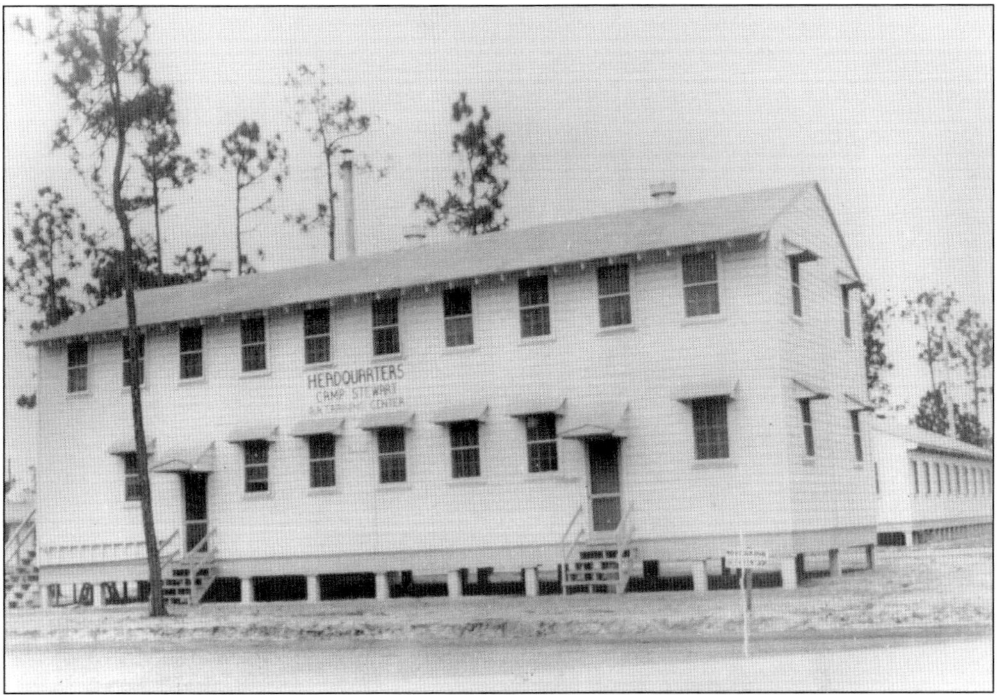

Building 01 at Camp Stewart was the Headquarters Building shown here. Constructed in 1940, the building was later flanked by two single-story buildings that were later connected to Building 01. The original building was torn down in the early 21st century. (Courtesy of U.S. Army Photographs.)

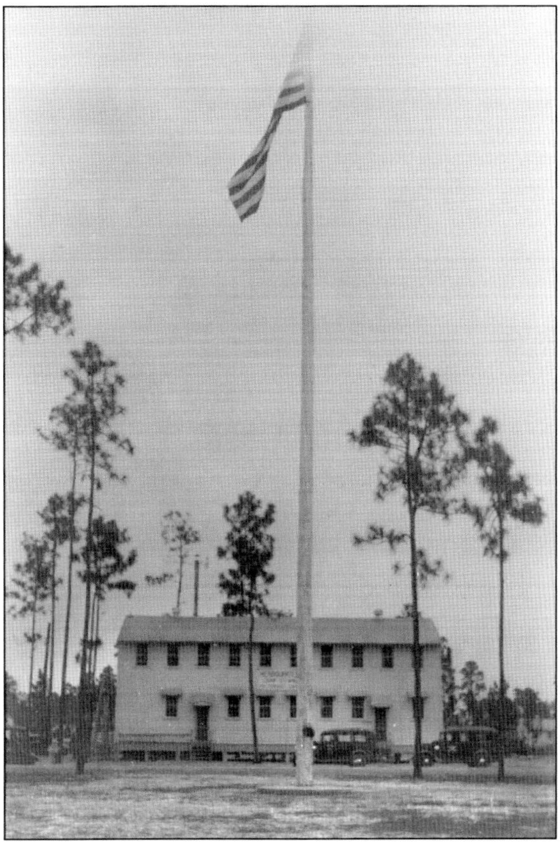

Another view of Camp Stewart Headquarters in 1941 shows the enormous flagstaff made from an area pine tree. (Courtesy of U.S. Army Photographs.)

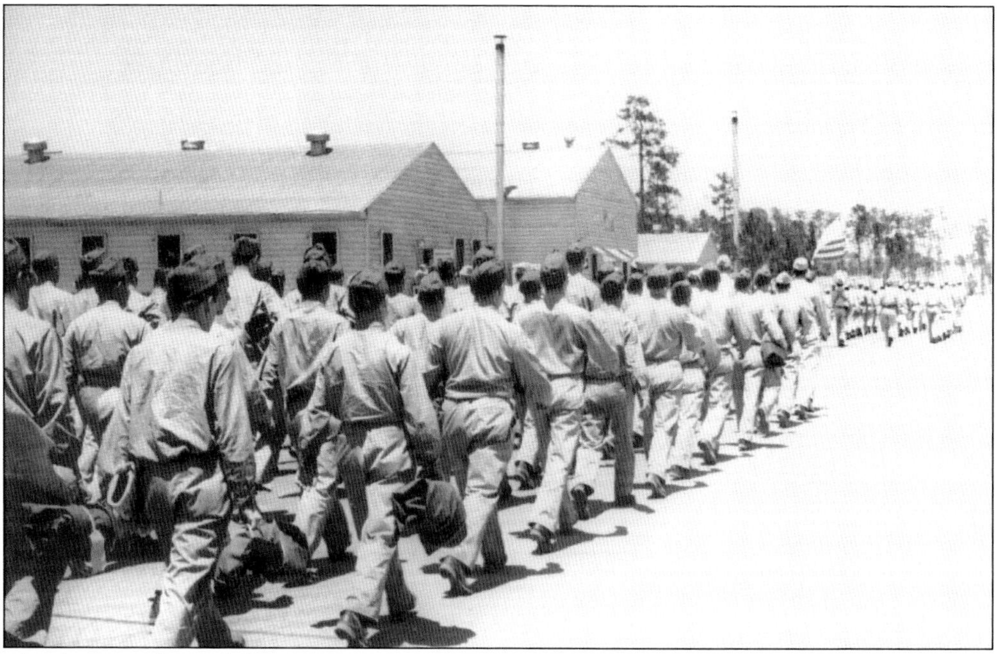

The first members of the regiment were volunteers, but with the onset of war, the draft was implemented. Shown in this photograph are the first men drafted into the regiment. When the troops arrived, the regimental band and one battery met their train. (Photograph by Robert Steinen; courtesy of the U.S. Army.)

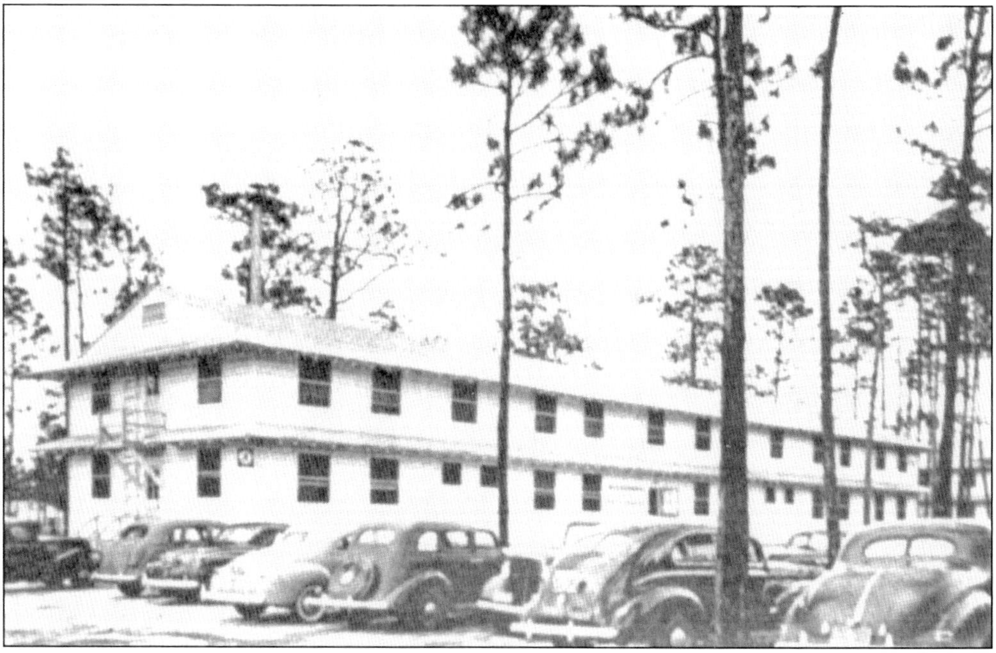

The U.S. Army housed the Land Acquisition Office for Camp Stewart in the building pictured here in 1941. Eventually, over 300,000 acres were acquired and over 1,500 families were relocated to make way for the largest military installation east of the Mississippi River. (Courtesy of U.S. Army Photographs.)

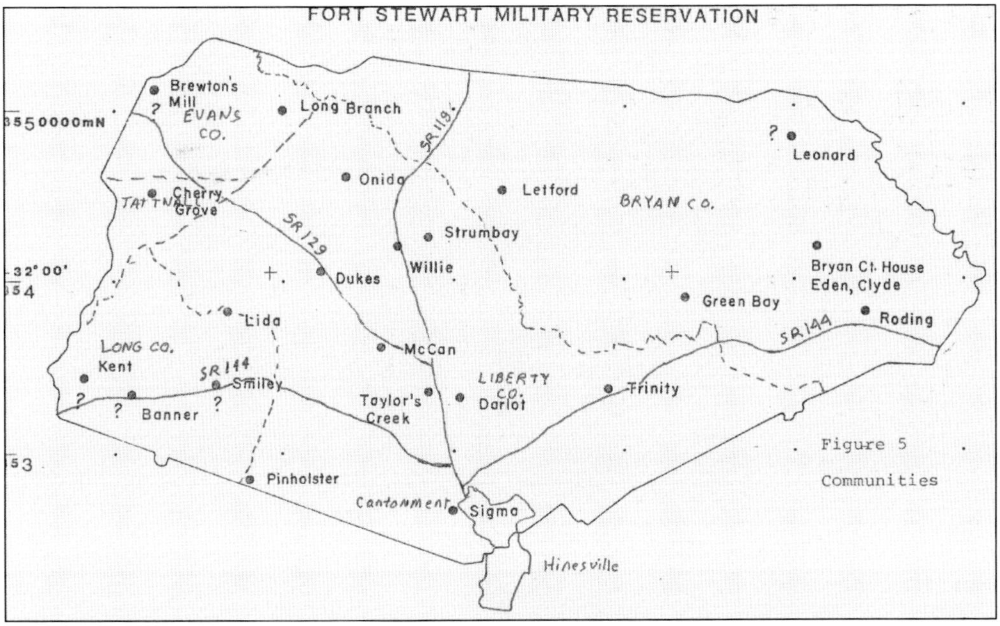

In the creation of Camp Stewart, the Land Acquisition Office targeted properties in Liberty, Bryan, Tattnall, Long, and Evans counties. This map from a later survey shows the extent of the reservation and the communities that were removed. Owners received payment for their properties, but the U.S. Army razed all buildings. Cemeteries were left undisturbed, and their perpetual care continues to be the responsibility of the U.S. government. (Courtesy of U.S. Army Photographs.)

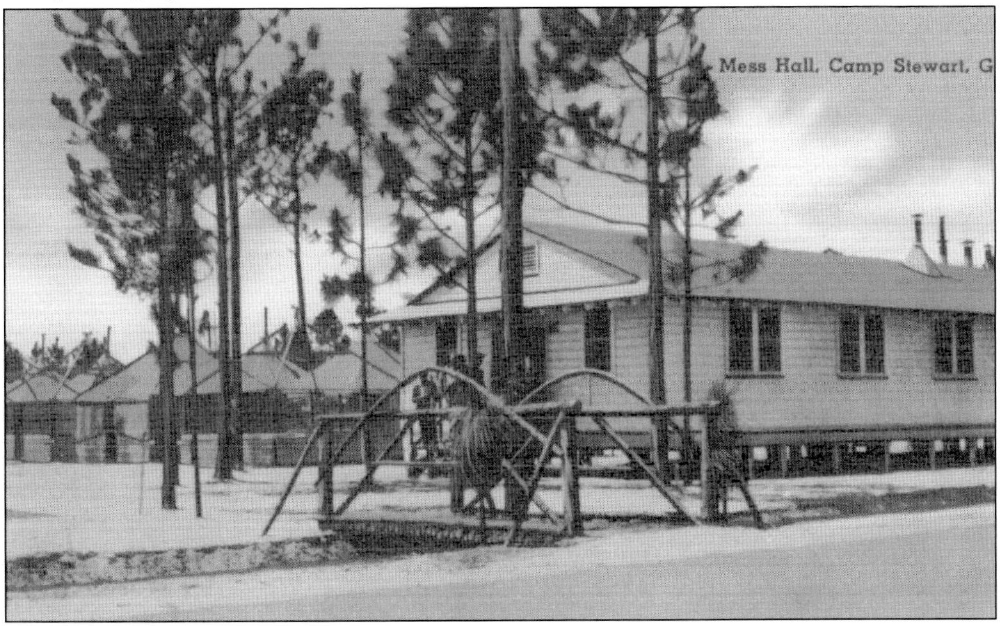

Camp Stewart was created in the midst of pine forests and old fields. Early buildings such as the mess hall depicted in this photographic postcard were constructed of lumber in very simple designs. Pine logs were incorporated into fences, curbing, and, in this instance, a decorative railing on the bridge leading to the mess hall. (Courtesy of the Springfield Legacy Foundation.)

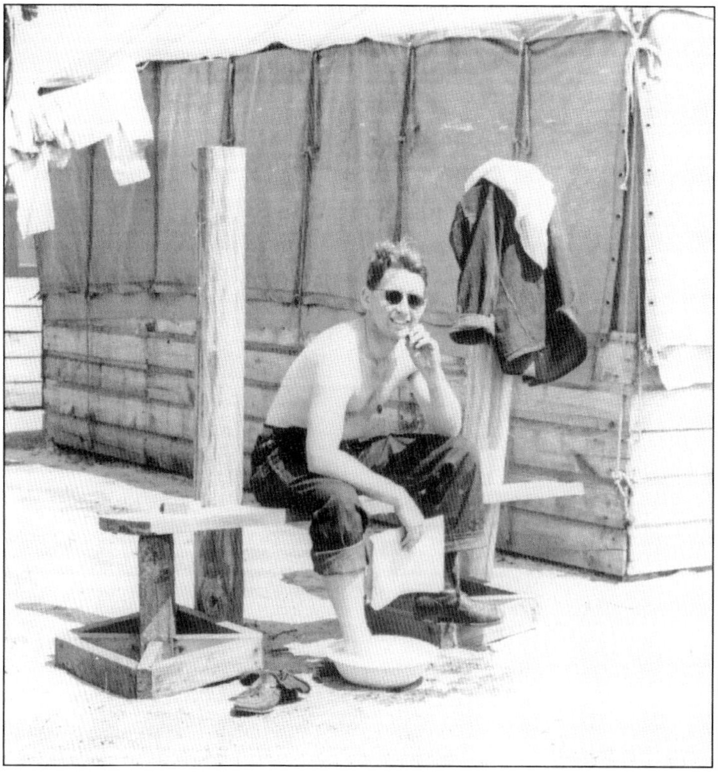

Compared to the barracks pictured here, the more permanent buildings were palatial. This photograph, titled "Oh, My Aching Feet!" shows Robert Steinen resting outside his barracks. Similar to field barracks seen later in Korea, the sleeping accommodations rested on the ground and were subject to flooding. Sometimes rainwater washed shoes out from under bunks. Screens kept biting insects out but did not keep out the heat and humidity of South Georgia. (Courtesy of U.S. Army Photographs.)

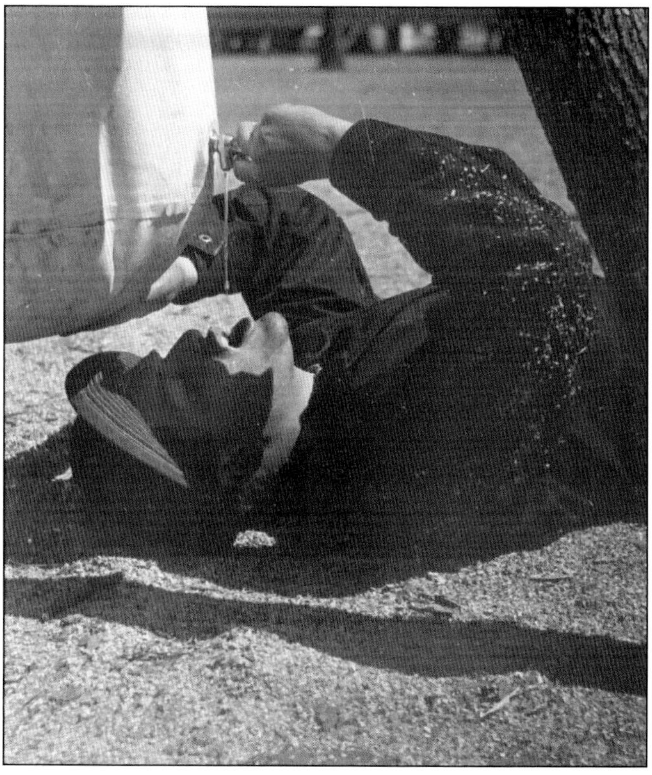

Here a soldier drinks from a Lister bag while lying on Battery Street, which was covered in pine sawdust. Used in the field and in permanent camps, Lister bags were the main source of water for drinking, cooking, washing, and bathing for U.S. Army soldiers. Named for Maj. William J. L. Lyster who used a solution of calcium hypochlorite in a linen bag to treat water, Lister bags were common from before World War I through the Vietnam War. (Courtesy of U.S. Army Photographs.)

Another example of pine usage, the C Battery bell rests on a frame of pine logs just outside the mess hall at Camp Stewart in 1941. (Photograph by Robert Steinen; courtesy of U.S. Army Photographs.)

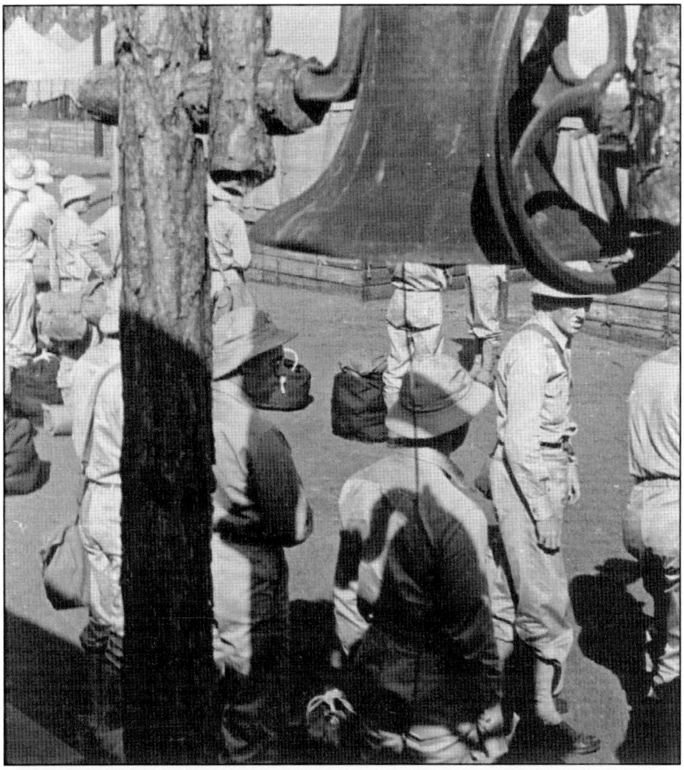

The mess hall became the place to catch soldiers for assignment to details. Here 1st Sgt. "The Eye" Quimby issues the day's orders to a young soldier, Mertens. (Photograph by Robert Steinen; courtesy of U.S. Army Photographs.)

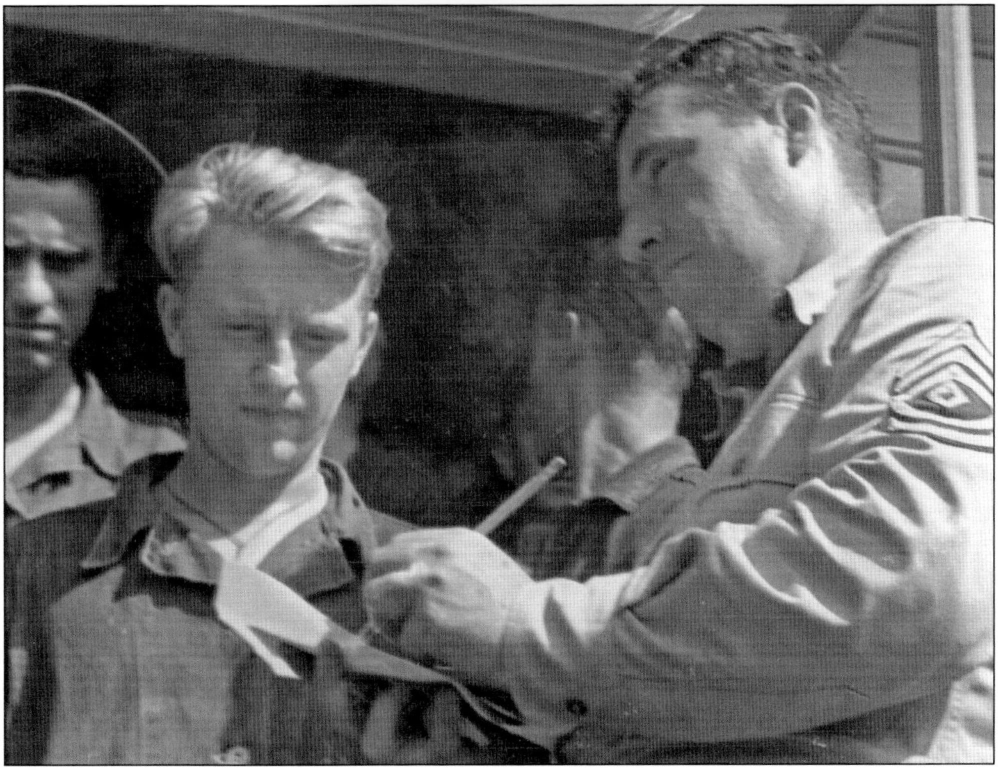

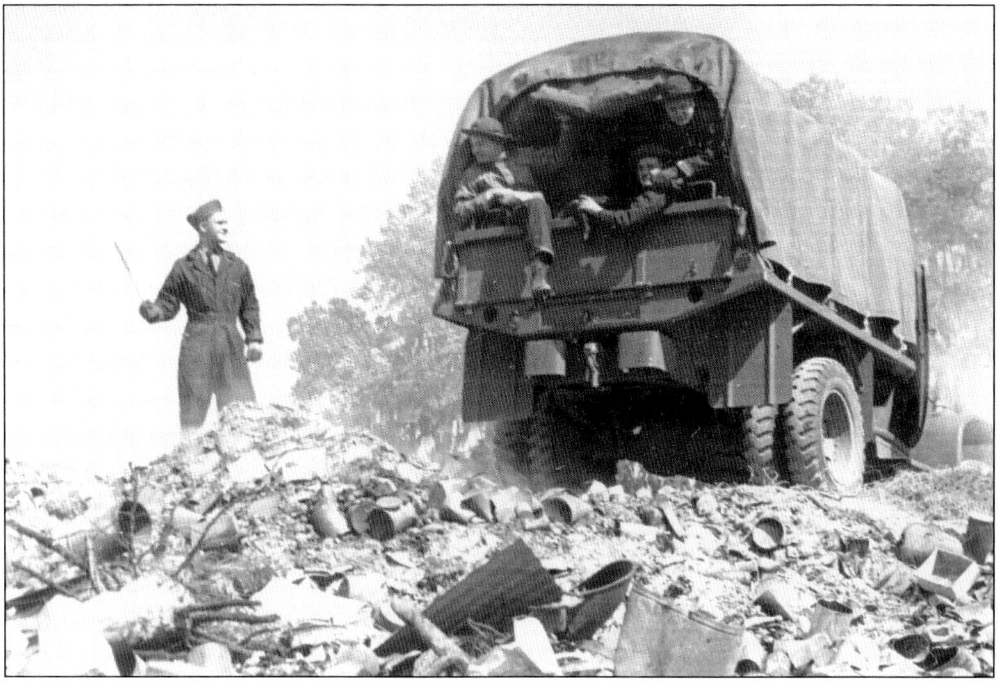

One common detail was delivering trash to the garbage dump. Soldiers at Camp Stewart in the early 1940s referred to this duty as "G-man detail." (Photograph by Robert Steinen; courtesy of U.S. Army Photographs.)

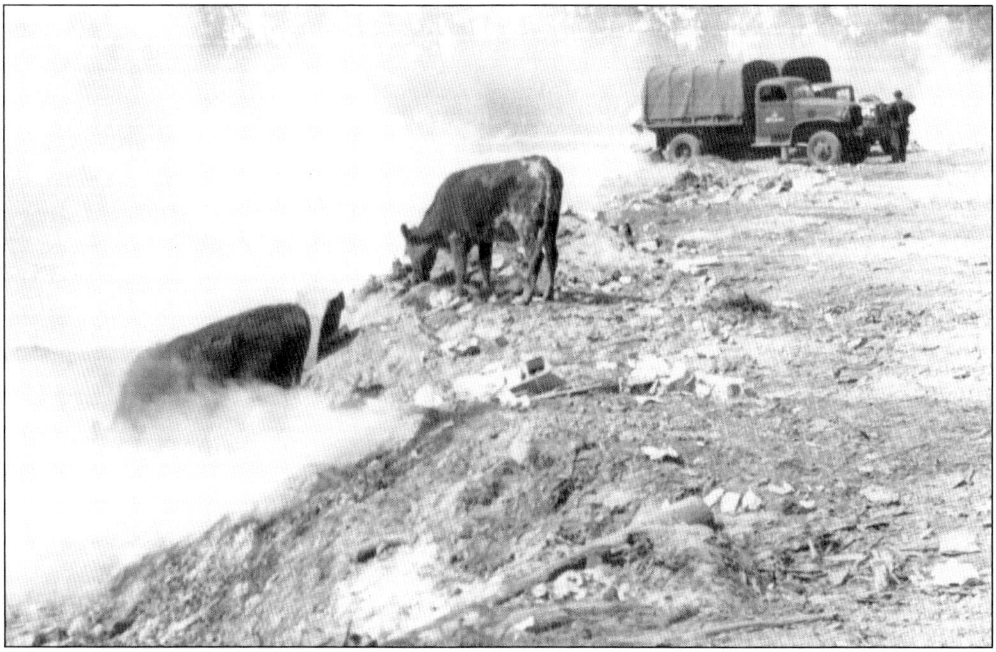

A clear indication of the collision of the new military presence with the old farming communities that existed before Camp Stewart was the common invasion of free-ranging cows foraging in the garbage dump. In the absence of fence laws, it was nearly impossible to keep the cows out of the trash. (Photograph by Robert Steinen; courtesy of U.S. Army Photographs.)

Early accommodations were primitive at Camp Stewart. In this photograph, Fred Taylor poses in a towel as he makes his way from the showers to the barracks across a dirt yard. After a heavy rain, trips from the barracks to the showers and toilets included a walk through the mud. Such conditions led the men to nickname Camp Stewart "Camp Swampy." (Photograph by Robert Steinen; courtesy of U.S Army Photographs.)

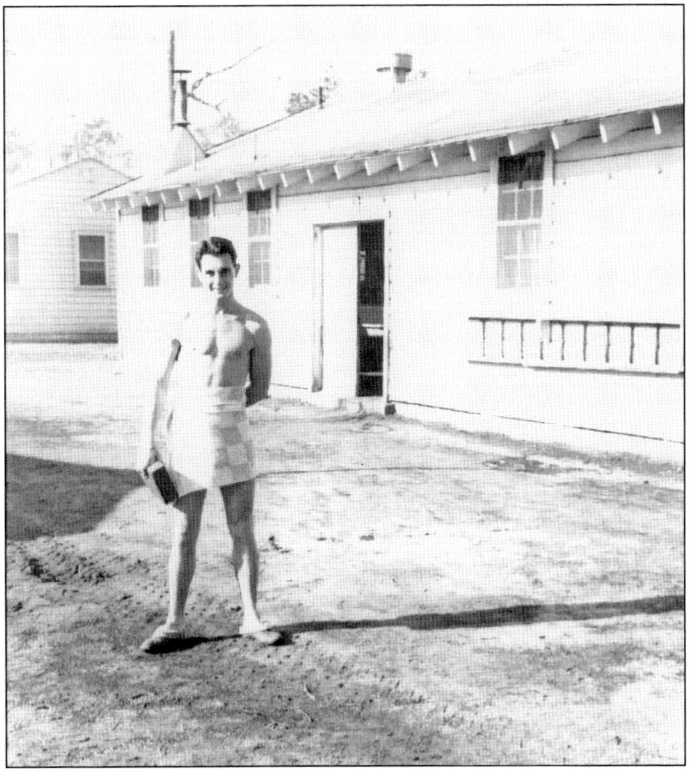

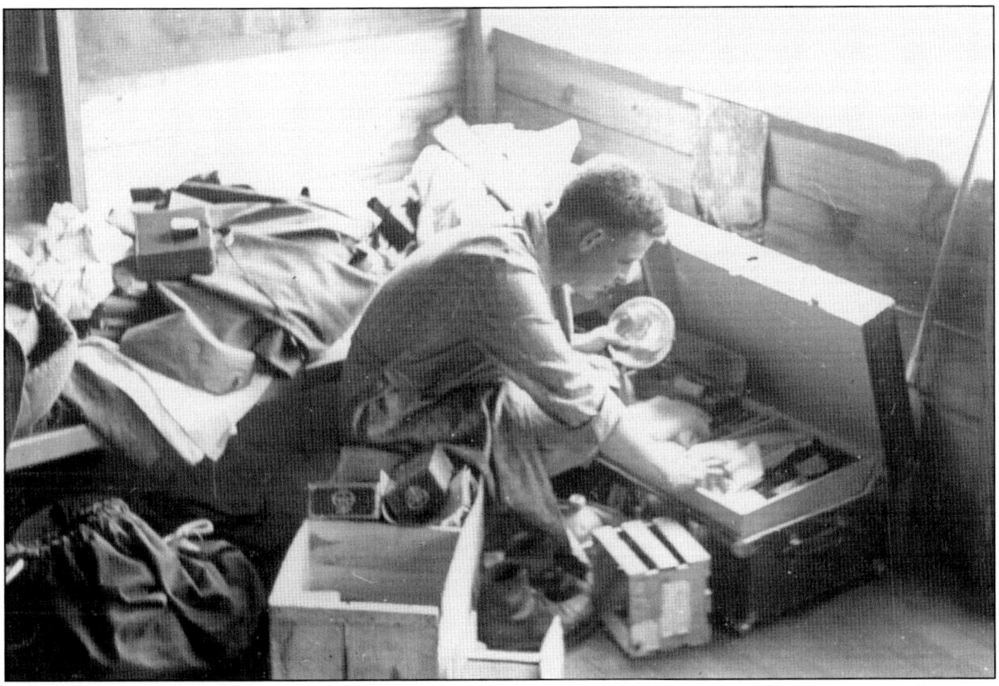

A rare view inside the barracks, an unknown photographer captures Robert Steinen cleaning up the mess. An editorial statement on the photograph adds, "High time!" (Courtesy of U.S. Army Photographs.)

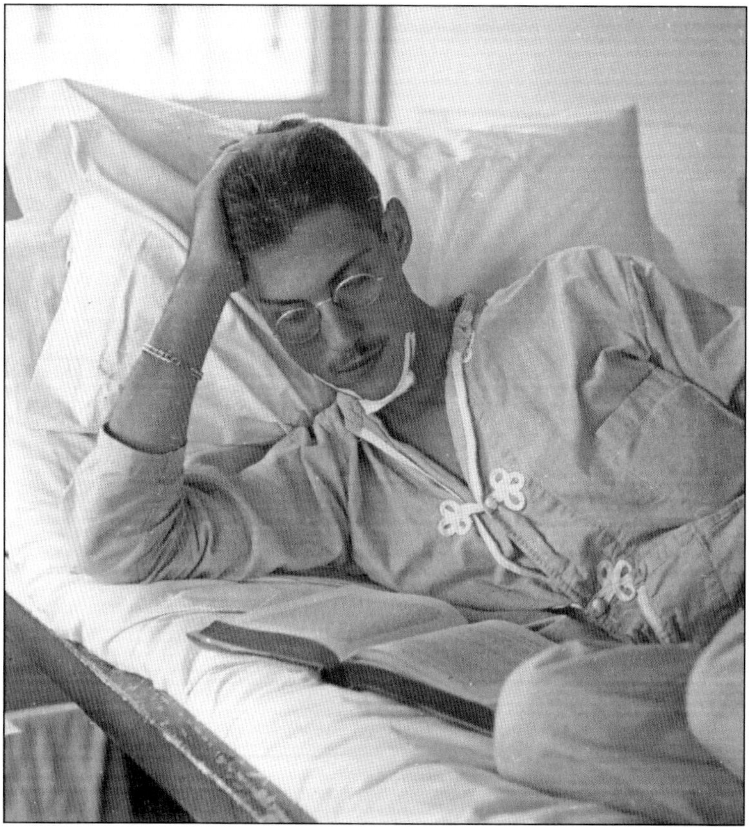

Stauber of A Battery relaxes by reading in his bunk while lounging in his pajamas in 1941. Leisure activities on base were limited in the first years of Camp Stewart. (Photograph by Robert Steinen; courtesy of U.S. Army Photographs.)

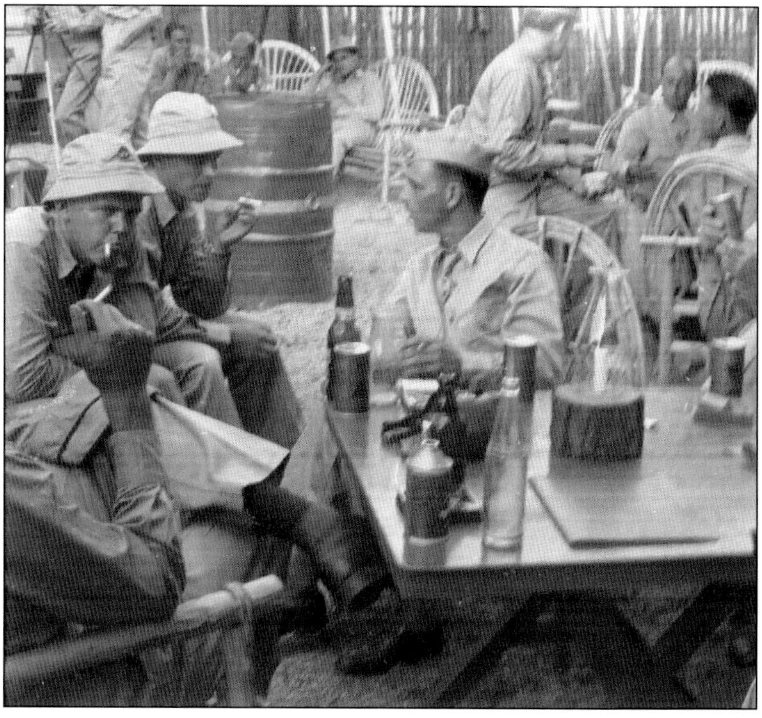

In the absence of a formal club, a makeshift beer garden sprang up next to the regiment post-exchange, or PX, in 1941. (Photograph by Robert Steinen; courtesy of U.S. Army Photographs.)

In the beer garden, Conklin stands with his motion picture camera, a rare luxury for the average soldier. (Photograph by Robert Steinen; courtesy of U.S. Army Photographs.)

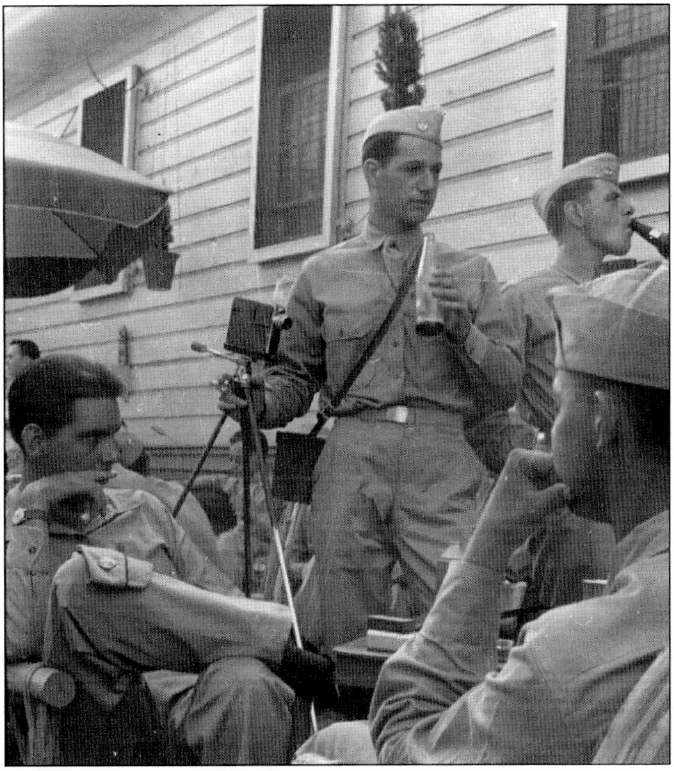

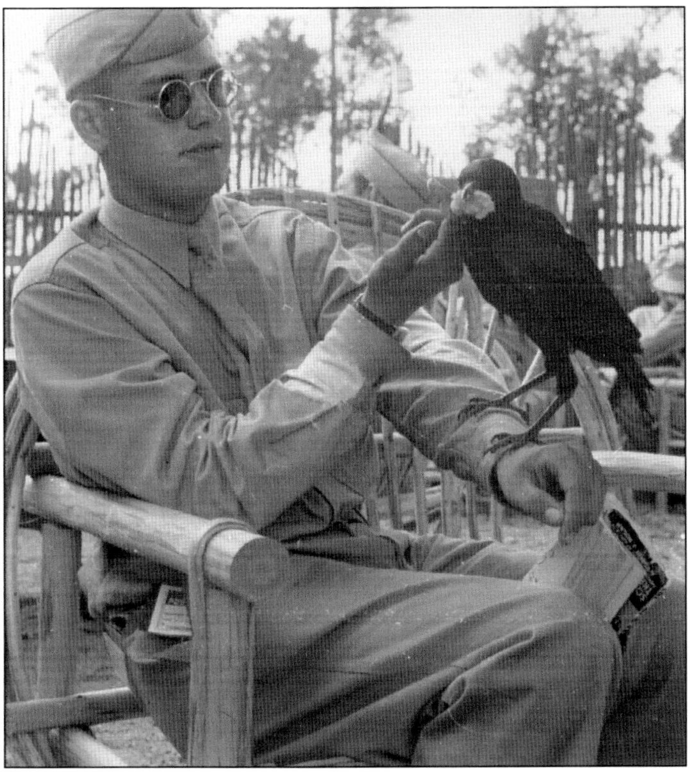

O'Connor sits with the regimental pet crow who frequented the beer garden. (Photograph by Robert Steinen; courtesy of U.S. Army Photographs.)

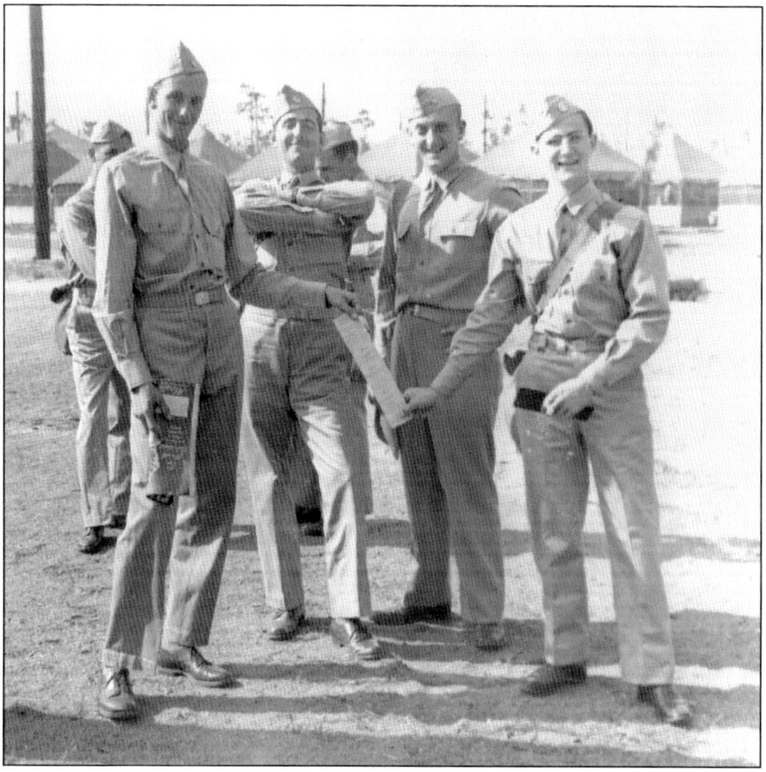

Men eagerly anticipated leave, and long 10-day furloughs allowed the men enough time to return to New York. In the summer of 1942, these four soldiers, including Limbacher, Penson, and Brenton, show off their tickets for the *Silver Meteor*, the train that operated between Miami and New York. (Photograph by Robert Steinen; courtesy of U.S. Army Photographs.)

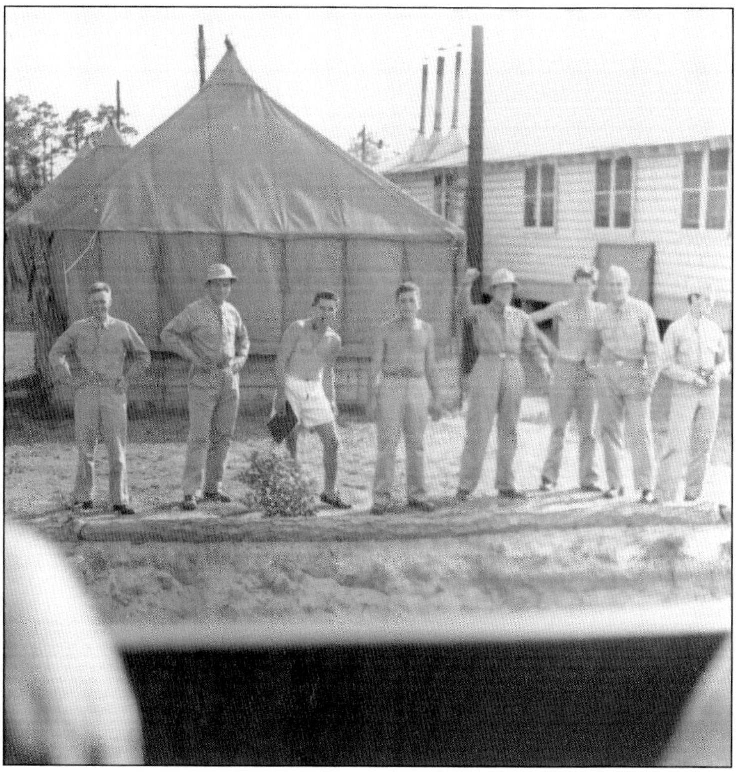

Naturally, not everyone furloughed at the same time. In 1942, Robert Steinen took this snapshot from the bus about to take him off for a pleasant weekend of rest and relaxation. Outside, the work detail left behind in camp makes their feelings known. (Photograph by Robert Steinen; courtesy of U.S. Army Photographs.)

Gnas (left) and Torrey (right) avoid work in the supply office at Camp Stewart in 1941. (Photograph by Robert Steinen; courtesy of U.S. Army Photographs.)

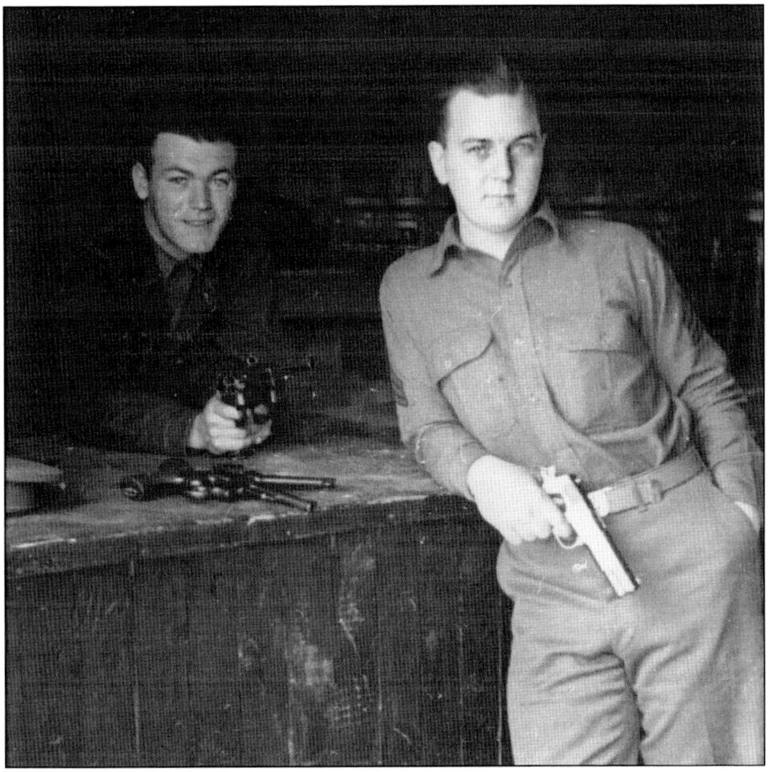

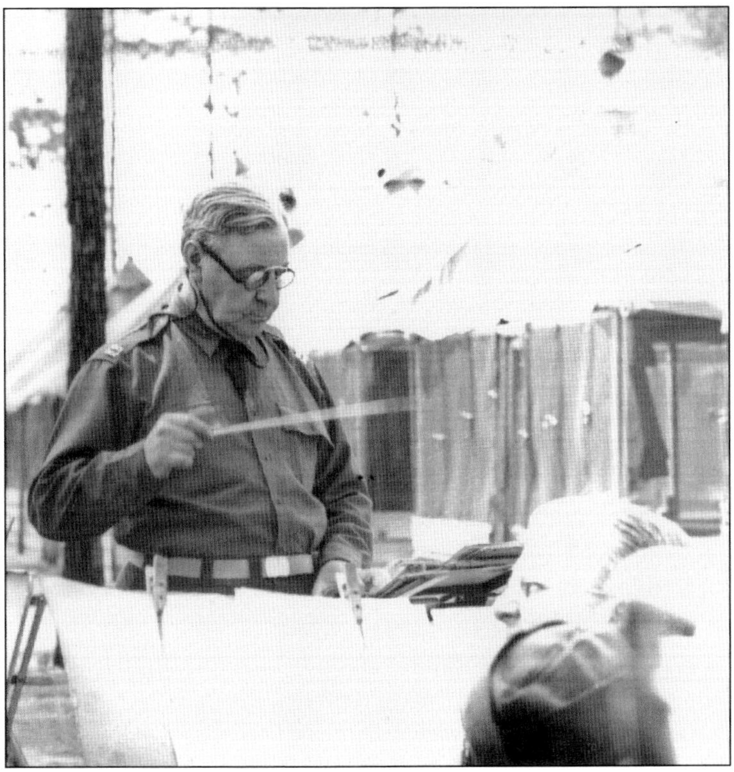

The regiment of New Yorkers was interested in music. In this photograph, bandmaster Captain Sutherland conducts his orchestra. (Photograph by Robert Steinen; courtesy of U.S. Army Photographs.)

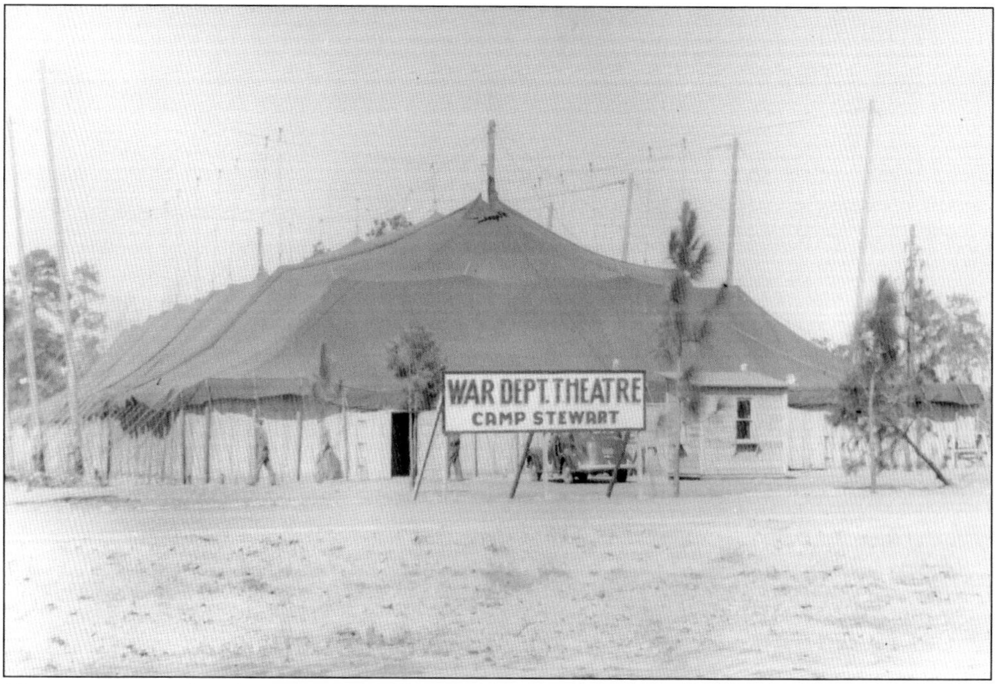

Movies were another diversion for soldiers at Camp Stewart. This enormous tent was pitched in 1940 for screening motion pictures. The tent was nearly destroyed by a storm in the winter. (Courtesy of U.S. Army Photographs.)

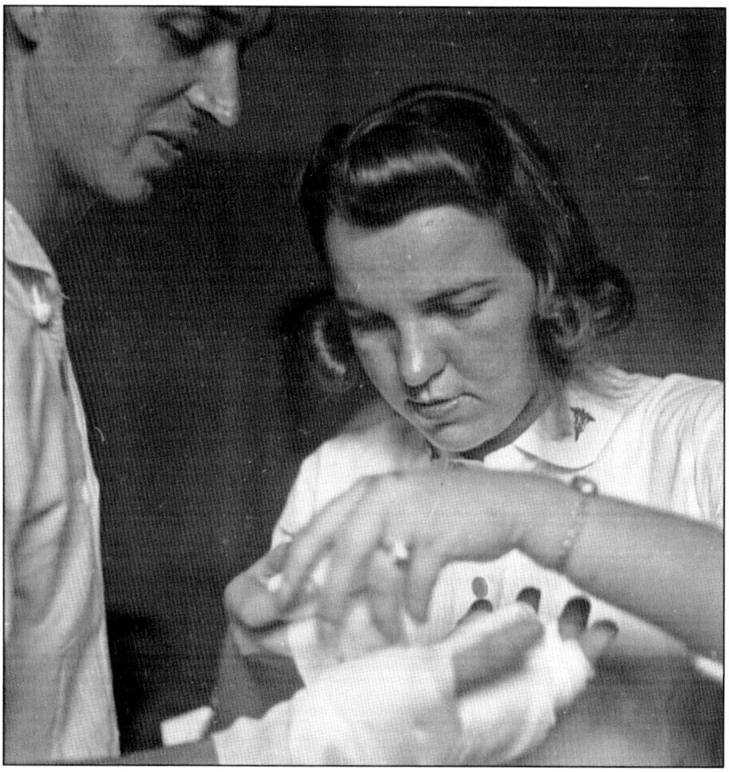

Women were also present at Camp Stewart. Here Lt. Helen Moore bandages a soldier named Wharton. Lieutenant Moore and Robert Steinen were later married. (Photograph by Robert Steinen; courtesy of U.S. Army Photographs.)

Maj. Gen. William H. Wilson assumed command of Camp Stewart from Brig. Gen. Richard Cox in March 1941. Major General Wilson served at Camp Stewart until December 1941. The army honored him by naming one of the main arterial roads leading from Hinesville onto post after him. (Courtesy of U.S. Army Photographs.)

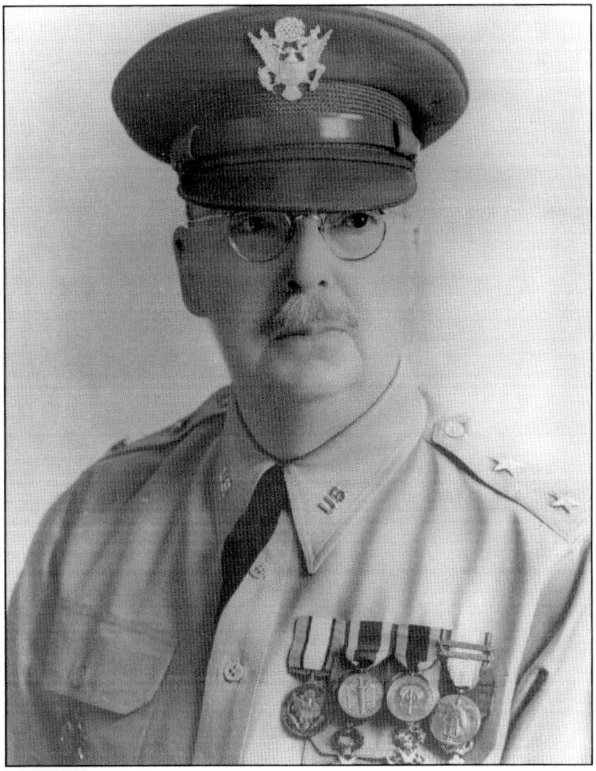

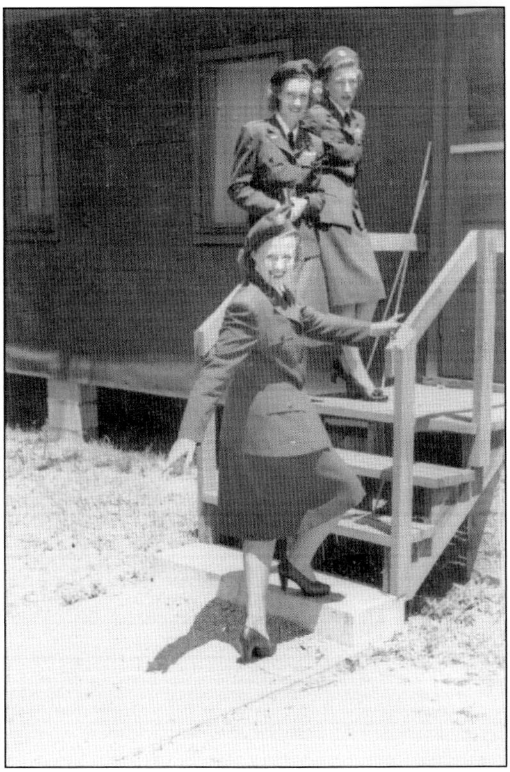

In addition to nurses, Camp Stewart was home to some of the first women trained to fly military aircraft. Women Airforce Service Pilots—WASP—were organized at the dawn of World War II to provide air support for combat operations. Showing off their humor more than their flying prowess, WASP, in this photograph taken in 1942, are, from left to right, Lydia Lindner, Eileen Roach, and Mary Clifford. (Courtesy of U.S. Army Photographs.)

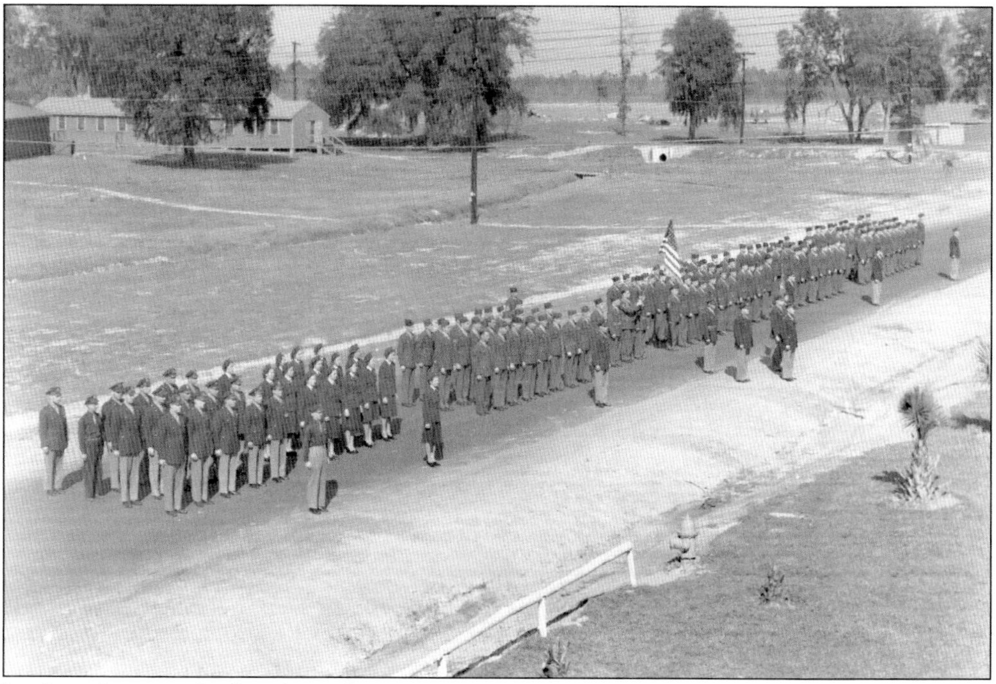

In this photograph, female and male members of the Army Air Forces–Air Corps Field Detachment stand for inspection at Liberty Field, Camp Stewart, in the early 1940s. (Courtesy of U.S. Army Photographs.)

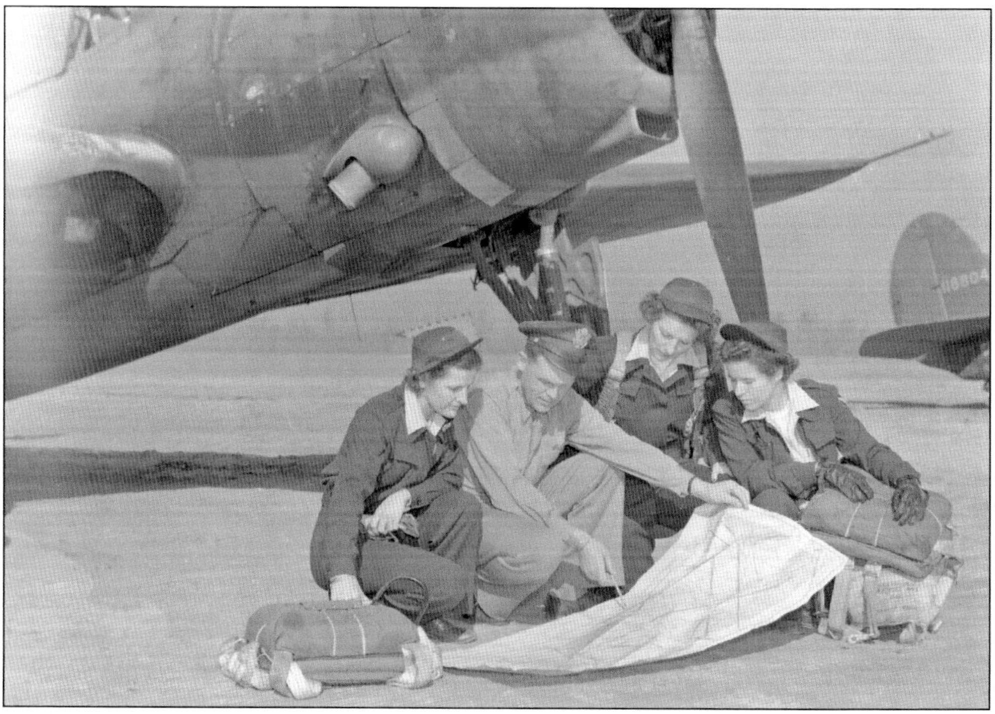

Unidentified WASP huddle over a training mission map on the tarmac at Liberty Field, Camp Stewart. (Courtesy of U.S. Army Photographs.)

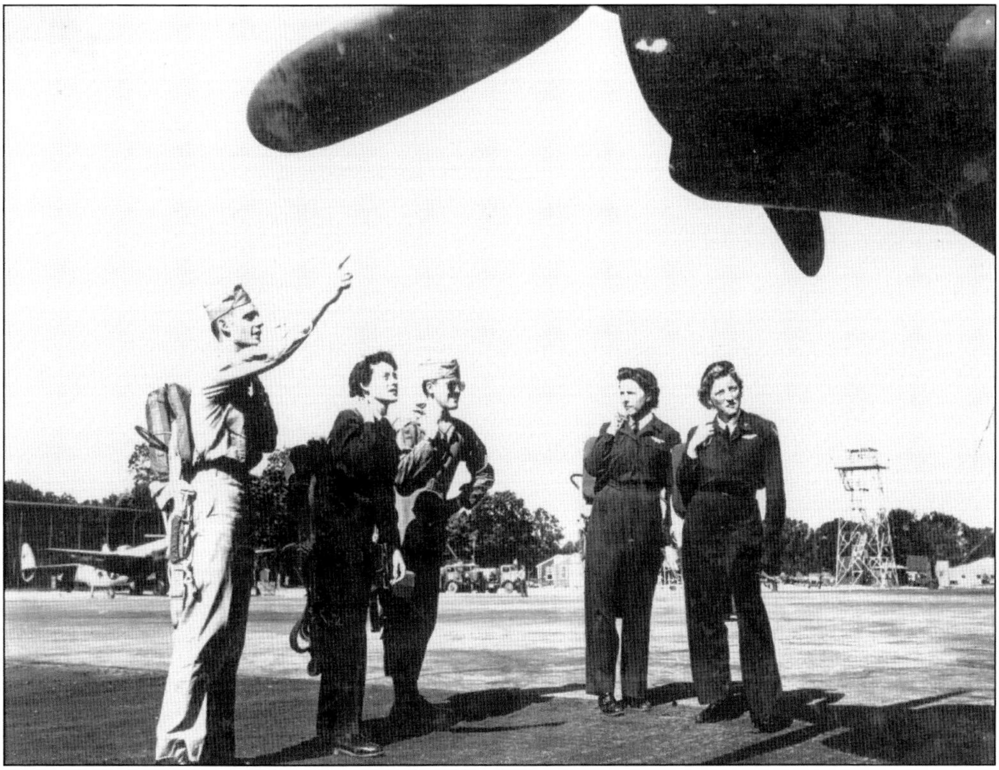

Recruited initially from women pilots who had more than 300 hours of flight time, WASP went through rigorous military flight training. Before the United States entered World War II after the Japanese attack on Pearl Harbor on December 7, 1941, many female pilots volunteered to fly for the British. While not flying combat missions, WASP were exposed to enemy anti-aircraft fire as they ferried food and other supplies into Europe and China. On the home front, WASP supported anti-aircraft artillery training at Camp Stewart by towing targets at which ground batteries would shoot. WASP prepare for the day's mission at Liberty Field, Camp Stewart (top). Ready to fly, WASP recruit Helen Wyatt Snapp (bottom) sits at the controls of her A-24 aircraft at Liberty Field, Camp Stewart. Originally thinking she would become a teacher, Snapp took flying lessons one summer and discovered her calling. When flight hour requirements were reduced for new recruits in 1943, Snapp was allowed to enter the WASP training program. By the time WASP disbanded in December 1944, Snapp had logged over 1,000 hours of flight time, most of which under fire. (Courtesy of U.S. Army Photographs.)

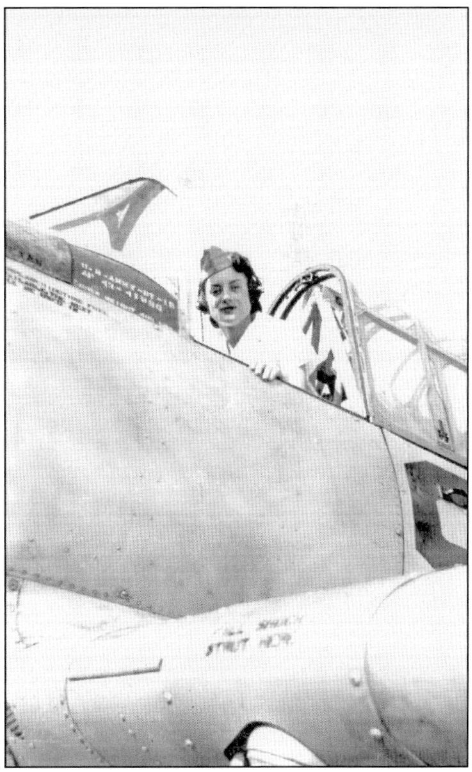

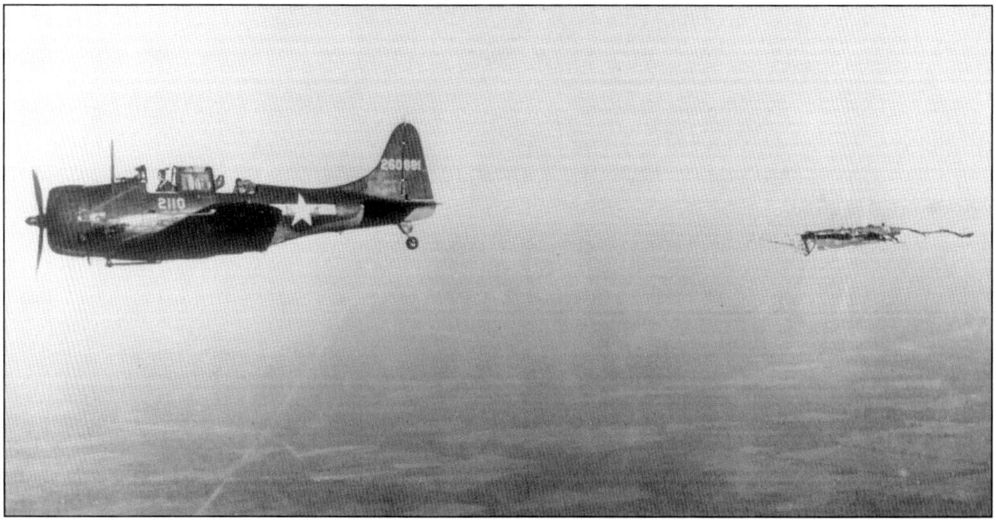

Helen Snapp is seen flying an A-24 towing a target while batteries on the ground fire anti-aircraft rounds. Despite their vital support of the war effort, WASPs served as government-service civilian employees and were not considered eligible for veteran status and benefits. Congress finally recognized WASP veteran status in 1977, and the U.S. Air Force followed with formal recognition of WASP veterans two years later. (Courtesy of U.S. Army Photographs.)

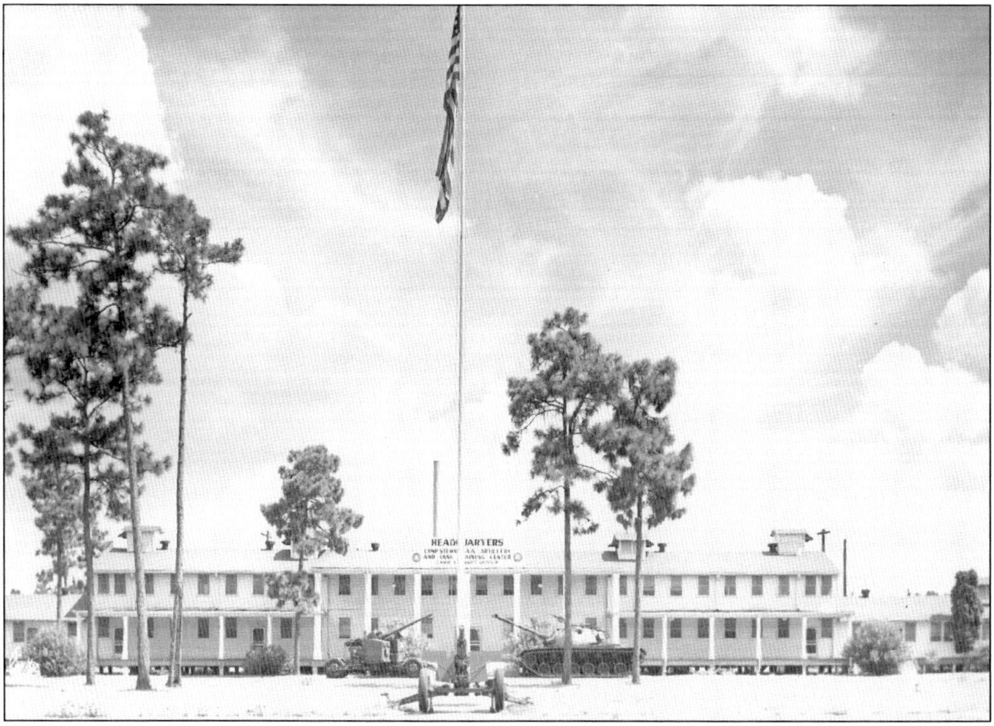

After World War II ended, Camp Stewart served as a U.S. National Guard training facility until the Anti-Aircraft Artillery Training Center was reopened in 1950. When this photograph was taken of Camp Stewart Headquarters in 1955, the base had expanded into tank training. This large facility actually joined old Building 01, seen at the center behind the flagpole, with two buildings, which flanked it. (Courtesy of U.S. Army Photographs.)

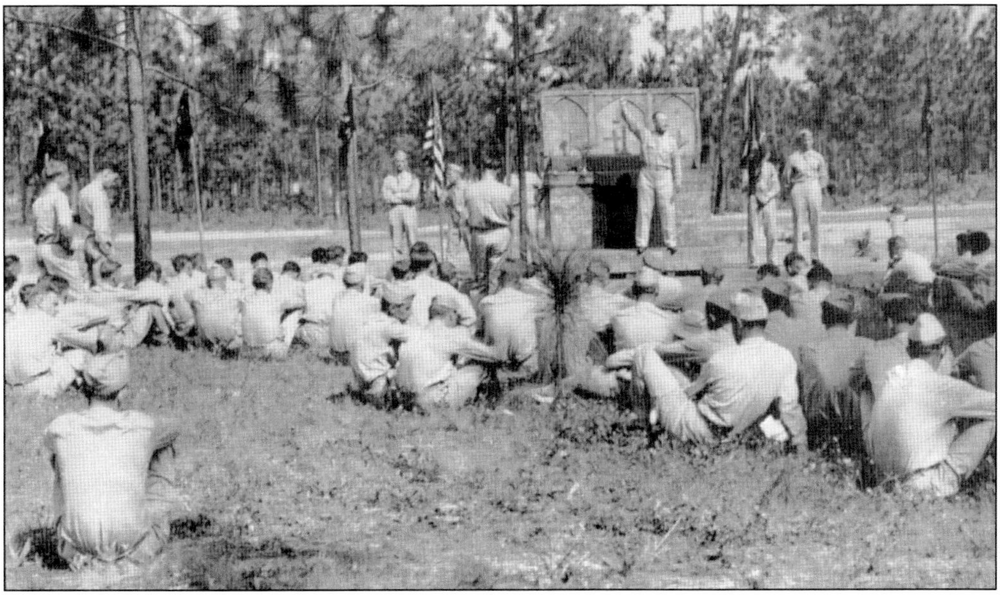

While a chapel was built at Camp Stewart, religious services were sometimes conducted in the field, as seen in this photograph in the early 1950s. (Courtesy of U.S. Army Photographs.)

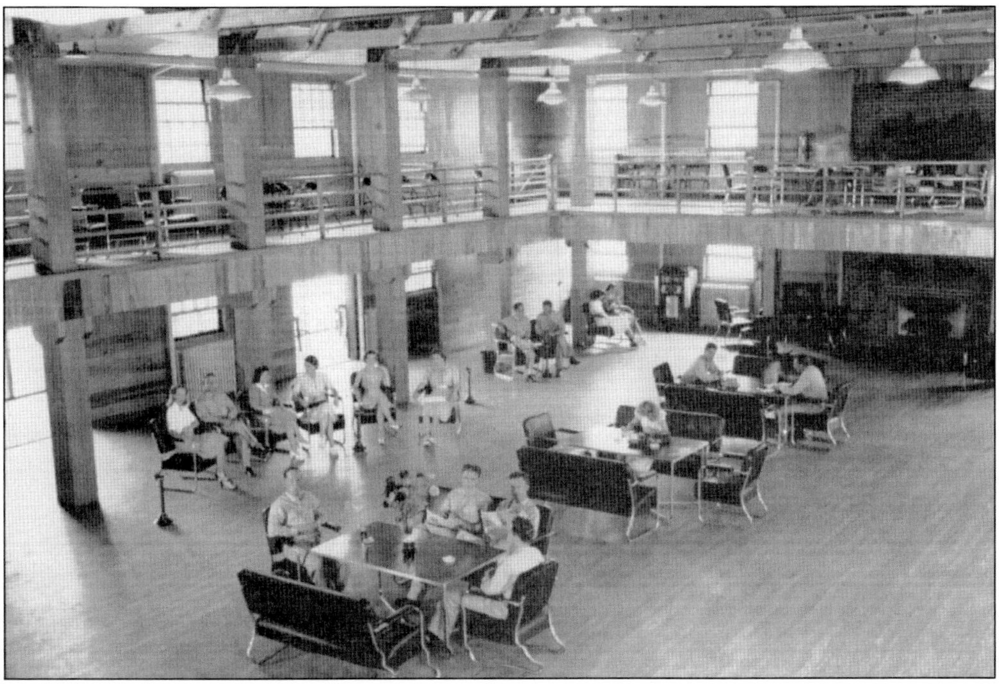

Soldiers stationed at Camp Stewart in the 1950s enjoyed more amenities than their World War II brethren. A popular retreat on post was the service club with lounge areas, a large multipurpose room, and balconies, which onlookers frequented during dance nights. (Courtesy of U.S. Army Photographs.)

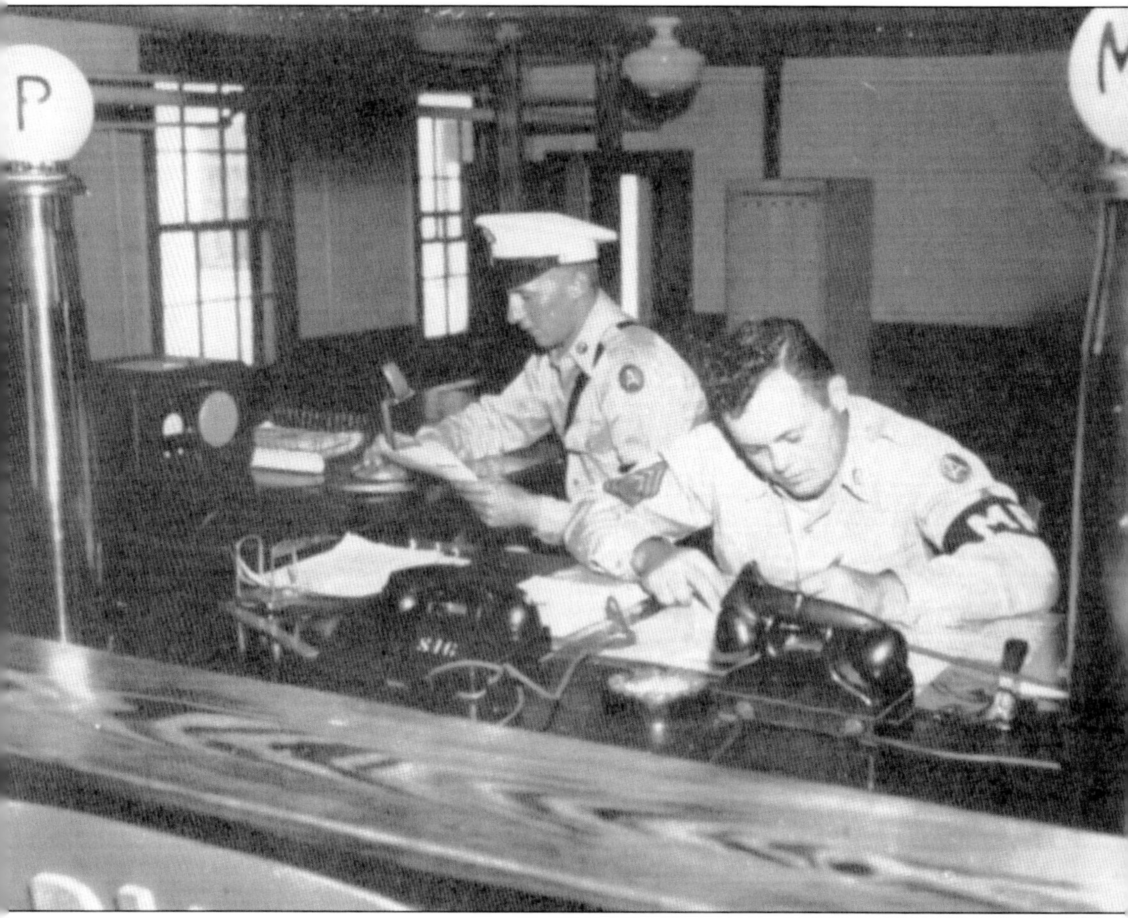

Unidentified desk sergeants at the military police station keep watch over Camp Stewart in 1953 when it was the headquarters for the 3rd Army AAA Training Center. In March 1956, Camp Stewart ceased to exist when it was renamed Fort Stewart. (Courtesy of U.S. Army Photographs.)

Five

Small Town Boom Town

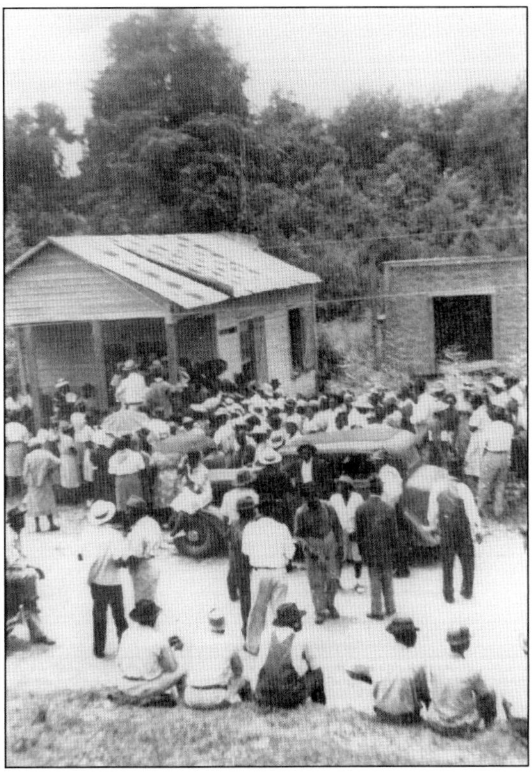

After World War II ended, President Truman looked at civil rights issues. In 1946, the U.S. Supreme Court ruled in a case affirming a black man's right to vote in Columbus, Georgia. The decision reversed 40 years of African Americans being denied the right to vote through poll taxes and other policies. Officials required black citizens to come in person to the Hinesville courthouse, and people walked or rode from all over Liberty County. Some citizens arrived with 40 years of poll tax receipts. At first, applicants completed an oral examination filled with complicated questions and nearly all passed the test. After several days and an intercession by a civil rights attorney, African Americans registered without taking the exam. The photograph shows African Americans in Liberty County at the polls in Riceboro voting in the July 1946 democratic primary. For several years, black voters were required to vote only in Riceboro regardless of where they lived in Liberty County. (Courtesy of Sallie W. Richardson.)

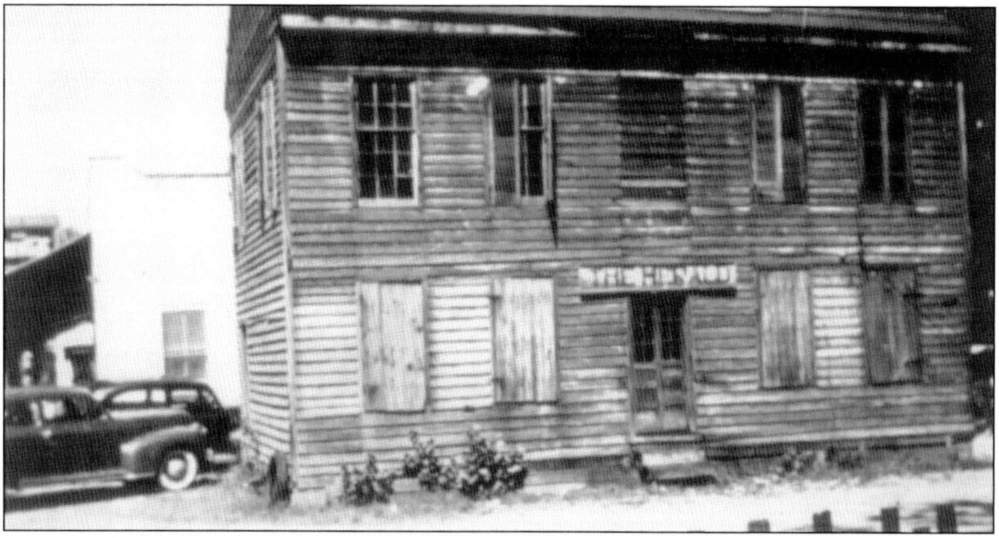

After purchasing the *Hinesville Gazette* in 1893, Robert "Bob" Moody Martin changed the name of the weekly newspaper to the *Liberty County Herald*. After the Martins, the Clark family owned, edited, and published the *Liberty County Herald*. The old Liberty County-Herald building, shown here in 1940, was located on Main Street. The same year this photograph was taken, the paper moved into a new building across the street. After M. F. Clark Jr. died in 1966, his widow, Lollie Gill Clark, continued publishing the paper, and their sons Marvin "Pete" Clark and Nicky G. Clark both served as editors until the family sold the paper in 1979. The newspaper was renamed the *Coastal Courier*. (Courtesy of the *Liberty County Herald*.)

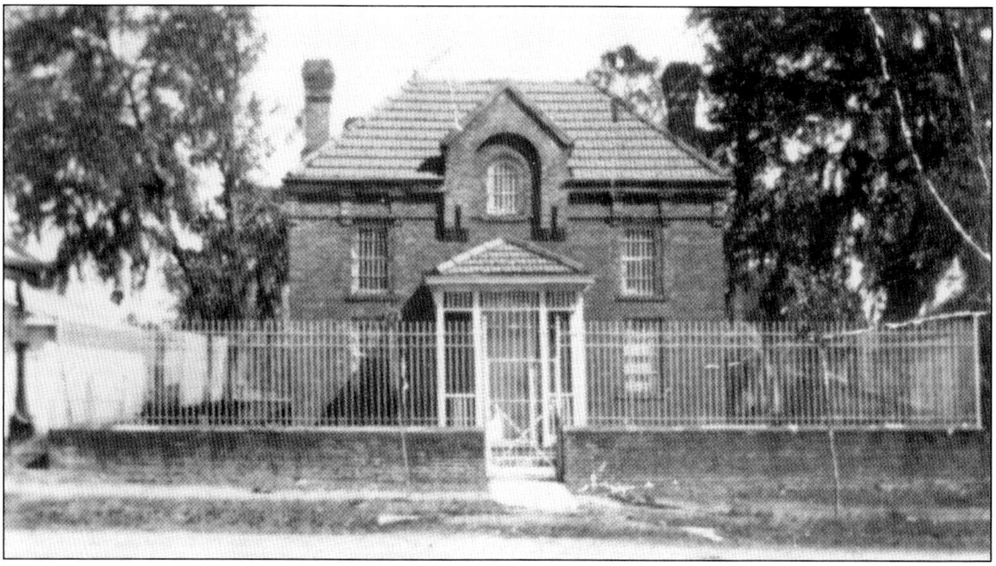

Built in 1887, 50 years after the county seat moved to Hinesville, the old jail held incarcerated prisoners and an occasional mental patient until the 1960s. Escapes were not uncommon. One colorful story was a known jail-escapee who promised Sheriff R. V. "Bobby" Sikes that he would not escape from his jail. The man broke out only to break back in, thereby keeping his word to the sheriff. In later years, the chamber of commerce used the building as an office, and the jail was restored in 2008 for use as a visitor center and museum. (Courtesy of the *Liberty County Herald*.)

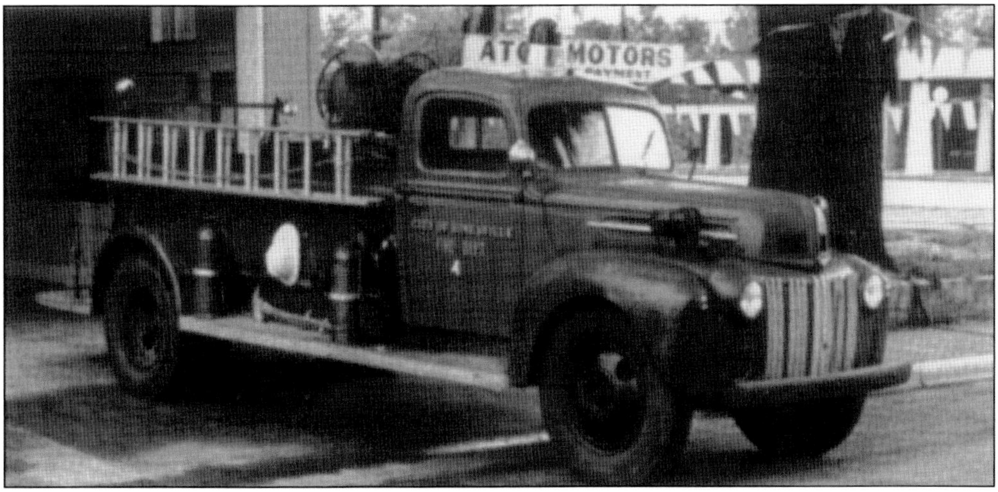

For many years, Hinesville had one fire truck. As the population grew, however, this old engine was replaced with newer vehicles and a professional fire department. (Courtesy of the *Liberty County Herald.*)

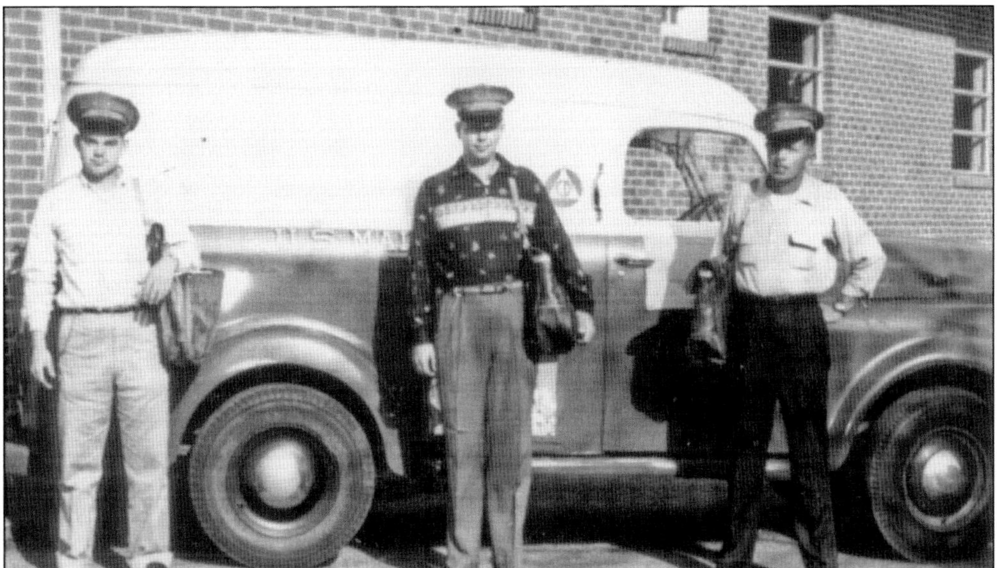

In November 1956, the Hinesville post office began to make home deliveries. Pictured here were the first three mailmen in town, from left to right, W. L. Salter Jr., James P. Argogast, and William P. Floyd. They are standing in front of Hinesville's only postal vehicle. (Courtesy of the *Liberty County Herald.*)

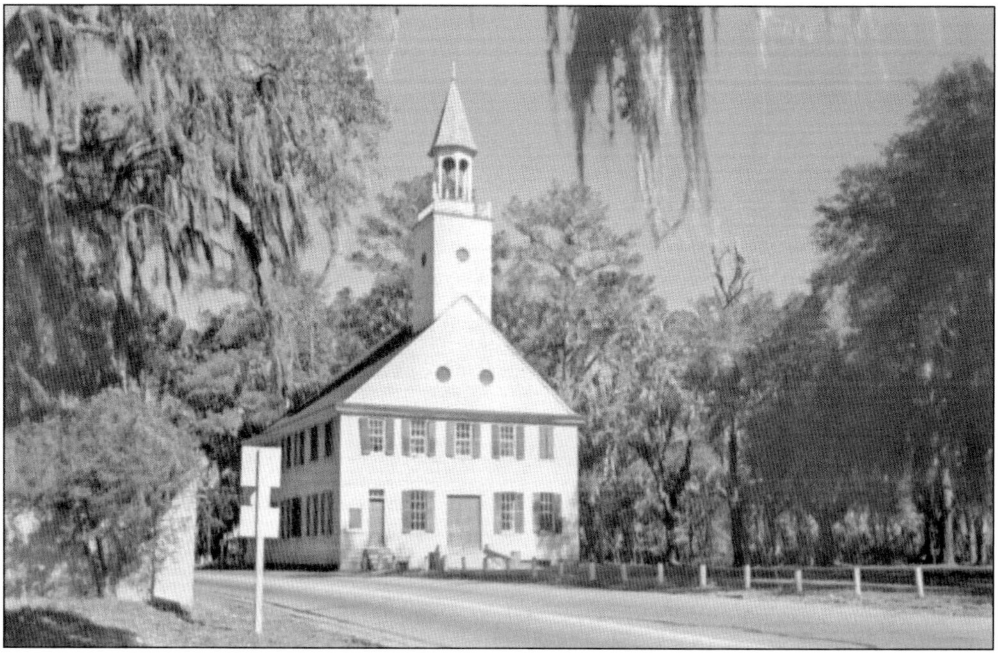

Continuing to be a focal point of Liberty County, the Midway Church became a familiar sight to tourists traveling between Florida and points north. As the sign above (top) indicated, those who wished to tour the historic building could obtain a key from the Gulf Station across the Old Sunbury Road from the church. The Midway Society continued to hold an annual service in the church, and selectmen were responsible for its upkeep. Beginning in the 1930s, however, a push was made to widen U.S. Route 17 to four lanes. To accommodate the widening, the church had to move. The church is pictured here (bottom) before it was moved. (Courtesy of the Springfield Legacy Foundation.)

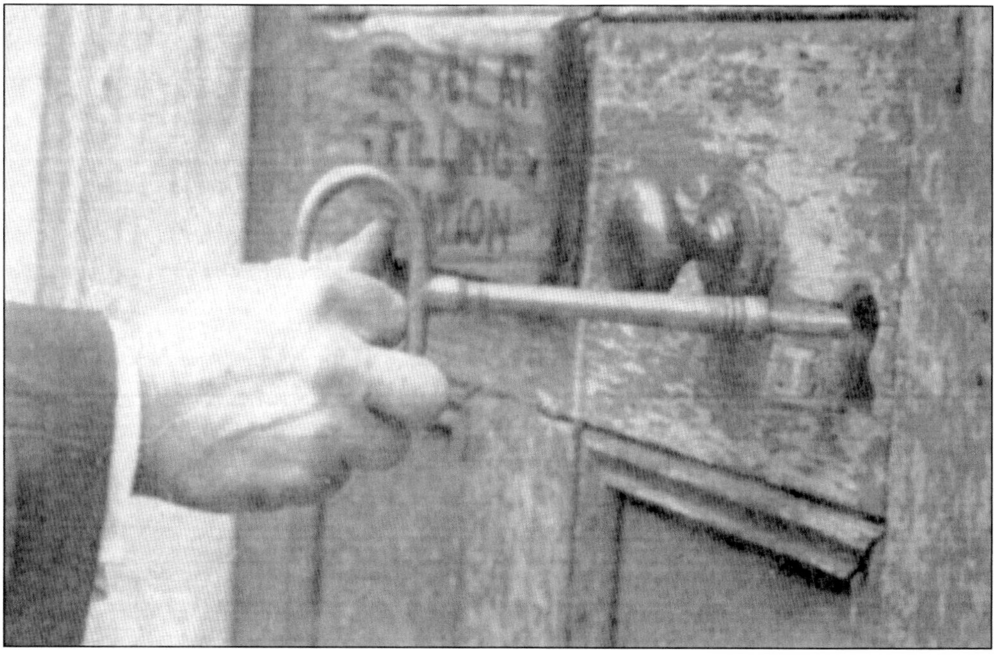

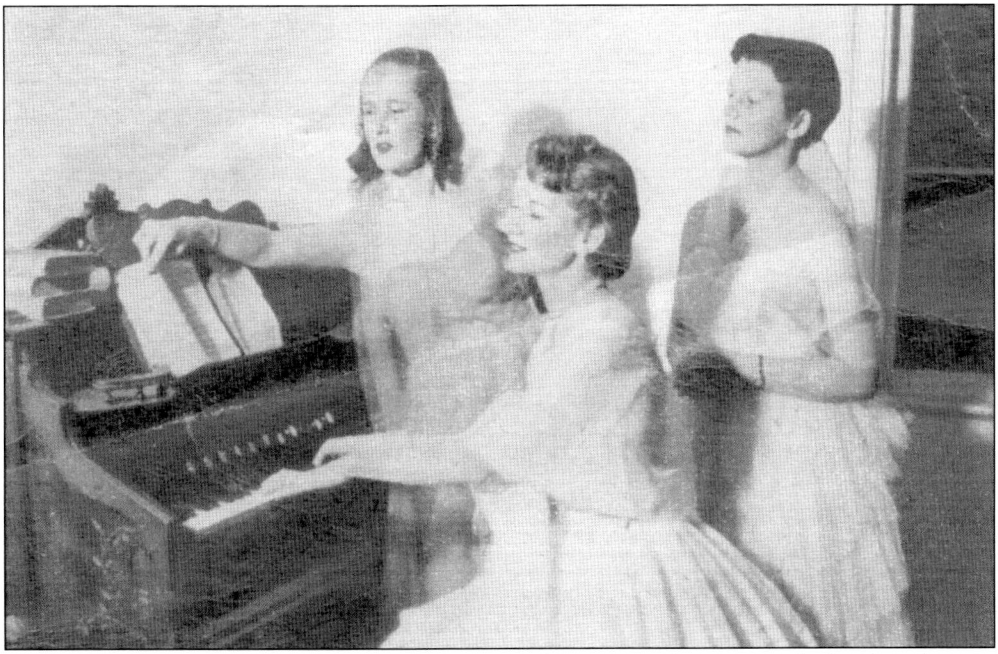

In 1954, the Midway Society looked forward to celebrating the bicentennial of its founding. In this photograph, descendents of Puritan settlers play the pump organ inside the Midway Church. (Courtesy of the Springfield Legacy Foundation.)

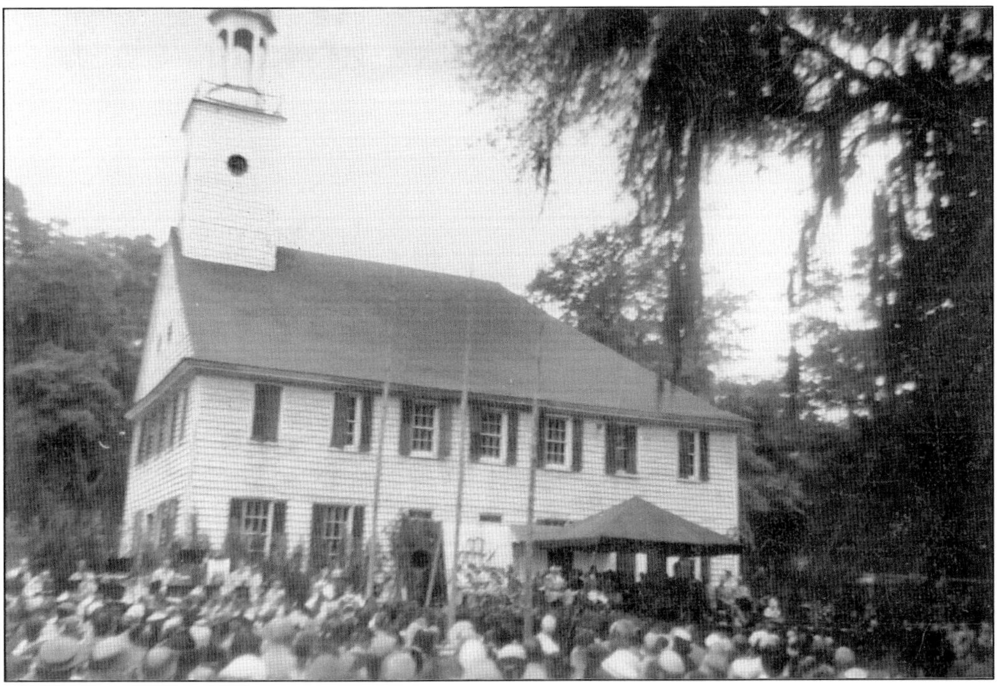

U.S. senator Richard B. Russell was the principal speaker at the bicentennial celebration of the Midway Society on April 24, 1954. While the Midway meeting always features a lunch under the oaks in the churchyard, the crowds were substantially larger than usual for this special event. (Courtesy of the Springfield Legacy Foundation.)

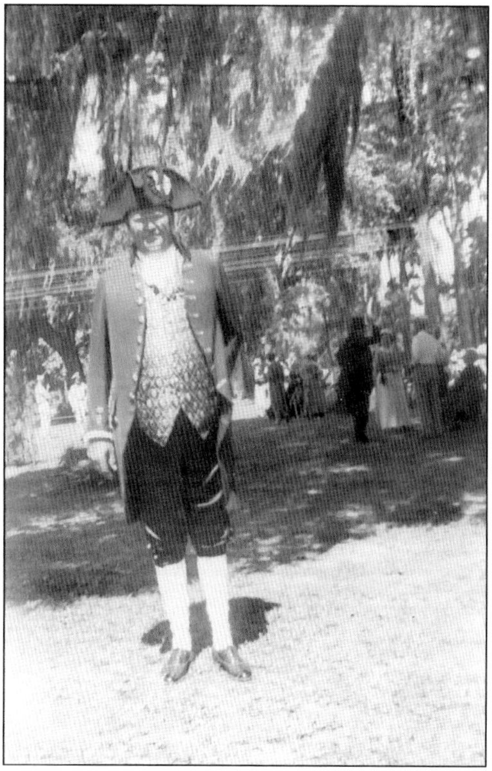

At the bicentennial celebration of the founding of the Midway Church in 1954, a pageant titled "A Charge to Keep," written by Josephine Martin and produced by Corrie McDowell Martin, presented a tableau of Midway's history. In this photograph, John Porter Stevens portrays his ancestor John Stevens, who gave the land for the meetinghouse in 1766. (Courtesy of the Springfield Legacy Foundation.)

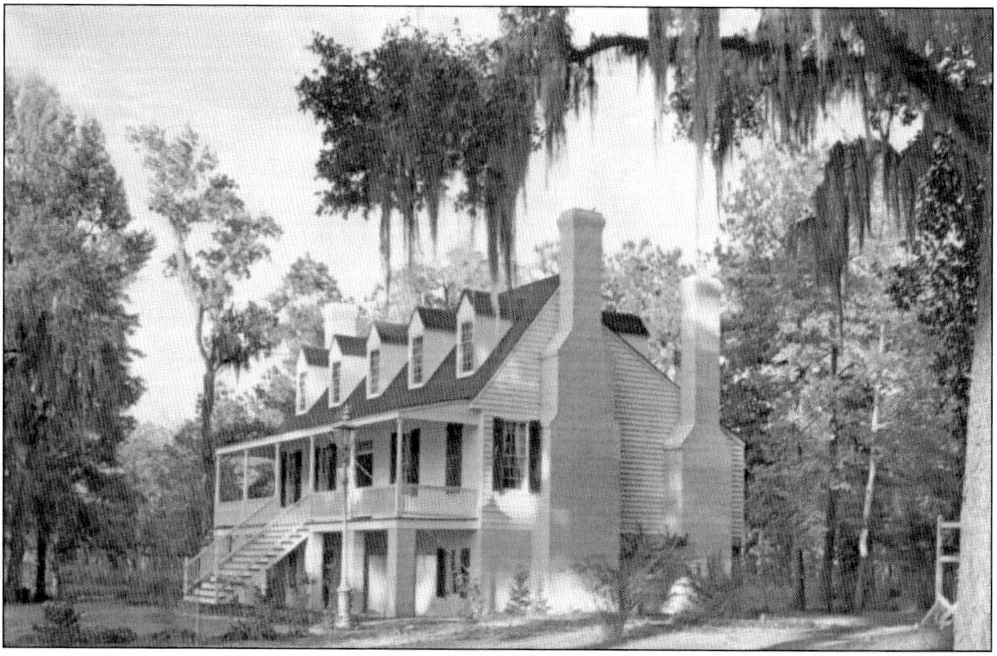

In the 1940s, a group of concerned citizens founded Midway Museum, Inc., to develop a plan to enhance the history of Midway. Designed by Thomas Little, architect for Colonial Williamsburg, the Midway Museum officially opened to the public in 1959. Modeled on 18th century local architecture, the building cost $50,000. (Courtesy of the Springfield Legacy Foundation.)

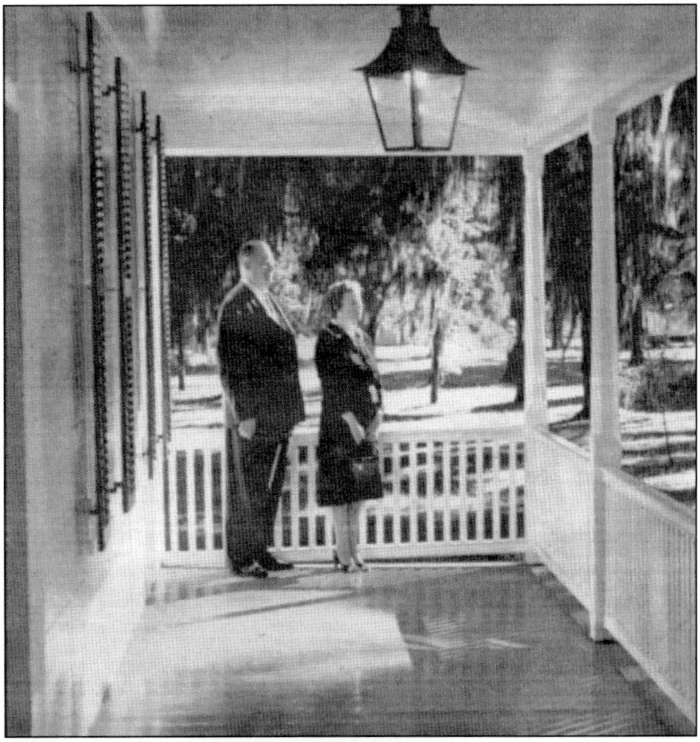

John Porter Stevens (left) and his wife, Martha Jefferson Randolph Stevens, (right) stand on the porch of the newly constructed Midway Museum. Having found a table belonging to Sen. John Elliott inhabited by chickens and flatirons at her mother-in-law's house, Martha Jefferson Stevens realized that, without immediate conservation efforts, much of Liberty County's history and artifacts would be lost. She helped establish Midway Museum, Inc., and worked tirelessly to bring the vision to life. (Courtesy of the Springfield Legacy Foundation.)

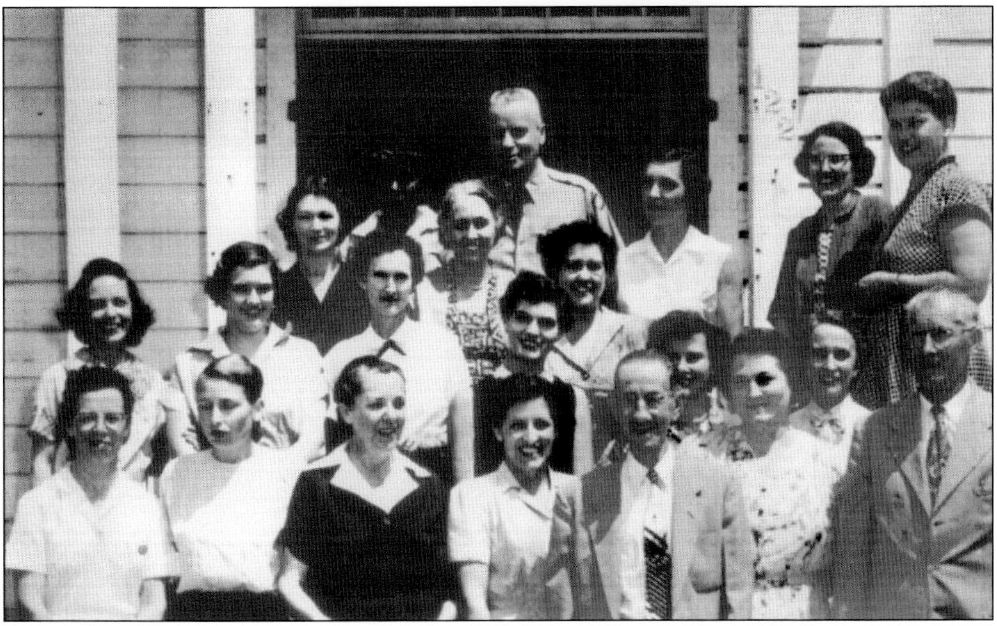

In addition to serving as a leading doctor in Liberty County from the 1920s through the 1950s, Dr. W. T. Welborn was mayor of Hinesville for several terms. These are participants in a Liberty County Health Center activity in the mid-1950s. Among those pictured are Mrs. Ann Dobbins, Mrs. Grace Warren, Dr. W. T. Welborn, Mrs. Jordye Bacon, Mr. Herbert Porter, Mrs. Virginia Fraser Evans, Mrs. Claudia Bacon Smith, Mrs. Mary Alice Walker, Mrs. Pat Tanner, Mrs. Hazel Jackson, and Mrs. Bailey. (Courtesy of the *Liberty County Herald*.)

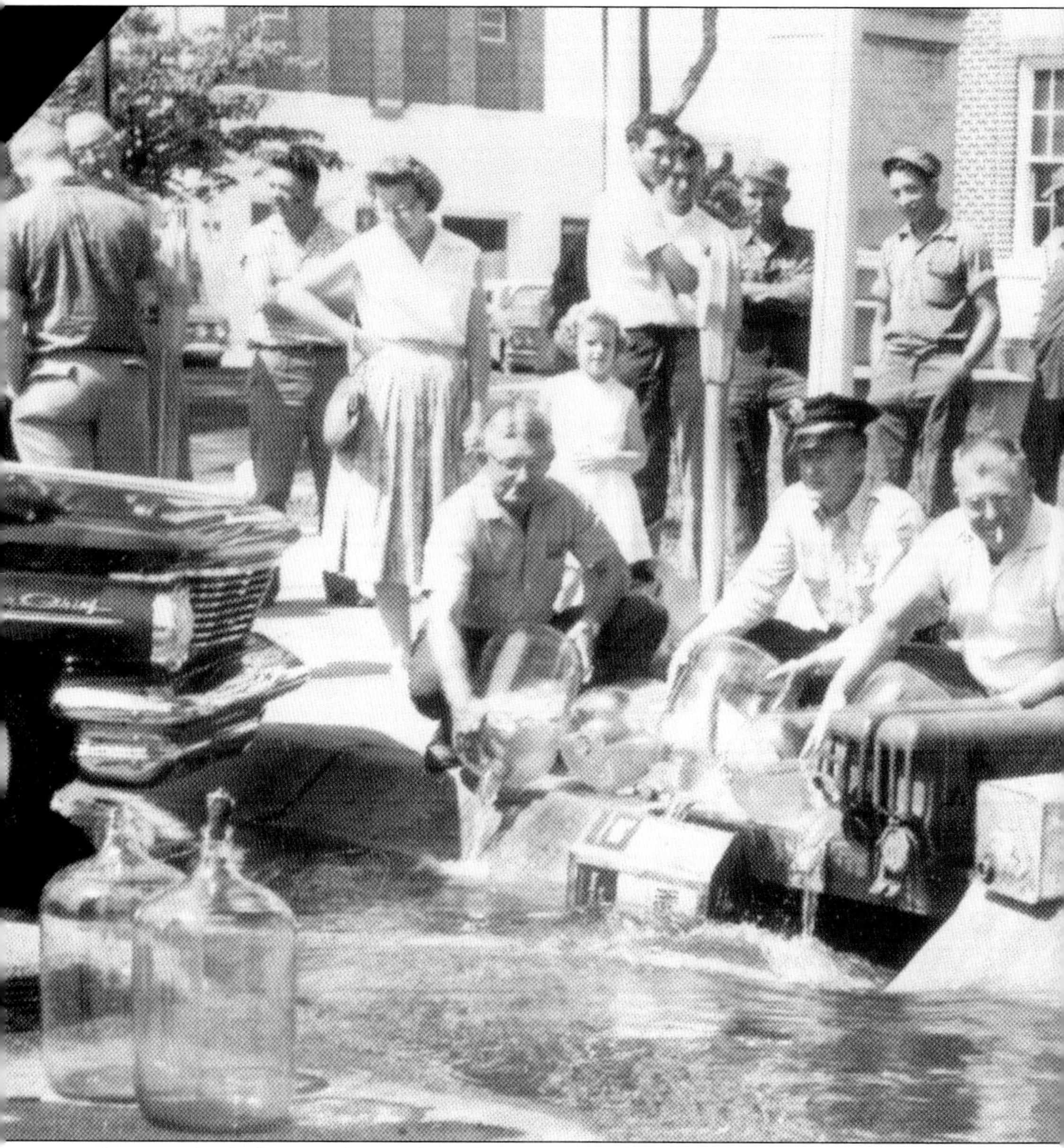

A group of onlookers watches in the early 1960s as Hinesville City Police and the Liberty County Sheriff's Department personnel pour confiscated illegal moonshine down the drain. Moonshine

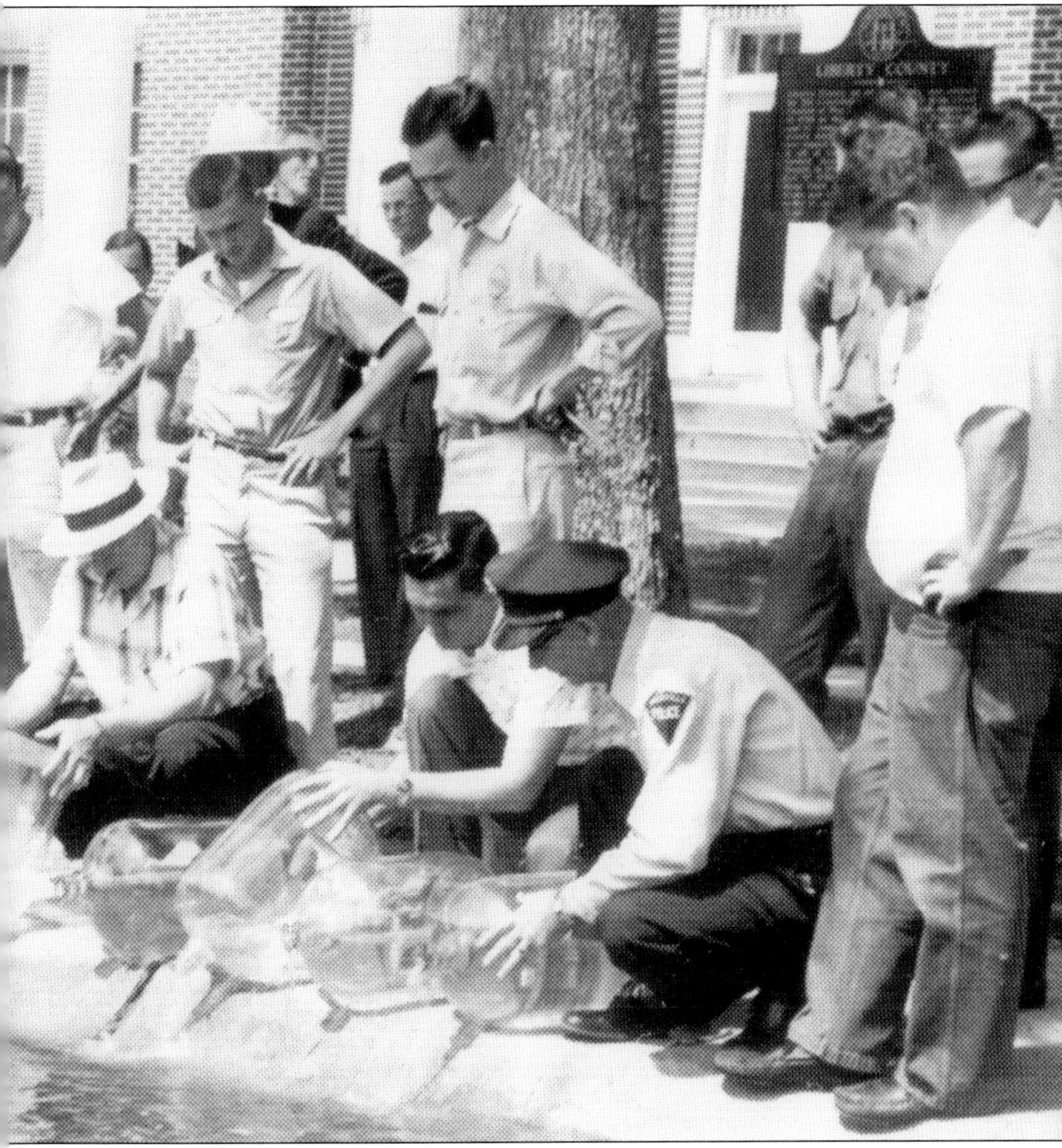

stills were part of the local economy for generations. (Courtesy of the *Liberty County Herald*.)

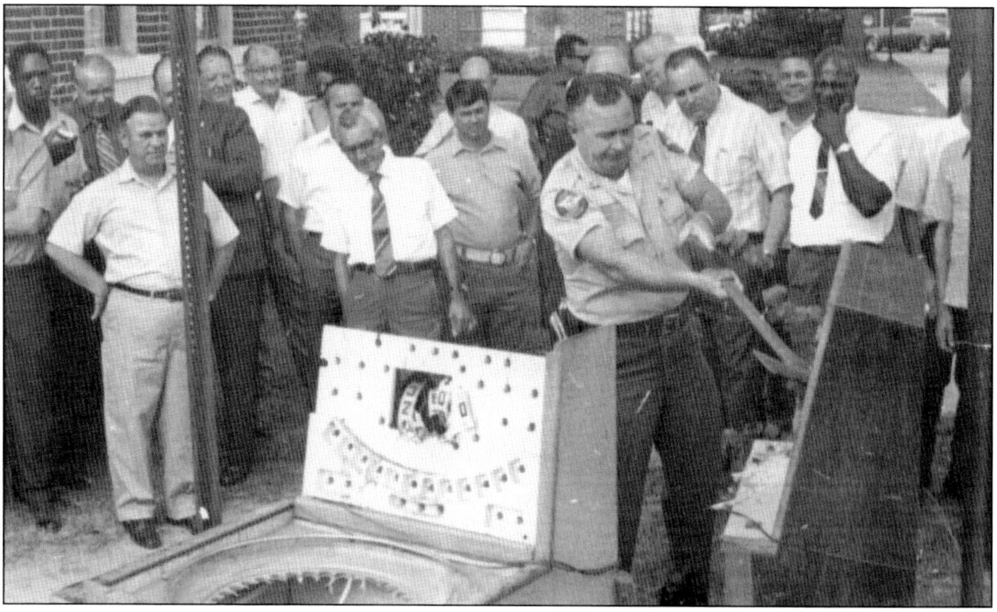

Liberty County sheriff deputy Miles Groover destroys gambling devices on the courthouse lawn as interested onlookers watch. (Courtesy of the *Liberty County Herald.*)

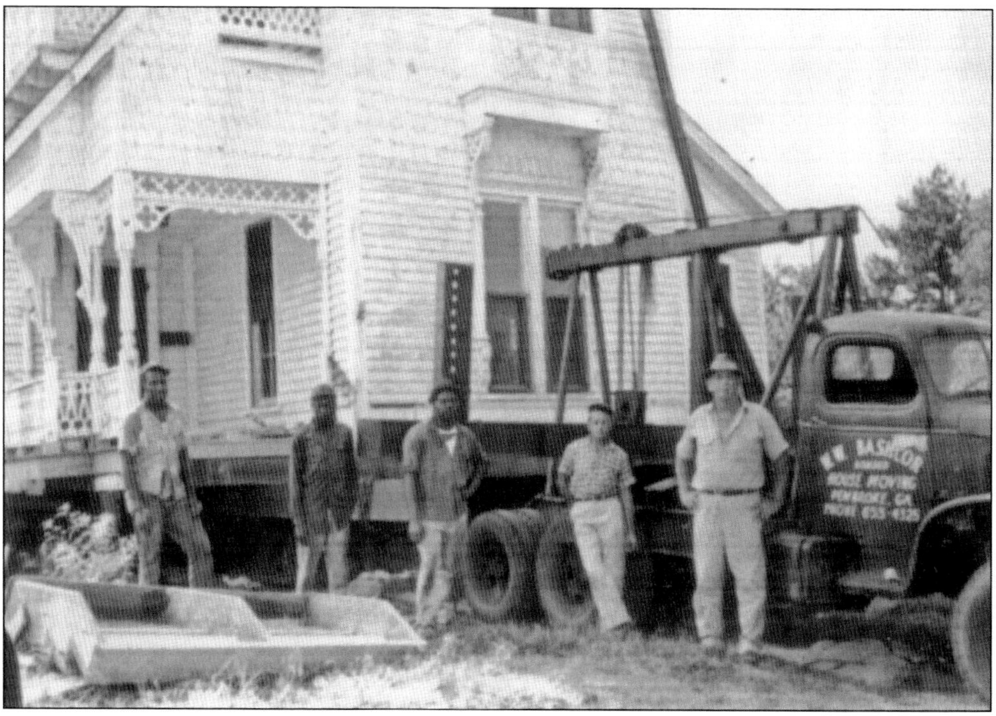

As Hinesville grew during and after World War II, older homes yielded to new commercial development. In this photograph, the Mingledorff home was being moved by Bashlor House Moving to provide space for the Hinesville Bank in the 1950s. (Courtesy of the *Liberty County Herald.*)

Blount Chevrolet stood at the corner of U.S. Highway 82—now U.S. Route 84—and East South Street in Hinesville from 1946 to 1966. Some of the Blount family is pictured above modeling a brand new 1958 Chevrolet convertible. Also on the lot are 1958 models of Oldsmobile automobiles and Chevrolet trucks. (Courtesy of the *Liberty County Herald.*)

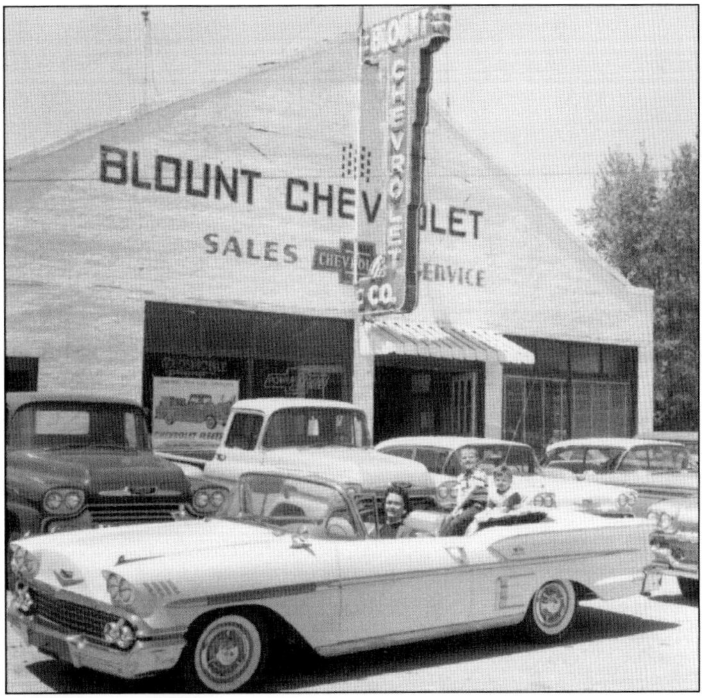

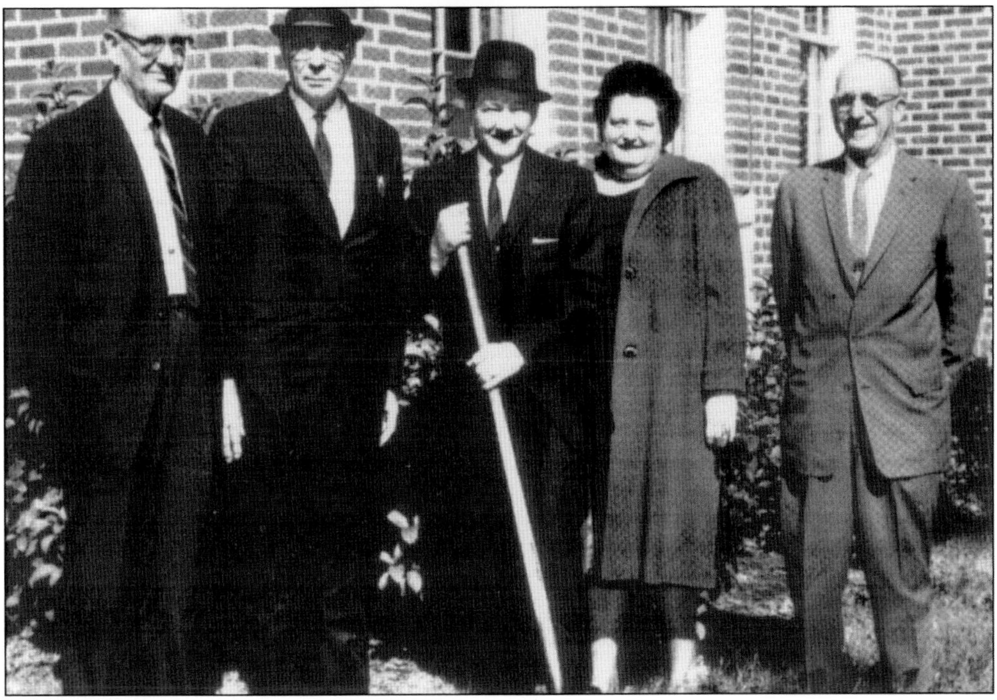

In the early 1960s, Liberty County commissioners broke ground for a new courthouse in Hinesville. From left to right, they are Commissioners Waller, Hook, Smiley, Carter, and Hoke Youmans. In addition to serving as Liberty County's first female commissioner, Hazel Carter was also the first woman licensed as a mortician in the state of Georgia. She and her family owned and operated Carter Funeral Home. (Photograph by Earl Elam; courtesy of the *Liberty County Herald.*)

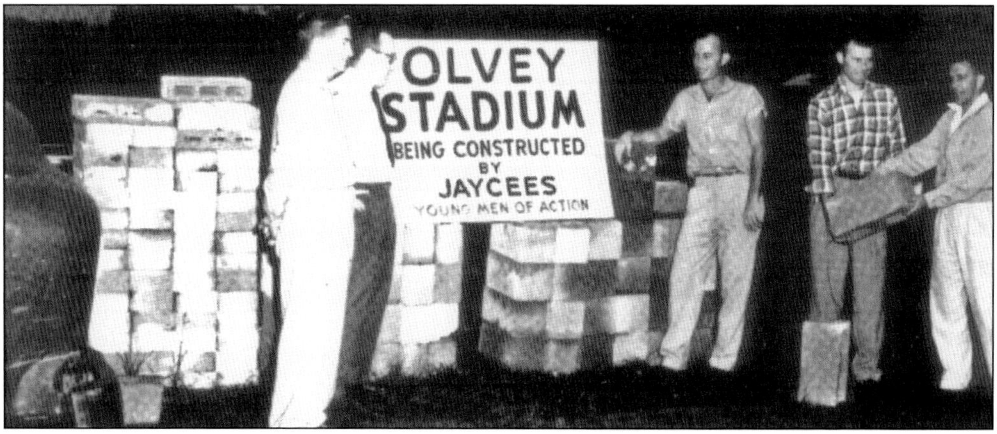

Concrete blocks were the beginning of Olvey Stadium in Hinesville named for Lee Donne Olvey, who graduated from Bradwell Institute with top honors. After graduating from West Point with ratings as high as Gen. Douglas MacArthur, Olvey was named a Rhodes Scholar and earned a Ph.D. in economics from Harvard University. Volunteers include, from left to right, W. C. Pafford, Joe Fraser Jr., Bruce Gaskin, Paul DeLargy, and Ed Edwards. (Courtesy of the *Liberty County Herald*.)

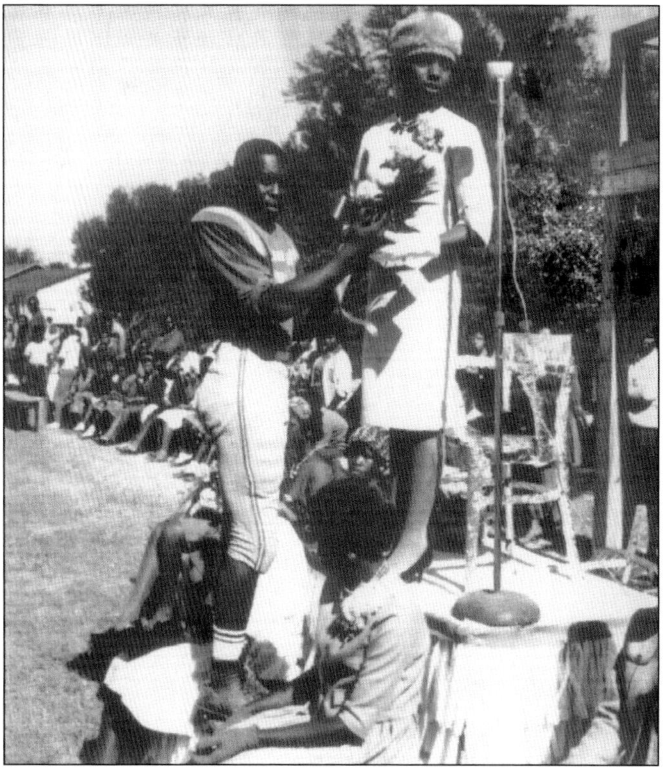

Booker T. Burley, captain of the 1962 Liberty County High School football team, presents homecoming queen Linda Quarterman with a bouquet of flowers. (Photograph by Earl Elam; courtesy of the *Liberty County Herald*.)

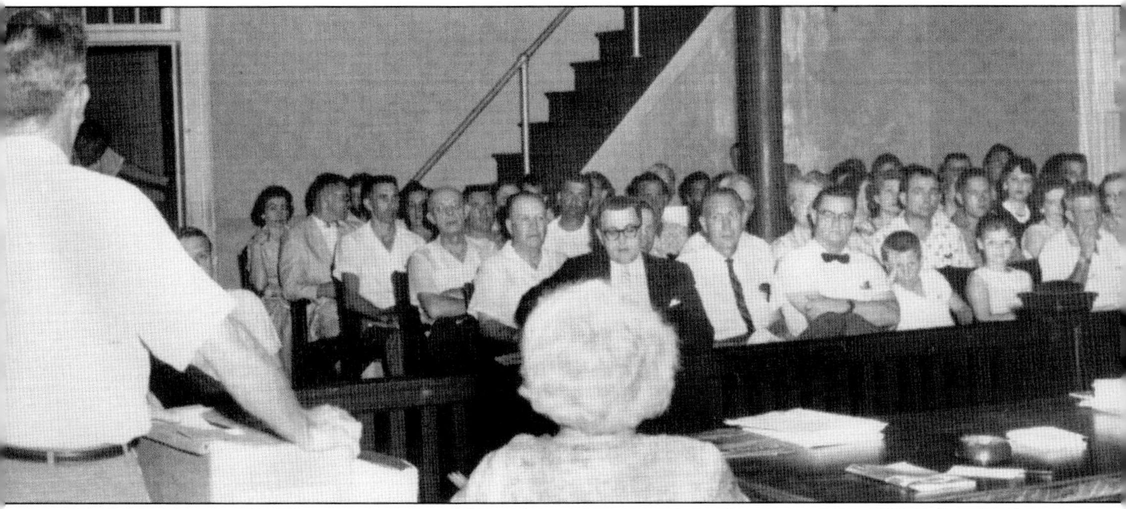

Citizens attend a civil defense meeting in the Liberty County Courthouse in 1961. With her back to the camera is Lucille B. Wood. (Courtesy of the *Liberty County Herald*.)

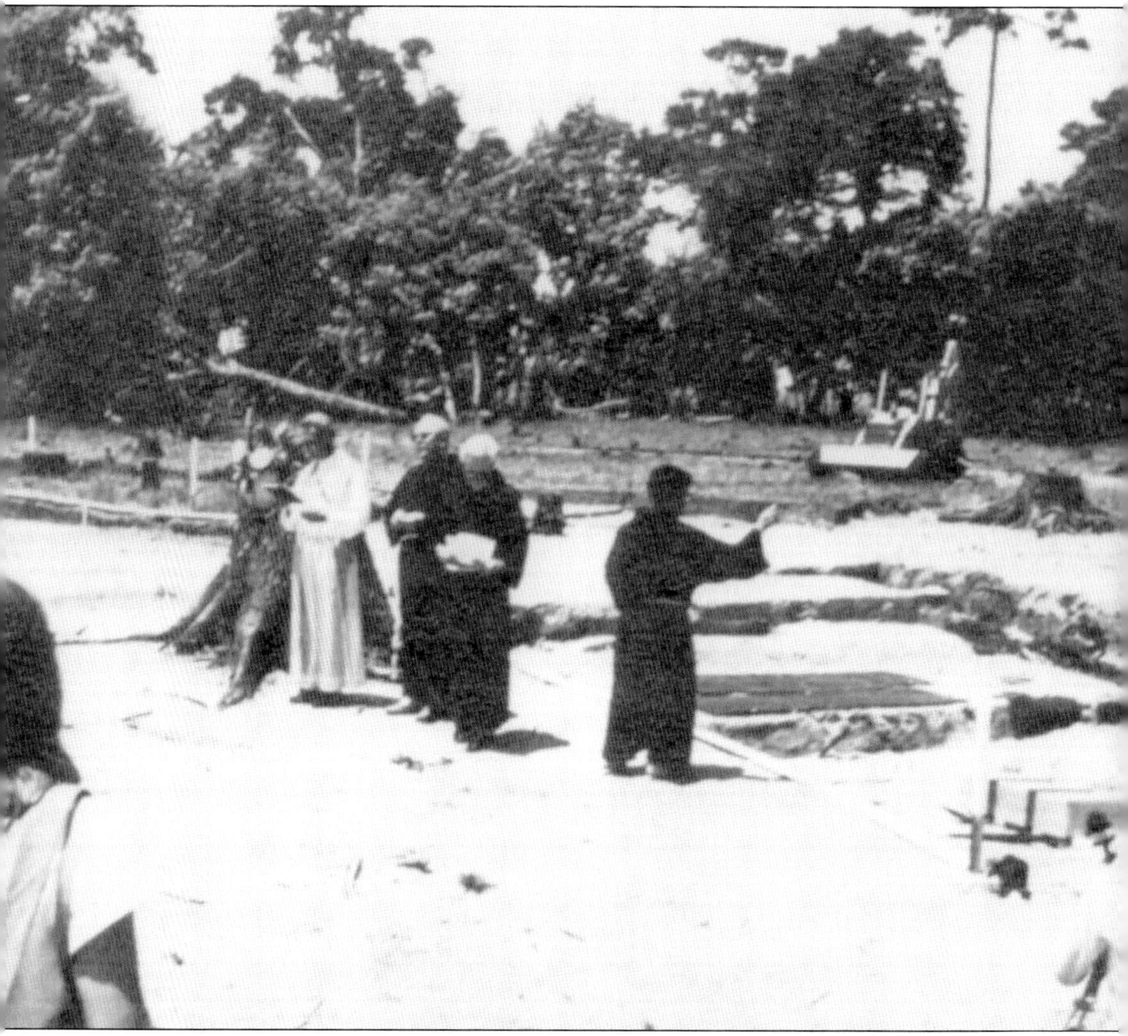

On St. Catherine's Island in May 1984, Catholic bishop Raymond Lessard and Franciscan fathers Adams, Wyse, and Morales conduct a service dedicated to "reblessing the ground and reburial of remains" at the Spanish Mission Santa Catalina de Guale discovered and excavated by eminent archaeologist Dr. David Hurst Thomas in the 1970s and 1980s. (Photograph by Dennis O'Brien; courtesy of the American Museum of Natural History.)

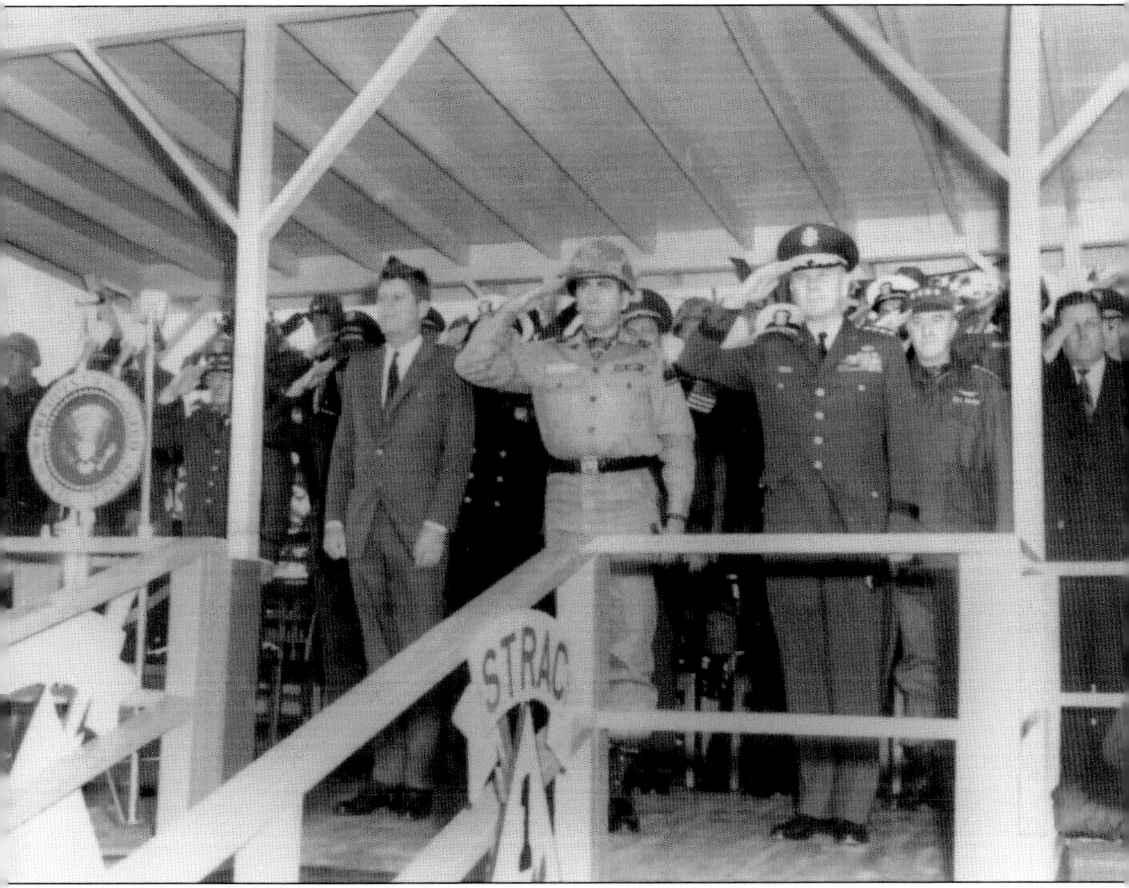

In 1963, Pres. John F. Kennedy visited Fort Stewart to thank members of the 1st Armored Division for their service during the Cuban Missile Crisis. From Fort Hood, Texas, 19,000 troops relocated to Fort Stewart in late 1962 to prepare for the possible invasion of Cuba. Once the Soviet Union removed its missiles from the island nation, the crisis passed. Standing, during a formal review of troops at Fort Stewart are, from left to right, President Kennedy, division commander Maj. Gen. Edwin Burba, and chairman of the Joint Chiefs of Staff Gen. Maxwell D. Taylor. (Courtesy of U.S. Army Photographs.)

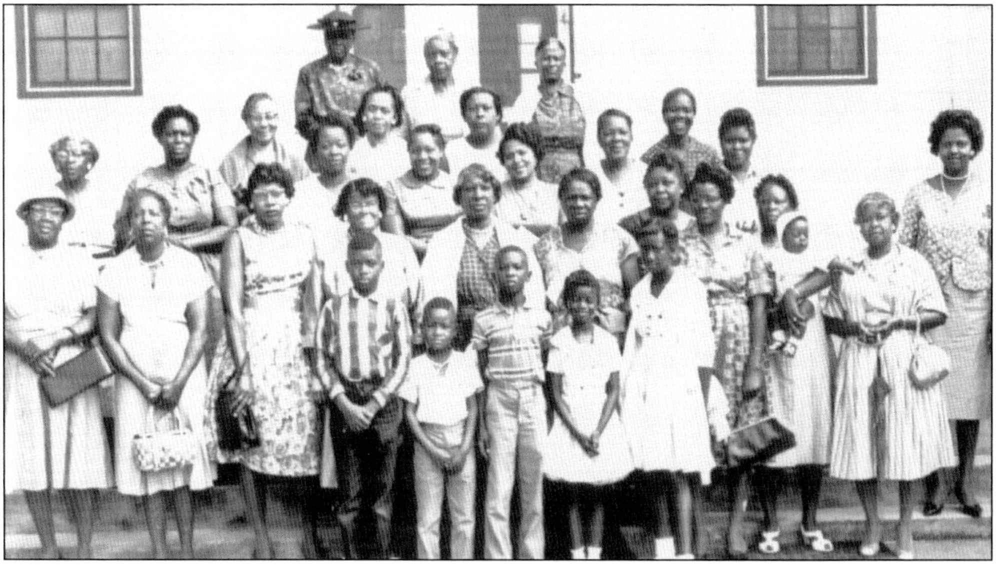

In 1962 during the National Home Demonstration Club Week, the Liberty County Home Demonstration Club toured Fort Stewart facilities. From left to right, in the first row, are Prince Ellis Wynn, Anthony Winn, Ridge Miller, Sidney Miller, and Patricia Miller. In the second row are Mary Etta Golden, Hager McIver, Thelma Baker, Viola Ripley, Mary Wilson, Catherine Hudson, Georgia Tate, Olner Noble, Ruby Hill, Rosemary Young, and Alfreta Adams, county extension agent. In the third row are Lucinda Simms, Florine Shellman, Ella James, Carlene Cummings, Henrietta Singelton, Ruby Smith, Carrie Fountain, Leona Miller, and Lulu Kennedy. In the rear are Cornelia Mullice, Bessie Williams, Nancy Cutty, Barbara Fraiser, and Ophelia Golden. (Courtesy of the *Liberty County Herald.*)

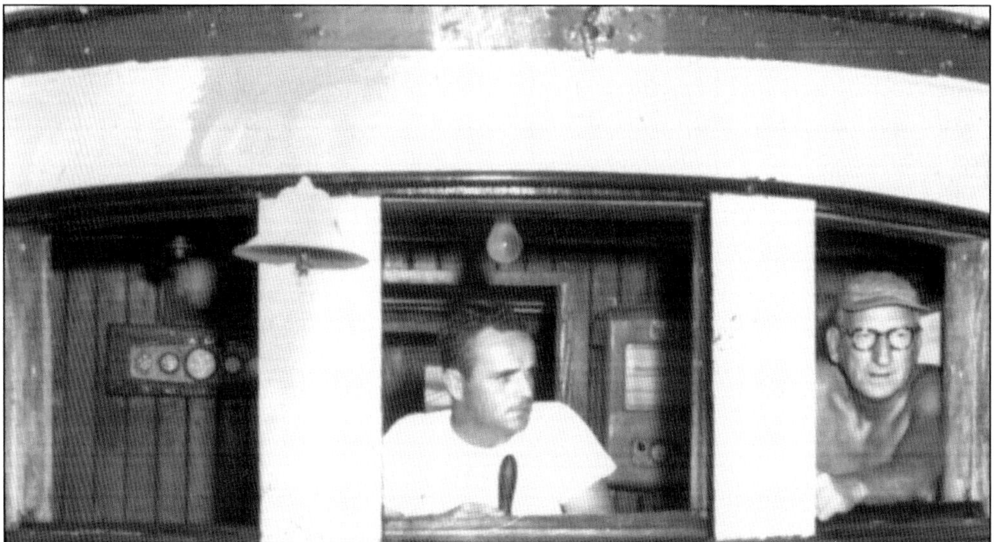

The marshes and sounds of coastal Georgia are a haven for shrimpers. One Liberty County shrimp boat, the *Green Seas*, is pictured here in the 1960s with Capt. Rod McCall (left). With him is T. R. Beach (right). At the beginning of the 21st century, fewer shrimpers ply the waters of Liberty County. (Courtesy of the *Liberty County Herald.*)

Once a common sight, this striker eats his lunch while working on a shrimp boat in coastal Liberty County. While most African Americans in eastern Liberty County owned land and raised food for their families, cash for taxes, clothing, and other necessities was difficult to come by. Men, women, and children performed domestic work or in the agricultural industries such as shrimping to pay for their families' needs. (Photograph by Earl Elam; courtesy of the *Liberty County Herald*.)

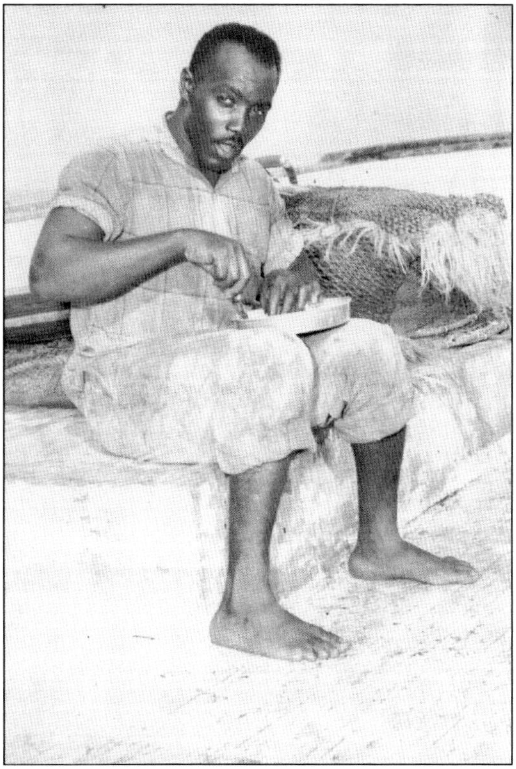

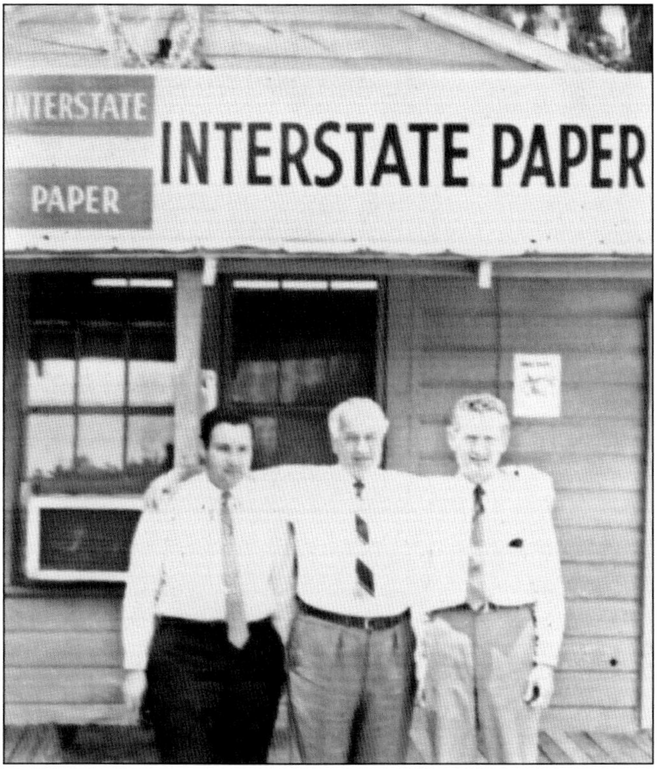

The first modern industry brought to Liberty County was the Interstate Paper Corporation that built a linerboard facility on the North Newport River at Riceboro. While completing construction on the factory, located on the former Montevideo Plantation once owned by Rev. C. C. Jones, Interstate Paper Corporation's owners, the Epsteins of New York, ran local operations from this building located on the site of an old sawmill and later owned by the Riceboro Chemical Company, which later became S. N. F. Chemtall Company, Inc. (Photograph by Earl Elam; courtesy of the *Liberty County Herald*.)

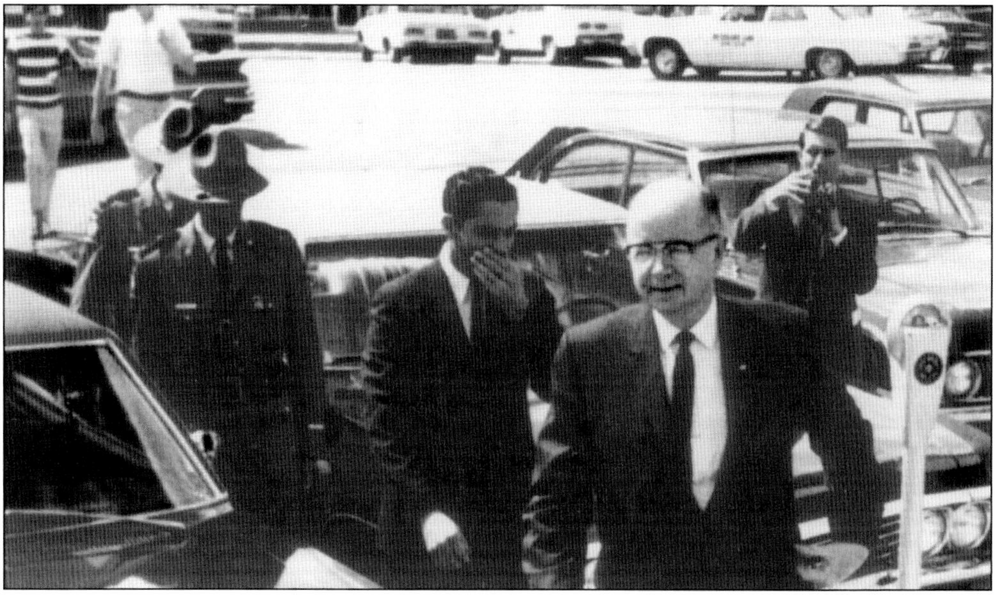

Liberty County played host to many of Georgia's governors. One of the most colorful and controversial men to serve in Georgia's highest office, Lester Maddox visited Hinesville many times throughout his career as lieutenant governor and governor of Georgia. In this photograph taken in the late 1960s, Sheriff R. V. "Bobby" Sikes, son of the late Sheriff Paul H. Sikes, and his deputies follow Governor Maddox as he walks through downtown. (Photograph by Earl Elam; courtesy of the *Liberty County Herald*.)

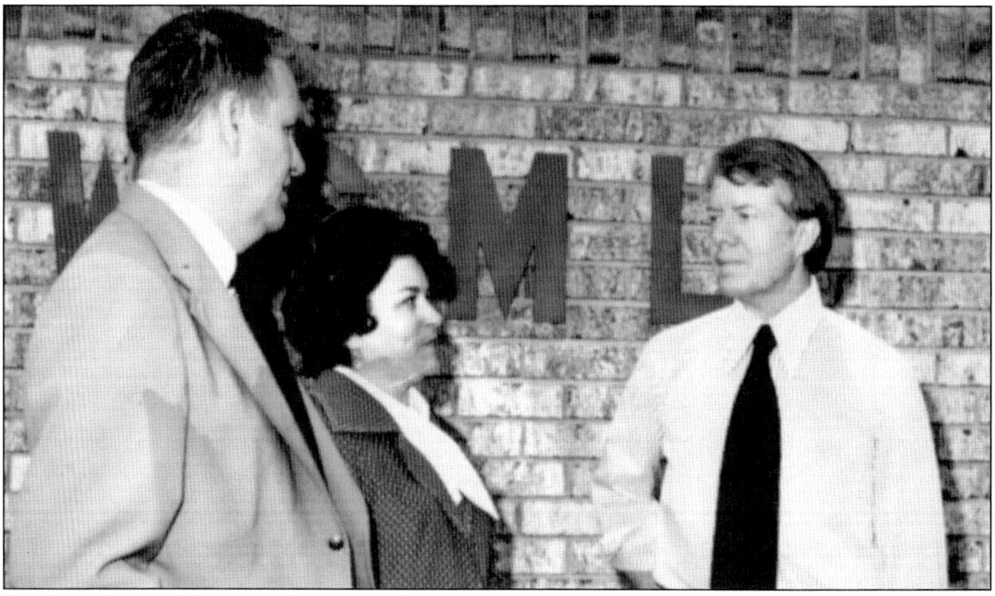

Future U.S. president Jimmy Carter, on far right, visited Liberty County while he was governor of Georgia in 1972. While in Hinesville, he met with Mrs. and Mr. Dave Steele, owners of WGML, Liberty County's first radio station. Founded in 1957 by Rep. Roscoe Denmark and Sheriff Paul H. Sikes, WGML derived its name from "Give Me Liberty." Gov. Carter recorded a message to celebrate the station's 15th anniversary. (Photograph by Earl Elam; courtesy of the *Liberty County Herald*.)

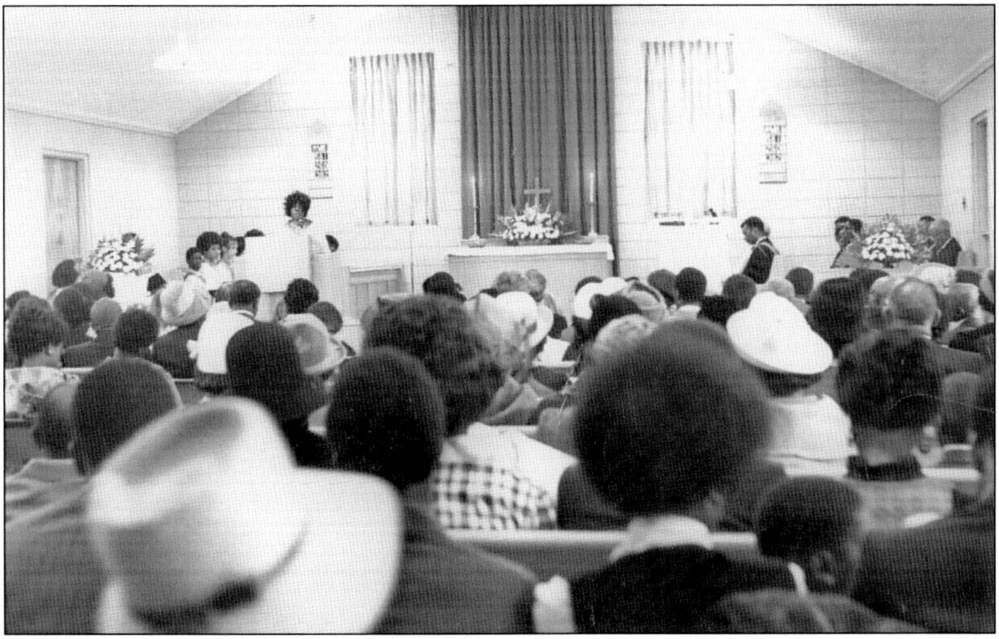

In 1972, Midway Congregational Church celebrated its 100th birthday with a special service. Founded in 1872 by freedmen who were communicants of the Midway Church, the congregation moved from the historic building to a new church built in Golden's Grove on land donated by William A. Golden for Dorchester Academy. Lillie Gillard (top), a local historian and preservationist, served as Midway Congregational Church's secretary for many years. In this photograph, she is making announcements at the Centennial Celebration of Midway Congregational Church. Leaders from Liberty County and elsewhere (bottom) paid their respects to this congregation and its deep history. Today the legacy of the Dorchester Puritans, who emigrated from Dorchester, England, in 1630, continues to live on in Liberty County. (Courtesy of Sallie W. Richardson.)

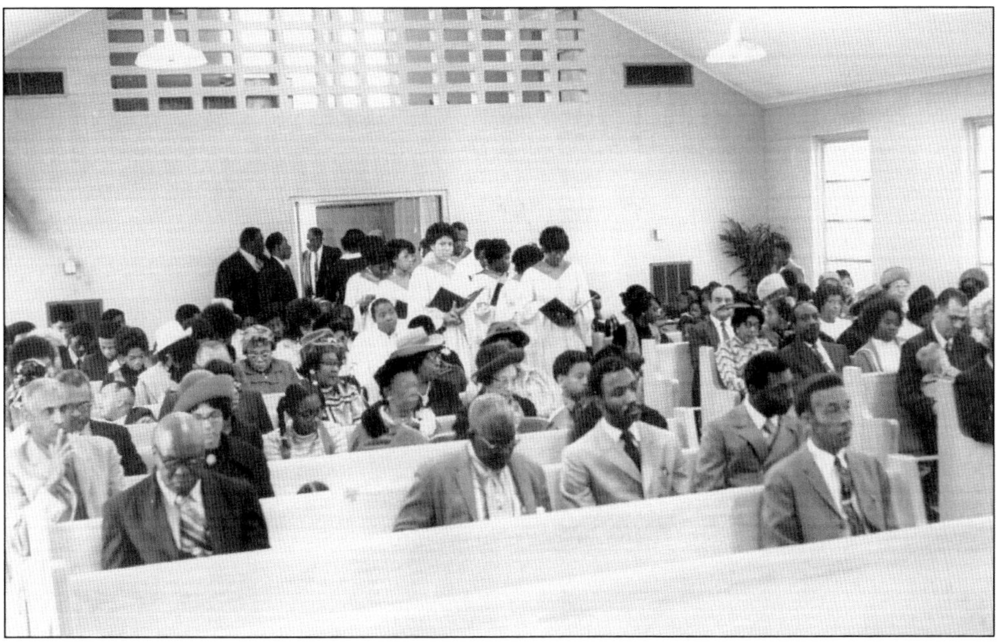